HITLER'S AIR WAR IN SPAIN

THE RISE OF THE LUFTWAFFE

HITLER'S AIR WAR IN SPAIN

THE RISE OF THE LUFTWAFFE

NORMAN RIDLEY

AIR WORLD

AIR WORLD

HITLER'S AIR WAR IN SPAIN
The Rise of the Luftwaffe

First published in Great Britain in 2022 by
Air World
An imprint of
Pen & Sword Books Ltd
Yorkshire – Philadelphia

Copyright © Norman Ridley, 2022

ISBN 978 1 39908 472 7

The right of Norman Ridley to be identified as Author of this work has been asserted
by him in accordance with the Copyright, Designs and Patents Act 1988.

A CIP catalogue record for this book is available from the British Library.

Typeset by SJmagic DESIGN SERVICES, India.

Printed and bound by CPI Group (UK) Ltd, Croydon, CR0 4YY

Pen & Sword Books Limited incorporates the imprints of Atlas, Archaeology,
Aviation, Discovery, Family History, Fiction, History, Maritime, Military, Military
Classics, Politics, Select, Transport, True Crime, Air World, Frontline Publishing, Leo
Cooper, Remember When, Seaforth Publishing, The Praetorian Press, Wharncliffe
Local History, Wharncliffe Transport, Wharncliffe True Crime and White Owl.

For a complete list of Pen & Sword titles please contact

PEN & SWORD BOOKS LIMITED
47 Church Street, Barnsley, South Yorkshire, S70 2AS, England
E-mail: enquiries@pen-and-sword.co.uk
Website: www.pen-and-sword.co.uk

Or
PEN AND SWORD BOOKS
1950 Lawrence Rd, Havertown, PA 19083, USA
E-mail: Uspen-and-sword@casematepublishers.com
Website: www.penandswordbooks.com

Contents

Abstract   vii

Chapter 1   Background to War   1
Chapter 2   International Reaction   4
Chapter 3   First Moves   18
Chapter 4   The Condor Legion   37
Chapter 5   Franco's First Attack against Madrid   53
Chapter 6   Foreign Aid Increases   63
Chapter 7   The Battle of El Jarama   79
Chapter 8   Franco's Drive into Vizcaya   90
Chapter 9   The Battle of Brunete   105
Chapter 10   Santander Falls   115
Chapter 11   Condor Legion at the Crossroads   121
Chapter 12   The Battle of Teruel   126
Chapter 13   Franco's Drive into Aragon   136
Chapter 14   The Ebro Offensive   150
Chapter 15   Strategy and Tactics   163
Chapter 16   The Spanish Civil War in the Context of Total War   168
Chapter 17   Lessons Learned and Lessons Ignored   179

Appendix   186
Notes   188
Sources   198
Index   201

In the wake of the Spanish Civil War, almost as much confusion existed over the role of aviation and armoured forces in battle as had existed before it began.

Richard P. Hallion

That the Spanish Civil War gave rise to significant changes in air doctrine, particularly in Germany and Russia, is axiomatic. This factor alone commends the Spanish conflict to the attention of the student of air power and its development.

John F. Guilmartin Jnr.

Abstract

Almost since the advent of warfare, civilians have suffered 'collateral damage' but the concept of Total War, a war without limits, had only surfaced in the early part of the twentieth century with the writings of theorists such as Gulio Douhet. Douhet's fundamental ideas, involving huge numbers of aircraft raining death upon defenceless cities, were seen by many as not only barbaric but, in practical terms, quite unrealistic given the logistical challenges that would have to be overcome in order to put them into practice. Any complacency over the threat, however, was rudely shattered on 26 February 1935 by the eruption onto the European military landscape of the German Luftwaffe and its blustering claims of irrepressible air power sending waves of panic rippling through ministries of war throughout the world.

Framing a realistic response to Hitler's propaganda offensive proved to be problematic given the lack of detailed knowledge of not only the numbers, but also the true performance capabilities of his new generation of aircraft and the ways in which they had expanded the boundaries of war. It was, therefore, of huge interest to all modern military establishments when these machines were deployed during the Spanish Civil War which broke out in July 1936. Notwithstanding the limited scope of this conflict, it offered, for the participating nations, a testing ground for new machines and, for the interested observers, a window into the future of aerial warfare in particular, although ground operations were also revolutionised to some extent by the advent of mechanisation.

When the war was less than a year old it had already seen the Luftwaffe employ air power in most of the ways that it would be used in the Second World War; not just airlifting troops, reconnaissance, interdiction, close support and strategic bombing, but also the deliberate targeting of civilians as a means of achieving military objectives. In this regard, despite the limited involvement of belligerents, it might well be seen as a laboratory for total war in which air power becomes the dominant factor.

This book looks at the conflict from the inside, through the words of those involved. Pilots, journalists and observers tell what it was really like to endure the roasting heat of the Spanish summer and the freezing cold of its winter; to fly in combat as predator or prey; to wait in the silent streets listening for the first distant drone of aircraft engines and then to feel the earth shudder under the crunch of bombs. All the significant aerial engagements of the war are clearly analysed against the background of a wider context, thereby fixing the place of the Spanish Civil War in the evolution of air power and the way in which its lessons were learned, or ignored, in the context of the much greater conflagration that was to come.

Chapter 1

Background to War

The circumstances surrounding the start of the Spanish Civil War bring into focus just how important aviation was right from the start. The war itself was sparked by an attempted military coup d'état on 17 July 1936 when garrisons at Madrid, Barcelona, Seville. Salamanca, Burgos, Valencia, Bilbao, Oviedo, Valladolid and Avila revolted, but the rebels failed catastrophically to straightaway grasp the handles of power and so condemned the insurrection to a prolonged and bloody war. When government forces held the capital Madrid by crushing the rebel troops in the Montaña barracks, and held most other major cities across the country, the rebel Nationalists found their forces widely separated with the bulk of their most effective troops in Morocco, far from where they were most urgently needed.

The plan was for General Francisco Franco Bahamonde to fly to Morocco from the Canary Islands at which point the 'Army of Africa' would rise up in revolt behind him. When the government got news that he had flown to Morocco without any specific order from Madrid it was greeted in the capital with equanimity and even when he called upon the Tetuan garrison to come out against the government, it was seen as little more than a 'ridiculous minor action, completely without significance'.[1]

It had been planned to get the Moroccan troops to the Spanish mainland by sea days before risings started in the main cities, but plans fell apart and naval ratings stayed loyal to the government by locking up their officers below decks. With the Straits of Gibraltar now patrolled by warships loyal to the government the only way to get those 50,000 troops onto the mainland was by air but Franco did not have anywhere near enough aircraft to do that. The vast majority of the aircraft available to either side at that time were little more than obsolete relics anyway and would not have lasted more than a few days before breaking down. It says much for the military ineptitude of the rebel generals that the isolation of the crack troops of Franco's 'Army of Africa' was a blunder of huge proportions and threatened to see the rebellion collapse in ignominious failure as others had done before it.

On the Spanish mainland the rebel forces were split between General Queipo de Llano in Andalusia, and General Emilio Mola in northern Spain, making any concerted move contingent upon uniting them, but telephone communications between the army in the North and that in the South were only possible through Portugal. Quiepo had taken Seville and secured it as a base to receive Franco's army if he could get them over the water. Mola wanted to bring a combined force to encircle Madrid and take it, which both he and Franco believed would destroy any resistance to the coup. The first of Franco's Moroccan troops crossed on 19 July in Fokker F-VIIs and Dornier-Wals seaplanes, but the numbers were small and more transport aircraft were urgently required. 'I have sent a commission to Rome to acquire the necessary Capronis', he told Mola on the 20th.[2] After some hesitation, the Italian leader Benito Mussolini agreed to help and when Hitler's Germany also agreed to supply him with a small number of aircraft, Franco might have breathed a small sigh of relief but he could not have imagined what these first small gestures of solidarity from fellow nationalist regimes would lead to.

When the Spanish Nationalists launched their coup d'état both they and the government forces were ill-equipped, poorly trained and led by generals whose appreciation of warfare owed little to tactics and strategy beyond what they had acquired during campaigns against primitive tribesmen in North Africa. Events leading up to the civil war had been bloody, savage and ruthless with many atrocities committed by warring factions within the deeply divided population and the war itself promised more of the same but on a whole new level. If neither side was able to win a swift victory the expectation of outside observers was that the conflict would be long, bestial and brutal with little common ground where moderation might gain a foothold.

Mussolini looked on with a haughty perspective and saw the possibility of exploiting the situation. Fascist power, he surmised, was ideally poised to move in and sweep Franco to an early victory over what he saw as a frankly primitive and fairly useless opponent in the left-wing government and in the process claim, as a reward, a few Italian naval staging posts on the Spanish Mediterranean coastline and a more secure outlet to the Atlantic. Surely, a beholden Franco could not deny him that. Germany, on the other hand, had no competing ambitions in the Mediterranean, but was only willing to see Italian influence increased to the point where it discomfited France. If Mussolini was going to make a power-play, then Germany would have to make some sort of a move to keep it in check.

Italy was first to send significant numbers of troops and aircraft after the initial supply of transports. Franco was staggered by the scale of the commitment, but while privately fuming at Mussolini's arrogant and excessive response which threatened to portray the Spanish Nationalists as helpless and needy, was unable to openly object even when the Italians chose to wage war very much according to their own agenda. After finding themselves succumbing to 'mission-creep', the Germans also chose to expand their role in support of Franco, but in a more controlled and cooperative manner. On the other side, the government, after frantically searching for any sort of help found a friend in Soviet Russia, whose motivations for being so were perhaps influenced more by political ambitions and a fortuitous opportunity to get their hands on significant amounts of foreign currency through control of the Spanish government's gold reserves. The result was that far from being just another primitive, provincial bloodletting, although it was certainly that also, the Spanish Civil War took on a whole new shape, characterised by the clash of modern war machines, strategies and tactics, and earned a place in the history of modern warfare that could never have been imagined on 17 July 1936.

Chapter 2

International Reaction

- Franco Appeals for Help
- Germany Responds
- Italy Responds
- France Responds
- Soviet Union Responds
- Britain Responds

Franco Appeals for Help

On 20 July 1936, the leader of the rebel Nationalist forces, General José Sanjurjo, was killed in Estoril in an air crash, while returning to Spain. He had chosen to fly in a small Puss Moth biplane aircraft rather than a much larger de Haviland Dragon Rapide, the same one that had transported General Franco from the Canaries to land at San Ramel airport in Morocco on the previous day. Sanjuro's aircraft, piloted by Juan Ansaldo who survived the accident, hit a stone wall on take-off and burst into flames. The three surviving leaders of the rebellion were Queipo de Llano, Mola and Franco, who outranked the other two and now became their preferred leader. On the same day that Sanjuro died, Franco flew from the Canary Islands to Tetuán in Morocco and took command of the Army in Africa, 'the one part of the Spanish army which was efficient, well-trained and ruthlessly led'.[1]

When Franco arrived in Spanish Morocco, he had not expected that the rebellion would take more than a few weeks to achieve its objectives and he certainly did not anticipate a full-scale civil war. However, within days it was clear that Queipo de Llano and Mola would be unable to force an early resolution without the help of Franco's Moroccan troops. The rebels on the mainland held about one third of Spanish territory which included the important Asturias mining district, but the government held a wide belt from the French border right across central Spain to Portugal as well as major cities like the capital Madrid, with all the Spanish gold reserves, Barcelona, Valencia and the entire Mediterranean coast. It also essentially retained control of the fleet, albeit one shorn of most of its officer class who had been removed by the crews and crucially, still controlled most of the Spanish Air Force. There was no clear border between the opposing forces and subsequently there were many isolated pockets within enemy territories. One such pocket held by the rebels was Seville with its Tablada air base and this would be the northern end of the shuttle that would bring Franco's army to the mainland. Less than half of the regular army on mainland Spain was under rebel control but many who were trapped in government areas had Nationalist sympathies and would defect in due course.

Franco's army in Morocco was comprised of about 5,000 soldiers of the Spanish Foreign Legion, 17,000 Moorish 'Regulares', and 17,000 Spanish conscripts, all of whom were regarded as the 'best-trained, best-led, best-equipped, most sternly disciplined and combat-worthy troops in the Army'. It had been planned to ferry these troops across the Straits of Gibraltar on board ships of the Spanish navy, but most of the Spanish seamen had remained loyal to the government and prevented the transfer. Franco managed to transport only a few hundred troops across before the sea route was blocked. The rebels on the mainland had no centralised leadership now that Sanjuro had gone and so lacked cohesion. The army in the South was struggling, with little success, to break out of the Seville enclave and drive north to join up with Mola's forces around Badajoz and Cáceres meaning that the prospects of a successful rebellion were looking bleak unless Franco could reach the mainland quickly and bring his Moroccan troops with him. It was a pivotal moment in the very first days of the revolt during which the scales threatened to tip decisively against the Nationalist effort and end it before it had ever quite begun.

Franco latched onto the idea of aircraft as his salvation; firstly to attack government airfields from which their bombers were striking at rebel areas and secondly to start moving his army bit by bit to reinforce the faltering and floundering main body of Nationalist troops on the mainland. Urgent, but ultimately fruitless, appeals went out through unofficial channels to Britain for the supply of aircraft, but Germany and Italy offered more hope. Franco had no official channels through which to contact the appropriate authorities in these countries but it was hoped that they would have political affinity to the cause of right-wing nationalism in Spain.

The Spanish Republican Air Force (Fuerza Aérea de la República Española) was equipped with a plethora of (mostly redundant) aircraft types, a large number of which had been previously built in and supplied by France. A programme of re-equipment and modernisation of the air force had begun in 1934 but procurement was mired in controversy and corruption with only ten of the 247 ordered being delivered before the coup. Breguet XIX light bombers of Grupo No 31, for instance, had been in service for some twelve years and the Nieuport Delage NiD 52 fighter was 'heavy and unresponsive' and prone to accidents.[2] More than half of the Breguets Grupo de caza No 31 and all of the Nieuports of Grupo de caza No 11 were at Getafe, near Madrid while those of No 13 were at El Prat de Llobregat, near Barcelona. Of the naval aircraft, the twenty-seven Vickers Vildebeests, seven Dornier Wal and nearly thirty Savoia S-62 seaplanes, remained loyal to the government at the San Javier, Barcelona and Mahón bases. A little over one-third of military pilots in Spain, around 215, remained loyal to the government with just over a quarter siding with the rebels, leaving the rest without allegiance to either. To compound the paucity of suitable aircraft, these pilots were inexperienced and poorly trained due to the cutbacks in military spending by the left-wing government of Manuel Azaña in the early 1930s. The only consolation for the Republicans at this time was that the Nationalist air force was in equally poor shape.

Spanish National Airline (Líneas Aéreas Postales Españolas) continued to operate in an intermittent and increasingly haphazard manner but many of the DC-2s, the fastest and most modern aircraft in Spain at the time which out-paced the Nieuport fighters, were immediately militarised and fitted with bombsights and even defensive machine gun positions, to be fired through the side windows. These proceeded to carry out important long-range bombing missions on the rebel air bases in North Africa, Seville, León or Logroño, as well as liaison flights to the northern coast of Spain, landing in Asturias and Santander.

Germany Responds

A request was duly sent, albeit with little hope of a positive response, to the Reich Foreign Ministry in Berlin for ten transport aircraft to be sent to Morocco and was, unsurprisingly, rejected out of hand. Hans Heinrich

Dieckhoff, director of the political section in Berlin at the time and a future ambassador to Franco's Spain argued that the German colony in Spain and German merchant ships and warships in Spanish waters would be under threat should it become known that Germany was supplying the rebels with weapons. It was also feared that international complications might arise if Germany interfered in a country with friendly links to France and Britain. The growing tensions in Eastern Europe, not to mention the German reoccupation of the Rhineland, was giving the German Foreign Ministry enough to think about. Franco, however, received an unexpected alternative option when, on 21 July, Johannes E.F. Bernhardt, the German manager of Wilmer Brothers, a German export firm in Tetuán, offered to facilitate communications between Franco and leading Nazis in Berlin. He had already tried to interest Berlin in selling Junkers transport aircraft on credit to the Spanish military but the Luftwaffe chief, Hermann Göring, unsure of his diplomatic ground both domestically and internationally, had prevaricated and refused to make a decision. Bernhardt persisted and was able to convince Franco, who was willing to follow any lead, however obscure, that he had connections with the Hitler's Deputy, Rudolf Hess; so with little to lose, Franco agreed that Bernhardt should carry his personal message to Berlin and try to get it into Hitler's hands. Despite Bernhardt having no authority to give any sort of undertaking to Franco, he proved to be the initial catalyst for Germany intervention in the Spanish Civil War and he eventually became one of the most influential Germans in Franco's Spain during the next decade.[3]

Bernhardt's mission met with stonewall resistance when he landed at Gatow on 25 July. Diekhoff, who was forewarned of the visit, instructed that 'the Nazi Party organisation should not permit the Spanish delegation to come into contact with the German political officials'.[4] Bernhardt, however, had contacts within the Foreign Organisation of the Nazi Party (Auslandsorganisation) and was able, at short notice, to make contact with Hess, who, in turn, arranged for him to meet Hitler at the Villa Wahnfried, where he was staying while attending the Wagner festival at Beyreuth. Hess mobilised a high-powered delegation of Nazi officials to accompany Bernhardt who was able to personally deliver a letter from Franco into Hitler's hands. Hitler was aware that the rebellion in Spain had stalled and, in a lengthy monologue, explained why it was doomed to failure. However, he was still sufficiently intrigued to call Göring and Wermacht chief, General Werner von Blomberg, into the meeting and quickly apprised them of the situation adding, to Bernhardt's astonishment, in sharp contrast to what he had said only minutes previously, that it was now his intention to respond positively and send aid to Franco. While von Blomberg offered no comment, Göring was adamant that Germany could ill afford to lose military equipment in such a risky venture and argued that German intervention could have negative international repercussions, but Hitler was adamant and brushed these objections aside at which point Göring abandoned his opposition and expressed wholehearted support.[5] Further discussion concluded that the military aid must be sent under a cover of absolute secrecy. It came as a great surprise and an indication of the disjointed Nationalist command structure after Sanjuro's death that a second, quite separate, delegation arrived in Berlin from General Mola with another request for aid. This was quietly ignored since it had already been agreed that all aid would go through Franco.

Exactly what diplomatic and strategic considerations were at the forefront of Hitler's mind at Beyreuth are the stuff of conjecture, but whether it was then or soon afterwards the implications of what was happening, or what might happen, in Spain led to consideration of the longer-term ambitions of the Third Reich. It might be threatened by the establishment, in Hitler's words, of a 'Bolshevik state' in Spain which would 'constitute a land bridge for France to North Africa' that would safeguard the passage of French colonial troops to the northern frontier of France thereby improving her strategic defence. German ambitions, however, did not include the establishment of a fascist regime in Spain which Hitler, in April 1937, described as impossible to achieve not to say 'superfluous and absurd'.[6]

Göring was given overall command of the aid operation to be called Untenehmen Feuerzauber (Operation Magic Fire), the Wagnerian connection no doubt resulting from the Beyreuth meeting (in the third act of Wagner's 'Die Walküre' Loge, the Norse god of fire, creates a magic protective circle of fire around the rock where Brünnhilde sleeps). Generals Erhard Milch and Helmuth Wilberg were hurriedly appointed to head a special staff, Sonderstab W, created to channel all military aid to Spain but exclusively through Franco. The speed with which Wilberg and Milch acted is remarkable given that they had no warning and had received precious little guidance from above. Neither can they have been wholly convinced about the viability of the whole enterprise when reports coming out of the German Embassy in Madrid said 'it is hardly to be expected ... that the military revolt can succeed'.[7] In a very short space of time, however, the necessary matériel was identified, packed and sent to Hamburg. Personnel were selected and made aware that their oath of secrecy over the mission would be enforced by the Gestapo. Customs at Hamburg were warned to turn a blind eye to what was going on at the port.

A private company, HISMA (Hispano-Marroqui de Transportes Sociedad Limitada) was registered in Seville on 31 July by Bernhardt, to handle all the operational details. This coincided with the departure of the first German ship, the Woermann Line cargo vessel SS *Usaramo*, from Hamburg with eighty-five German 'civilian' technicians, including the future military head of HISMA, Major Alexander von Scheele. The cargo included aircraft (ten Junkers Ju-52s and six Heinkel He-5Is), anti-aircraft guns, bombs, ammunition, and various other pieces of equipment all stripped of any insignia that might indicate their origin. The aircraft had, in fact, been requisitioned from the civil airline Lufthansa, Göring having decided that the operation did not warrant putting at risk any of his precious Luftwaffe machines. At the same time, a further ten Junkers Ju-52S were already on their way to Nationalist Spain under their own power. On 2 August the first of these aircraft landed in Seville. From there they proceeded straightaway to Tetuán and immediately began transporting Franco's troops to Jerez de la Frontera and Seville.[8]

On 27 July, the pilots of the Luftwaffe's fighter units, the He 51-equipped I./JG 132 'Richthofen' at Döberitz and the Arado 65- and Arado 68-equipped I./JG 134 'Horst Wessel' at Dortmund, received an appeal for 'volunteers' to join a mysterious expeditionary force destined for an unidentified foreign country. In a similar procedure that had been followed during the clandestine military collaboration with the Soviet Union at Lipetsk, all those who responded to the call resigned their commissions and were put on the reserve list but remained under 'strict military orders and military law'.[9] As far as their comrades were concerned, they 'suddenly vanished into thin air [and after six months] returned sunburnt and in high spirits'.[10] Von Scheele was given strict orders forbidding any of the pilots to fly combat missions other than escorts for the transports. One of the 'volunteers', Oberleutnant Hannes Trautloft of 9. Staffel of II./JG 134, at Köln-Butzweilerhof recalled:

> On 28 July 1936, while serving as an oberleutnant with 9./JG 134 at Köln, I received a telephone call from my Kommandeur, Hauptmann Horst Dinort. His first question was 'Are you engaged to be married?' I stated that I was not. He then swore me to secrecy and began to explain to me about the situation in Spain and the need for well-trained pilots in that country. Before he even had the chance to ask me if I would be prepared to go there, I said to him 'I volunteer!'
>
> Dinort then told me to get ready to travel to Dortmund within the next two hours, where I would receive orders directly from a Geschwaderkommodore. He also ordered me to maintain absolute discretion about the whole thing, for it would not be easy to explain to my comrades what I was doing when they saw me hurriedly packing my bags![11]

Italy Responds

Since 1932, the Fascist government of Italy had toyed with the idea of supporting right-wing factions in Spain in at least two abortive military coups, but had actually done little of a practical nature faced with opposition from the French and British governments which had important economic interests in the country. Neither had the Italian 'Duce' Benito Mussolini developed much admiration for Spanish anti-government conspirators who failed to live up to his own ideals of decisive, fascist leadership. The two regimes may have shared an interest in nationalism and authoritarianism, but they had little in common otherwise. On 31 March 1934, the Italian government had signed the a 'Treaty of Friendship and Neutrality' with Spanish monarchists pledging arms, financial support and training facilities to support an overthrow of the Republican government, but the deal was scrapped by Mussolini a year later when it became obvious that there would be no insurrection. Instead, Il Duce began subsidising Falangist groups in Spain in the hope of promoting fascism there.

By early July of 1936 the prospect of a successful Nationalist coup d'état had increased considerably and the mood in Italy was becoming more interventionist especially when it became clear that the British and French had seemed to abandon the Republican government to its own devices. Franco had urgent need of aircraft. His first-hand experience of air power in the Rif wars of Morocco had shown him how important aircraft had become in modern warfare and the parlous state of the Nationalist air resources prompted him to authorised his close aide and press attaché, the journalist Luís Bolín, who had flown with him to Morocco, to urgently 'purchase aircraft and supplies' wherever he could find them.[12] Bolín, who spoke a little Italian, went first to Rome on 21 July to ask Mussolini for twelve transport and three fighter aircraft with bombs and ammunition while Franco made contact with the Italian Consul in Tangier. At first, Mussolini rejected these advances simply scribbling 'NO' at the bottom of the note handed to him from Franco, but after receiving erroneous reports that France was sending aircraft to the Republican government in Madrid, on 27 July he softened his views and authorised the transfer of twelve fast, well armed, modern Savoia-Marchetti SM.81 (Pipistrello) tri-motor bombers with crews and relevant specialists that took off from Elmas military aerodrome near Cagliari in Sardinia on 30 July. The nine that survived the journey arrived at Nador and became the first unit of the Aviación de El Tercio and twelve Fiat CR.32 fighters followed by sea on 14 August. Italian pilots and support staff who accompanied the aircraft were listed as 'volunteers' in the Tercio Extranjero (the Spanish Foreign Legion) and issued with false identities. Mussolini's decision to intervene was based partly on Franco's personal assurances to the Italian Minister Plenipotentiary, Pier Filippo de Rossi del Lion Nero, and his Military Attaché, Major Guiseppe Luccardi, that victory for the rebels would be certain and quick, and he flattered Mussolini by saying that he intended to establish 'a Republican government in the fascist [Italian] style adopted for the Spanish people'.[13] All the aid was offered on credit with very favourable terms.[14] As well as aircraft, the transport ships *Araujo, Ciudad de Alicante,* and *Ciudad de Ceuta*, carried 4,000 men, four artillery batteries, two million cartridges, and twelve tons of other munitions to mainland Spain. Encouraged by the success of this first operation, Mussolini began sending a steady stream of munitions, personnel, and supplies under the name of Aviazione Legionaria.

Both Italy and Germany acknowledged the possibility of a left-wing government in Spain forging close ties with the Soviet Union and saw common cause in giving sufficient aid to the Nationalist rebels to prevent it happening. Ulrich von Hassell, the German Ambassador at Rome noted 'a sudden increase in the warmth of German-Italian cooperation' when he met the Italian Foreign Minister, Galeazzo Ciano on 25 July.[15] He reported to Berlin that 'victory for the Spanish government is regarded as the equivalent of a victory for Communism. Such a development is abhorred in Italy for ideological reasons.' Later, on 7 September the Hungarian Minister in Rome, Baron Frederick Villani, in conversation with Ciano would report that Hitler, in a recent conversation with the Hungarian Prince Regent, Admiral Miklós Horthy, had personally spoken of the need for good relations between Italy and Germany in support of General Franco.[16]

France Responds

For the Nationalist side, in the early hours of 20 July the newly appointed Prime Minister of the Spanish Republic, José Giral, sent a personal telegram to the, not quite so newly appointed, left-wing French Prime Minister Léon Blum: 'We are surprised by a dangerous military coup stop beg you arrange assistance with arms and planes stop fraternally Giral.'[17] The two countries had historic ties as well as current politically aligned socialist governments and there were already military agreements in place between them. Indeed an Accord of December 1935 had actually bound Spain to buy a substantial quantity of French arms. On 24 July, Giral, citing legitimate international treaties between France and Spain, again petitioned Paris for military aid in the form of guns and ammunition and, while they were at it, twenty Potez 54 bombers with bombs. Blum and his Air Minister Pierre Cot were sympathetic but constrained by strong British counsel not to interfere in the Spanish conflict. Neither was Cot enthusiastic about letting go of the few Potez 54s he had, preferring instead to palm the Spanish off with seventeen Potez 25s which were unused but had been in storage for three years. Right-wing sympathisers in the French government were quick to let Berlin know what Cot was up to but the Germans seemed uninterested. Meanwhile Spain had shipped a quantity of gold sovereigns to Paris to show they meant business but the French Cabinet, after heated debate which threatened to crush a weak and hesitant Blum, was 'unanimous' in rejecting the appeal for military aid. When the Soviets publicly and loudly declared that they did not have the slightest intention of intervening in Spanish affairs, the Spanish government quickly found itself isolated diplomatically and France was unable to make any sort of public statement of support without going out on a limb. As a compromise, the French Cabinet, drawing a fine line between international condemnation and Spanish approbation, agreed to send the Potez 25s stripped of all armaments, bomb racks and bomb sights to Spain unofficially in a 'private' deal financed through a complicated arrangement between the government and Potez-Bloch CAMS. The deal crashed when it was discovered that only seven of the aircraft were airworthy and someone had alerted the French right-wing press, whose fierce condemnation pressured the government into an immediate cancellation of the deal.

Blum, pursuing a policy of 'relaxed non-intervention' took urgent steps to replace the Potez but few French companies were willing to sell arms to the Spanish government. Amiot refused a request for six Amiot 143 bombers, but Loire-Neuport were less fastidious and agreed to supply the first six Loire 46 fighters, from an order of sixty, but delivery could not be made for many weeks. Only fourteen Dewoitine D.372s, originally destined for Lithuania, were available straight away but at a price 28 per cent above the Lithuanian contract valuation, and to these were added six Potez 54s made available by Cot, which also went through at a hugely inflated 73 per cent above normal price. After all that, when the Dewoitines arrived in Spain they were without any spare parts and all cockpit signs and instruments were in Lithuanian.

While the Nationalists had been given immediate aid from the authoritarian Italian and German governments without any discussion of payment, the Republican government had been forced to plead with democratic governments, operating under the scrutiny of a free press and parliament, and who, not only dealt in evasion, deception and broken promises, but demanded payment in advance from the Spanish gold deposits now in Paris. When aircraft were delivered, they were 'few [and] without arms or the means of installing them and unsupported by maintenance back-up, trained pilots or anyone to train them'.[18] The few French personnel who accompanied the aircraft were not popular with Spanish commanders who found them 'disruptive'.

Soviet Union Responds

Hitler's renunciation of the Rapallo Treaty which had been the basis of Soviet-German collaboration since 1922 had threatened the Soviet Union with diplomatic isolation. As a consequence, the Soviets had adopted a charm offensive to persuade the Western powers that it posed no military threat and was pursuing its anti-fascist agenda by peaceful means. However, the Soviet economy had been on a war footing since 1934 and when the Spanish Civil War broke out, Soviet intervention seemed to align with its greater European strategic ambitions. While its sympathies were naturally very much with the socialist government in Spain, the Soviet Union had no historic or major current economic ties with the Spanish state. Britain and France, to a lesser extent, were unnerved by the presence of anarchists and communist elements in the Spanish government and made it clear that any Soviet intervention would be considered a violation of international law.[19] Abandoned by Germany and rebuffed by Britain, the Soviets had little to lose by helping the Spanish government as long as it could do so clandestinely.

The Soviet Union had been made aware of Germany's decision to help Franco through the Schulze-Boysen spy ring operating within the Luftwaffe which fed intelligence back to Moscow. They were therefore probably not surprised when Giral reached out to them for help in early August, but their public response was that, while the Soviets would be politically supportive of the Republican government, no direct military assistance from that quarter was possible. They would, however, eagerly encourage communist volunteers across Europe and the United States to become involved by going to Spain to join the government forces. When the level of German, and especially Italian, military assistance became clear however, the sheer volume made imminent defeat of the Republican cause a distinct possibility. The Soviet Politburo weighed up the options and at the end of August decided that on a philosophical level, it was not prepared to stand aside and see the grass-roots of communism in Spain scotched by Nazi and Fascist power and, on the political level, it would be to their advantage if, by prolonging and expanding the conflict into what would become a 'proxy' war with his fascist enemies, it might distract Germany from pursuing their ambitions in Eastern Europe. On 16 September the 'Transportation of Special Goods to Our Friends in "X" [Operation X]' was established to administer all aid going to Spain.

The Soviet aid operation was placed under the control of Marshal Kliment Voroshilov in the foreign department of the Soviet Secret Police (NKVD) and Soviet military intelligence working out of Odessa but it is clear that Stalin retained a firm personal control over the whole operation, for the first year at least. One of his first instructions was that none of the equipment sent to Spain should be traceable back to the Soviet Union so all sales had to be through a 'neutral private firm'.[20] Stalin authorised the first shipment of antiquated rifles, machine guns and ammunition which left Feodosia in the Crimea on the SS *Campeche* and arrived in Spain on 4 October. The most stringent precautions were taken to maintain a blanket of secrecy over the docks there and at other Black Sea ports. Documents showed the arms to have been loaded in Turkey but when the ship passed through the Dardanelles the German embassy in Ankara became aware of the cargoes. Two reports by the German military attaché there gave a complete picture of Soviet arms shipments to Spain between September 1936 and March 1938. This detailed information gave figures for each month and must have come from a German agent with access to Turkish records.[21]

It was clear to the Turkish customs that the cargo was from the Soviet Union and this intelligence found its way to Berlin. After this first shipment – and clear proof that Spanish gold was on its way to Moscow to pay for it – the Soviet Politburo voted to increase aid in the knowledge that they would receive full payment. A further motivation, given the prospect of significant sales of military matériel at a price controlled by them (much of it superfluous and obsolete stock) was the intelligence reaching them that after the fall of Toledo, Franco's forces were poised to take Madrid and bring the war to a rapid conclusion. Because of Stalin's earlier prevarication time was of the essence. Urgency now gripped Voroshilov and between 12 and 28 October, in a hurried and frenzied operation, he sent fifty T-26 tanks, thirty Tupolev SB Katiuska bombers and twenty-five Polikarpov I-15 'Chato' fighters. The first week of November saw shipment of a further fifteen Chatos and thirty-one Polikarpov I-16 'Ratas'.

The chaotic nature of the operation was made unavoidable by the huge difficulties of procurement and transport of the arms from all across the great expanse of the Soviet Union. Urgent demands were received without warning at arms depots and military establishments. Most of the guns and ammunition were relics of the First World War and of many different types, which made the matching of guns and ammunition an obvious problem.

All identification marks had to be filed off, according to Stalin's orders. The NKVD commandeered 1,000 railway trucks. Often the cargo, such as crated aircraft, assigned to a particular ship was too big to go through the hatches and the choice of ships in the Black Sea ports was not great. When the SS *Komsomol* was sunk by the Nationalist cruiser SS *Canaris*, the Soviets decided that all Soviet ships should be replaced by Spanish vessels. Once through the Dardanelles, the ships were subject to interception or attack, as in the case of the SS *Timiryazov* and SS *Blagoev*, so they were disguised by elaborate means until they were clear of the Algerian coastline and ready to run the Nationalist coastal blockade to Cartagena, Alicante and Valencia.

Britain Responds

Britain looked on the Spanish insurrection from a position of Europe's leading political power with extensive economic interests in the country and a strategically vital naval base at Gibraltar. Reports of a military conspiracy were taken seriously, even though there had been a number of failed coup attempts in the recent past. A Republican-Socialist coalition government in Spain in 1931 had raised eyebrows in Whitehall, but it was not until February 1936 with the coming to power of the Popular Front government backed by Communists and Anarchists that the Foreign Office's alarm bells started ringing. Beyond Spain, Britain's diplomatic efforts in the Mediterranean at this time had been mainly focused on establishing a stable relationship with Italy to forestall that country's alignment with Nazi Germany and Japan, and to prevent tensions in the Mediterranean from escalating out of control. The potential involvement of Italy in the Spanish war and the implications for Gibraltar could not be taken lightly, especially since Britain had placed great emphasis on forging a friendly relationship with Mussolini in order to dissuade him from establishing an understanding with Hitler in a wider European context.

Contradictory reports reached Britain after the 17 July coup; one to the effect that the rebels were firmly in control, albeit in Tetuán and not the mainland, and another that the rising had been crushed in Barcelona. Clearly the insurrection would not find immediate resolution and the prospect of civil war loomed large although, given the state of the inexpert and poorly supplied government militias as opposed to the professional soldiers of the rebel forces, the war promised to be of brief duration. The Foreign Office view was that an extreme right victory was likely to be embarrassing in respect of British foreign policy and interests, given its stance on Germany, while an extreme left victory might encourage potential left-wing revolutionary movements at home. For the Conservative-dominated British government of 1936 the choice was obvious; its sympathy lay with the Nationalists who, supported by landowners, Church and Army, were pledged to stem the tide of extreme radical socialism. The Spanish government was likely to forge strong ties with a left-wing government in France which risked the spread of extreme political ideologies and it was fear of the spread of communism, above all else, that informed British foreign policy. It was important, however, not to be seen to take sides in the war, although there was a clear expectation that other foreign powers would not remain aloof. Past experience suggested that Italy would help the Nationalist cause and it was likely that Germany would not stand aside if the Soviet Union got involved. Britain could not allow its democratic credentials to be besmirched by speaking out against the legitimate elected government of Spain, but it was not about to make a fuss about covert military aid going to the rebel Junta. One thing was made quite clear, however, when the British Prime Minister Stanley Baldwin declared that, 'On no account must [Foreign Secretary Anthony Eden] bring us into the fight on the side of the Russians.'[22] Tacit and unconditional neutrality was the publicly declared policy as long as the risk of a communist government in Spain was avoided and British trade with Spain was unaffected. The intervention of Germany and Italy were not seen to be of major concern, but it was vital that the war should not escalate beyond Spain's borders. To this end, French neutrality was considered vital, as Churchill put it to Eden: 'to make Blum stay ... strictly neutral, even if Germany and Italy ... back the rebels and Russia sends money to the government'.[23]

On 26 July Hitler told Joachim von Ribbentrop, before he left for London to take up his post as Ambassador, that a victory for communism in Spain would in short time result in the 'Bolshevisation' of France. The Permanent Under-Secretary at the British Foreign Office, Sir Robert Vansittart, visited Berlin soon afterwards and found the Germans to be obsessed with events in Spain and the threat of Bolshevism. The possibility of a strengthening of links between the radical governments of France and Spain was a common concern of both Britain and Germany.[24]

Chapter 3

First Moves

- Morocco Airlift
- First Aerial Engagements
- Bombing of Civilians at Tetuán and Zaragoza
- Franco Marches on Madrid
- Bombing of Madrid
- Non-Intervention Agreement
- Hitler Names His Price for Helping Franco

Morocco Airlift

When Hitler authorised the supply of aircraft to airlift Franco's forces over the Straits of Gibraltar he had thrust upon the nascent Luftwaffe a responsibility for which it had never planned and probably had never even considered. When the first Ju 52s arrived in Morocco, the ground personnel were thrown into the deep end and had to improvise in accordance with the scanty orders they had been given. Already some troops had been ferried across by Spanish aircraft, so the template was set and the airport at Seville was ready to take the men, but the Ju 52s were only designed to take a dozen passengers. Showing great ingenuity, the ground crews stripped out all superfluous fittings and converted the Ju 52s for troop transport so that as many as thirty-five men could fit in at any one time and the transfer of Franco's men to Seville started without any further delay. While the German contribution to the transfer operation was substantial, especially in terms of heavy equipment transported, it should be noted that nine Italian and a number of Spanish transports were also involved in what was undoubtedly one of the most important actions of the war, without which the Nationalist rebellion would almost certainly eventually have failed. By 5 August, more than 1,500 colonial troops had been landed in mainland Spain along with their leader, Franco, who set up his headquarters in Seville, but the operation was far from straightforward. Few of the Moroccan troops had flown before and the turbulent air currents over the Straits coupled with instability of the aircraft due to overloading, caused a great deal of air-sickness which was extremely unpleasant for everyone in the cramped aircraft. Intermittent anti-aircraft fire from two Republican warships was also a serious matter. Fortunately for Franco, the Republican leaders completely misread the situation in the south and fighter aircraft that could have given the transports a hard time were kept at Getafe in Madrid, because, as an official communique stated, 'The Republican battleships have complete control over the Straits [of Gibraltar] so that any attempts to bring troops [across] is quite impossible.'[1] It is no surprise that an operation launched at such short notice and conducted so far away gave rise to logistical headaches. Fuel was soon exhausted and all flights had to be grounded for two days until a tanker was brought in. That was only half a solution because there were no pumps to transfer fuel from bowsers to aircraft, forcing ground crews to refuel by hand using cans under the blazing North African sun.

On 8 August the SS *Usaramo* with the first contingent of German volunteers had arrived at Cádiz and docked the next day. They offloaded six crated He 51s while the port was under a Republican air attack and took them by train to Seville. The German pilot Oberleutnant Trautloft captured the mood when he said,

> The next morning we found ourselves at Seville airfield, a frequent target for 'red' airmen. On the 9th of August we started the job of rebuilding our six He 51s – a real piece of teamwork involving pilots and ground personnel. The Spanish personnel were quite surprised to witness us work with such energy, but we really were getting quite impatient and wanted to get our machines into the air as soon as possible.[2]

By the 10th, the aircraft were ready for action and the Germans were quickly getting acclimatised to their new surroundings. Oberleutnant Herwig Knüppel slept 'in the full glare of the sun ... when not flying or else had language tuition with Spanish crews'. Wolf-Heinrich von Houwald, however, found 'the airfield was so poor that we were worried whether our

Spanish comrades would be able to fly our aircraft from there', and he was right about that. When, 'full of enthusiasm and idealism', five Spaniards proudly climbed into his aircraft and took it up for a spin they promptly crashed it on landing.[3] On 13 August the SS *Kamerun* left Hamburg, followed by the SS *Wigbert* on the following day loaded with aviation fuel, bombs, ammunition, and two Junkers Ju-52s later unloaded in Lisbon; which would become a valuable link in the Nationalist supply lines after they had captured the border town of Badajoz on the 14th.

Acting on his own initiative following an instruction from Berlin to 'protect the transports', von Scheele authorised two of the Ju 52s to be converted to carry bombs so that they could ward off the Spanish ships firing on the transports as they crossed the Straits of Gibraltar.[4] On the 13th, one of the ships, *Jaime I*, was bombed outside Málaga harbour. Incensed by the death of forty-seven crewmen, Republican sailors on board the vessel, in revenge for the attack, shot their officers who had been held captive since the start of the insurrection.[5] The bombing of *Jaime I* was an event that was to mark the first escalation of German involvement as other German aircrews, elated by the strike, petitioned von Scheele for permission to follow suit. Berlin was unwilling to criticise von Scheele's action, which it saw as legitimate in terms of his responsibilities, but still refused to sanction more widespread involvement of German personnel. This ambivalent response encouraged von Scheele to find other ways of satisfying his aircrews' calls for action that would not fall outside his brief. On 23 August he authorised Ju 52s to fly over the besieged fortress of Alcázar de Toledo to drop food and medical supplies to Nationalist supporters inside.

Many Spanish airmen had been forced to choose sides after the coup and the indications were that the rivalry between the two sides, which had caused so much bloodshed even before the rising, was about to escalate. The ferocity of the civil war that pitted former comrades against each other was evident when a Republican Breguet XIX of 1a Escuadrilla of Grupo No 1 of the Fuerzas Aéreas de Africa, based at Tetuán, flown by Sargento Félix Urtubi Ercilla landed at Getafe airfield in Madrid carrying the body of teniente Juan Miguel de Castro Gutiérrez. Ercilla explained,

> We left Tetuán at 0600 hrs today. We were ordered to strafe
> and bomb the government column travelling from La Línea.
> There were three aircraft. At an altitude of 1,000 ft over the

Straits of Gibraltar I turned to the teniente and shot him four times – in the forehead, in the chest and through the mouth …
I was ready to do anything. I'd rather die than surrender to the traitors.[6]

The Spanish pilots, on both sides, were very keen to get their hands on some of the more modern aircraft starting to come in. Ten of the German Ju 52s had been handed over to the Spanish and a small number had formed themselves loosely into what they called the Escuadrilla Rambaud, named after Captain Luis Rambaud, at Escalona del Prado. On 23 August, three He 51s escorting Spanish-flown Ju 52s attacked Getafe airfield outside Madrid. It was still considered too risky to send German airmen flying over the Spanish capital in case they were shot down and paraded before the world's press. The Spanish pilots, however, had some problems with the He 51 during the landing since the fighter had a tendency to bounce and veer once on the ground. The Germans, eager to get into the action, demanded of the Nationalist air chief Alfredo Kindelán y Duany that they, alone, should be allowed to fly the Heinkels. This was agreed upon and the Escuadrilla Rambaud was disbanded at the end of the month, but it now meant that German crews began flying regularly in combat missions and claiming aerial victories against Republican aircraft which were flown by significantly less well-trained pilots. The Spanish pilots, Captain Joaquín García Morato and Rambaud however, continued flying operationally in German aircraft which encouraged the Germans to train more Spanish pilots.

Meanwhile, the Italian military build-up gathered pace. Rome dispatched a further twenty-seven fighter aircraft, five tanks, forty machine-guns, and twelve anti-aircraft guns as well as ammunition, bombs, aviation fuel, and lubricants to the rebels on 7 August.[7] At dawn a week later, the Italian freighter SS *Nereide* docked at Melilla, on the Mediterranean coast of Spanish Morocco and discharged twelve Fiat CR.32 bi-plane fighters, which had been embarked in the Italian port of La Spezia a week earlier. The Fiat CR.32 was a robust, highly manoeuvrable biplane fighter powered by the excellent Fiat A.30 R.A. V12 engine which gave it a top speed of over 350km/h. It had been operational with the Italian Air Force for just over a year. Almost 400 of these fine aircraft would be operational in Spain before the end of the civil war. Also on the ship were eighteen volunteer airmen from the Regia Aeronautica with false passports. The Fiats were assembled at Nador (Melilla) over the course of several days and eventually transferred by air to Tablada (Seville), in southern Spain. They were incorporated into the Aviación del Tercio and these, the first fighter unit of this force became the Primera Escuadrilla de Caza de la Aviación del Tercio (1a Escuadrilla de Caza del Tercio) commanded by Capitano Dequal. The aircraft were given defensive duties for Nationalist forces in Andalusia against the numerically superior Republican air force in the early weeks of the war.

First Aerial Engagements

The Spanish Civil War would see air operational practices that had been employed since the First World War, but they would now be witnessed on a whole new scale. Air power would be manifest in a number of ways, none of which would have surprised observers but the technological advances since 1918 meant that the effectiveness of various aspects of military aviation were essentially redefined in an enhanced combat environment. A new level of sophistication both in performance and tactics were the most obvious developments.

By the end of August three more CR.32s had been sent to Mallorca and nine more were offloaded in the port of Vigo de Galicia, on Spain's Atlantic coast, from the Spanish ship SS *Ebro*. The latter had been renamed *Aniene* in Italy so that it could run contraband under a flag of convenience. The aircraft were assembled at Tablada and formed the Segunda Escuadrilla de Caza del Tercio. The three CR.32s sent to Mallorca were unloaded from the Italian steamer SS *Emilio Morandi* at Palma de Mallorca during the night of 27th and stationed at Son San Juan airfield. On the Republican side, a number of Breguet XIXs were moved south to Andújar and Herrera del Duque to provide air cover to the Republican units retreating from Franco's columns advancing on Madrid. Twin-engine French Potez 540 bombers arrived at El Prat de Llobregat, in Barcelona, in early August, where they equipped the international Escadre Espana and fourteen Dewoitine D.372 parasol-winged fighters arrived soon afterwards. Republican pilots, however, were loath to fly except in groups because of the overwhelming number of enemy CR.32s in the area. The Potez 540 was a relatively new aircraft but its design was distinctly antiquated. Its top speed of just over 300km/h was significantly less than that of the Fiats and its vulnerability earned it the sobriquet 'Ataúd Volante'(flying coffin). The Dewoitine D.372 was much faster at around 400km/h but its design was poor and it was not popular with pilots.

The Nationalist aim was to take Madrid and bring the war to a swift end but Mola soon realised that he had too few troops and gave up on the idea, preferring instead to hold all the main arterial roads until Franco's army could arrive. The first few Moroccan Foreign Legionnaires who had crossed in the three Fokkers and two Dornier seaplanes immediately started to move north from Seville towards Mérida to begin clearing the way to Badajoz and opening up a link to Portugal, through which supplies would be brought. On 5 August, however, they met Republican forces with aircraft at Almendralejo and were temporarily forced to halt their advance. Nationalist aircraft interceded, bringing terror and panic to the defenders and the advance was quickly resumed under the overall command of Lieutenant Colonel Juan Yagüe y Blanco, a 'chunky, tall [man] with a leonine mane and the look of a short-sighted hunting animal'. He was a veteran of the Rif Wars given to bouts of almost insane temper and, as villages were overrun on the road to Madrid, he sanctioned the brutal and merciless killing of enemy prisoners and civilians alike. Villagers who fled across the border were herded back by the Portuguese authorities and murdered.[8]

The character of the war was further defined at Badajoz on the Portuguese border when a Nationalist force comprising Foreign Legionnaires and Moroccans, commanded by Yagüe, took the city on 14 August with the aid of DC2s, Italian-piloted SM.81s and Spanish-piloted Ju 52 bombers that had dropped incendiary bombs on the defenders on the ancient city walls over a three-day period of bombardment. The Nationalists sacked the city. Murder and mass rape continued for days earning Yagüe the sobriquet of 'The Butcher of Badajoz'. A shocked Italian observer reported that 'all prisoners were shot after a fierce and brave defence'.[9] The massacre of an estimated 2,000–4,000 civilians was excused by Yagüe in the following terms: 'Of course we shot them … what do you expect? Was I supposed to take 4,000 reds with me as my column advanced, racing against time? Was I expected to turn them loose in my rear and let them make Badajoz red again?' Badajoz became a tool of Republican propaganda as a symbol of Nationalist barbarism. The German contingent soon learned to treat Yagüe with kid gloves and not to be too offended by his, often intemperate, comments such as when he referred to the Germans and Italians as 'Beasts of Prey'.[10]

Bombing of Civilians at Tetuán and Zaragoza

Kindelán began issuing directives to his air force which essentially hardly existed at all as a force given the antiquity and paucity of its machines but, nothing daunted, he described the ways in which the various types of aircraft should be used. In anticipation of receiving the Savoia-Marchetti SM.81s promised by Italy, he applied his mind to the concept of strategic bombing and ordered that these tri-motor bombers should be employed to strike at bridges, fortifications, airfields and rail junctions as well as munitions factories deep behind enemy lines where they should be escorted and protected by fighter aircraft.[11] Aerial bombardment of civilian areas was a feature of the war right from the start. Which side started it, however, is a matter of dispute. Each accused the other, and apparently with some justification. As early as the first week of the struggle, Franco was quoted as having accused the Madrid government of 'sending its planes to bombard cities and towns without defence, killing women and children'.[12] This referred to the reported bombing of the Spanish military stronghold of Tetuán in Morocco on 20 July 1936 which claimed twenty victims, three of them children.

An alleged attack upon the Moroccan port of Ceuta in late July is often cited as equally conclusive evidence of the Republican's culpability in this context. Another incident often alluded to as evidence that the Republicans were first to use aerial bombardment as an offensive weapon was the accusation that Catalonian aircraft raided Huesca and Zaragoza on 21 July, but since Huesca was an important outpost protecting the vital rail and distribution centre of Zaragoza, these raids may have had legitimate military objectives.

A British correspondent, H.G. Cardozo, was in the town of Soria, north of the Guadarama mountains outside Madrid, which he claims was hit by an air attack in July. He reported that aircraft dropped 'small and clumsy' bombs which killed a score of individuals in the village.[13] Such actions were not without wider consequences. The first evidence of the reaction of civilian populations to aerial bombardment of predominately non-military areas is from a Scottish zoologist living in Málaga at the time, Sir Peter Chalmers Mitchell, who reported in his book *My House in Málaga* that Franco's aircraft bombed a working-class section of Málaga, killing 40 and wounding 150, mostly women and children. So great was the anger of the town's populace that a mob marched to a local prison, took out forty-five inmates who had been incarcerated as Nationalist sympathisers, and shot them as a reprisal.[14] The reaction of civilian populations to aerial bombardment had been a subject of much debate ever since the Italian military theorist, Guilio Douhet had expounded his ideas of 'total war' in his seminal book *The Command of the Air* in 1922. He had concluded that the massive indiscriminate bombing of cities would quickly erode morale and cause the population to rise up in revolt and demand that their government capitulate to the aggressor. Spain was now the laboratory in which experiments to test that theory would be carried out. It can be shown that the results would initially vindicate Douhet, but over the course of the war would change and begin to cast doubts on his conclusions. Initial reactions were mixed and graphically described in the English Aviation periodical *Flight* on 20 August 1936 when reporting on the bombing of Zaragoza in July:

> so far from intimidating the people of the town, the raiders have proved to be excellent recruiting sergeants. The townsmen have been infuriated and have hastened to enlist. That may be because the damage done by bombs has been small. It may be that, if a city were subjected to a systematic bombing by a large force of regulars, the people would clamour for surrender. If so, it would be the first time in history that a virile nation had been beaten by frightfulness.[15]

Republicans without a sizable and loyal army and navy could only hope to retake ground lost to the rebels by ground and sea action by disrupting their transportation and communications to prevent Franco concentrating his widely separated armies and it was accepted that the most effective way to do this was by aerial action. At this stage, Franco seemed less willing to use air power to attack the government strongholds of Valencia, Barcelona, and the Basque provinces in the north, but that may well have been because he did not have the aviation resources to do it. He may also have judged that he would not win the popular support of government-controlled regions by devastating their infrastructure. It was the government that elected to take the risk of being the first to resort to aerial bombardment of centres where civilians might suffer from the results. It was soon clear, however, that bombing of civilian areas would become an actual, if not admitted, part of the strategy of each side and a pattern was set.

Rebel aircraft would appear over the north Spanish resort and summer capital city of San Sebastian several times in August and on the 13th, 'five new Italian planes bombed the town'. There is no record of casualties or other effects, but the commanding officer of the local garrison 'threatened to shoot five prisoners for every person killed by bombardment from air or sea. Everybody laughed at this war of counter-threat; all except the prisoners.'[16]

Franco Marches on Madrid

The Germans were finding that the Spanish climate was somewhat different to the one back home. On the afternoon of 25 August the German fighters under the nominal command of Oberleutnant Kraft Eberhardt, made their first operational flight in support of the drive on Madrid. Trautloft was feeling the heat as he 'sat in [his] aircraft in shorts and a T-shirt – [his] tennis clothes!' but was still able to claim the first aerial victory by a German pilot in Spain when he sent a Breguet spiralling 'towards the earth in a steep, uncontrolled dive [smashing] into the ground north of the village of Comenar'. On the following day flying over Madrid, Eberhardt and Knüppel each claimed a Breguet XIX. Knüppel then came up against 'a French parasol monoplane ... sitting on my tail. Just as I was about to turn onto him, he shot upwards. I was unfortunately unable to catch him, as his aircraft climbed better and was faster.' Trautloft had also quickly understood that they were in for a fight when 'it was clear that our aircraft were not superior enough for us to feel completely safe from the enemy'.[17] Italian SM.81s, meanwhile kept up a constant aerial bombardment on Málaga and Toledo where ammunition factories were the target.

There were indications that air power was going to play a significant role in the war when Republican forces invaded the Balearic islands of Mallorca and Ibiza. After a largely unopposed landing at Porto Crispo, the invading troops saw little need for urgency and were caught in the open without air cover when Italian fighters and three bombers launched a concentrated bombing and strafing attack against them. Nationalist aircraft were unable to break through the Italian fighter shield and the 8,000 Republican troops were subjected to incessant air attack over two days before being thrown back onto the mainland in disarray. At Irún, the *Times* reporter George Steer witnessed Nationalist bombers striking the undefended town as the occupants fled, but defending Anarchists set off demolition changes which destroyed the town centre. This gave the Nationalists a narrative that they could resort to later when towns were bombed blaming the devastation on the destructive actions of the Leftist and Anarchists.[18]

Bombing of Madrid

As Franco's troops closed on Madrid, the city took the threat of night bombing seriously as the Ministry of War ordered a nightly blackout after eleven o'clock, as well as a prohibition against any but essential street traffic after that hour, but the stations of the municipal subway system were to remain open as refuges for the city's population in the event of air raids. Private homes could still be lighted, but windows were to be covered to prevent the lights from showing in the streets, and all public gatherings as well as visiting in private homes and apartments was to cease after eleven in the evening. Reports of a large number of bombers arriving from France and being assembled at Getafe and Cuatro Vientos brought calls for SM.81s and a number of Ju 52s now released from transport duties to bomb the airfields but von Scheele was not keen to see his operational theatre expanded so far north without official permission from Berlin.

As the war progressed and more areas were lost to the Nationalists, aerial bombardment became more concentrated and practically one-sided. Republican aircraft appeared with less frequency over the rebel-held towns and rarely dropped bombs on civilians. The German and Italian fliers operating on behalf of Franco, however, intensified their efforts and the world came to take for granted that any report of an air raid upon a Spanish city was a rebel attack by German or Italian pilots on a Republican city such as Madrid, Barcelona, Valencia, Bilbao, or some other town which found itself the target of Franco's bombers on one day and part of a headline the next.

In what was to become a recurring and horrifying consequence of aerial bombardment, on 22 August an air raid causing severe damage in the Argüelles district of Madrid provoked mob violence when armed militiamen surrounded the local prison and demanded that right-wing prisoners be handed over to them. Ignoring pleas from the Minister of the Interior, General Pozas, they stormed the prison in a mood of 'murderous fury' and took thirty prisoners into the cellars where summary 'trials' were held before all were shot. This murder of prisoners was far from unique as both sides committed a sickeningly virulent and widespread campaign of extra-judicial killings, but aerial bombardment would now act as a catalyst to inflame the pent-up anger of civilian populations under attack. The Republican government was appalled by the atrocity and tried to temper the 'revolutionary excesses', which it managed to do to some extent but only slowly.[19]

The Spanish Civil War proved to be a breeding ground for mass atrocities, carried out by belligerents eager to eradicate their ideological opponents. Long before the Moroccan uprising of 17 July 1936 kick-started the Spanish Civil War, political-inspired murder and ex-judicial executions were horrifically common throughout the country and these proliferated thereafter on what Martin Baumeister called 'the home front as a war zone'.

The War itself was characterised by massive political violence, carried out by both sides on the battlefield and on city streets. The Nationalists included the right-wing monarchist Carlists, Falangist fascists and traditional conservatives who were fiercely anti-Bolshevik. Nationalist Moroccan troops, who had little emotional connection with the occupants of the Spanish mainland and who were instrumental in preventing an early government victory, together with units of the Spanish Foreign Legion whose reputation for extreme violence and lack of restraint was legendary, operated almost without restraint by observing none of the terms of the 1929 Geneva Convention on the treatment of prisoners of war.

On the third day of the revolt, General Franco had threatened that unless the Madrid government capitulated he would bomb the headquarters of the Republican politicians in the capital. His bluff was called as the government held firm, forcing Franco to deny his threat and tell a correspondent of the *Petit Parisien* on 16 August, 'I shall never bomb Madrid – there are innocent people living there whom I have no wish to expose to danger.'[20] It was only a few days later, however, that the emptiness of that promise was exposed. Over a period of three days on the 27th, 28th, and 29th, bombs were dropped on the city but little damage resulted, except in the last of these raids when seventeen people were wounded. The first German airman to strike at the capital was Oberleutnant Rudolf Freiherr von Moreau, who bombed the Republican Air Ministry with a Ju 52 on 28 August.[21] According to one account the 'air bombing … was carefully worked out with a view to frightening the Cabinet into surrender if possible without inflaming the people of Madrid'.[22] A correspondent, H.E. Knoblaugh, asserted that

> Franco notified the Loyalists that he would respect a zone 'which he outlined, roughly a mile square, and asked that all women and children be sent to that part of the capital'. The government's reply, according to Knoblaugh, refused to recognise such a zone 'but almost immediately it transferred most of its barracks and munitions to points within it'. Franco did not attack this zone until later.[23]

The intensification of bombing of the capital brought the population to a state of 'popular fury' whipped up by rumours of a 'fifth column' of traitors working within the city and resulted in very many executions of suspected Nationalist spies and sympathisers.

Non-intervention Agreement

When twelve Savoia-Marchetti SM.81 bombers, one of which had Bolin on board, had flown from Elmas aerodrome and landed at Tetuán, the world had been witness. Unlike the Germans and the Soviets to come, the Italians had not shrouded their support for Franco in secrecy. The front-page news of their arrival in Morocco prompted feverish diplomatic exchanges in European capitals. In Paris, Prime Minster Blum, who had wanted to help and had seen no problem with sending military aid to a legitimate friendly government, had looked to London for support but was met with a cool rebuff. The British government's wish, as explained to the Italian embassy, was 'to see the rebellion triumph', while simultaneously preserving the veneer of British neutrality.[24]

While parading their neutral credentials to the world, however, the British interpretation of neutrality included stationing the battlecruiser HMS *Queen Elizabeth* in Algeciras Bay to ward off attacks on the port by the Republican battleship *Jaime I*, and days later allowing a convoy of small Nationalist vessels to enter the port and discharge troops and guns. Furthermore, the British secure communications network centred on Gibraltar was made available to Kindelán for the purpose of coordinating Nationalist air operations in the early days, which would have been so much harder had he been obliged to rely on the antiquated and malfunctioning Spanish network. Spanish government requests to Britain for munitions was officially 'treated in exactly the same way as a similar request from any other friendly government', but in reality the Foreign Office was instructed that 'all plausible means be found to delay or refuse export permits'.[25] The Republicans, however, in the form of 'little men in black suits with bags of gold', were allowed to buy twelve 'unsaleable second-hand aircraft [that] were being hurriedly furbished up' at Croydon and Heston and flown to Spain; a deal that apparently fell outside the arms export regulations. Furbished up in this context was something of a misnomer since prior to shipment many engines were replaced by 'nearly worn-out' ones, and the deal was concluded at 'more than twice the market value'.[26] Any Spanish pilot flying these aircraft over the high Sierras was unlikely ever to return.

The British denied pressuring the French, but Winston Churchill, albeit not in government at the time, had privately warned that French intervention in Spain on the side of the Republicans would push Britain to support the Nationalists. Blum, already weak and fearful of being isolated diplomatically, opted instead to hide the little aid he did send and publicly follow Britain's lead by calling for all countries to stay out of the conflict and abandon whatever plans they had in place to supply arms and war matériel. The two countries in Blum's sights were, of course, Germany and Italy, both of whom appeared to pay diplomatic attention to the request but ignored it in practice.

The French Foreign Minister, Yvon Delbos, made 'an appeal to the wisdom of the European nations, which would lead to the adoption of common rules of non-intervention'. This resulted in the spectacle of Delbos, on behalf of the non-interventionists in the French government, engaged in a frantic round of diplomatic negotiations to secure the acceptance of a non-intervention agreement by the principal European Powers, while Blum, Cot, and Daladier, on behalf of the interventionists, did all they could to help the Spanish government before any such agreement could be reached.[27]

On 3 August, the French Ambassador in Rome met Italian Foreign Minister Ciano and suggested that, to begin with, any non-intervention agreement should be restricted to Britain, France, and Italy. Ciano would only 'take note' of the suggestion. On the following day, the French Ambassador in Berlin met the German Foreign Minister, Baron Konstantin von Neurath, and asked him whether Germany was prepared to take part in a joint declaration of non-intervention in Spain. His reply, clearly showing that the Germans were willing to reduce the policy of non-intervention to the level of farce, was that the German government had no need to do any such thing since it did not intervene in Spanish internal political affairs and disputes. It was, however, willing to discuss preventing the intervention by foreign powers as long as all the interested countries, particularly the Soviet Union, signed up to such an agreement. On 5 August, the French chargé d'affaires in Moscow met the Soviet Commissar for Foreign Affairs, Maxim Litvinov and was told that the Soviet Union subscribed to the principles of the agreement but insisted that Portugal should be included. The French had originally proposed Britain, France, and Italy. Britain had asked for Germany to be added, Germany for the Soviet Union, and the Soviet Union for Portugal. All the countries eventually agreed to sign up to a joint declaration of non-intervention but the exercise was deeply flawed since the agreement had no force in law and almost all countries considered themselves justified in circumventing the restrictions on the grounds that all the others were doing the same thing.

In late August, an international agreement of 'non-intervention' was drawn up and subscribed to by twenty-seven nations, including France, Great Britain, Germany, Italy and the Soviet Union. Signatories were prevented from supporting either side in the Spanish conflict through the provision of military equipment. The draft declaration contained three points. The first involved a ban on all exports of war matériel to Spain and her overseas possessions. The second extended this ban to orders that had already been placed, and the third pledged the signatory Powers to keep each other informed of the measures they were taking to implement the declaration. The Italians had 'most considerable reservations', while the Germans stressed the difficulties of enforcement and claimed that, in any event, the Soviets could not be trusted to adhere to it. The Germans and French acrimoniously accused each other of sending arms to Spain. It was agreed to set up a Non-Intervention Committee which met for the first time on 9 September 1936. In November, plans were adopted to post observers to Spanish frontiers and ports to prevent breaches of the agreement although it was already clear that the whole thing was a façade behind which countries continued to breach its terms.

By the end of August, the Spanish government had lost a large quantity of their weapons and munitions captured by Yagüe's men as they marched towards Madrid. Their French aircraft were still without armaments and governments across the world were publicly refusing to sell them any weapons, forcing them to delve inexpertly into the dangerous and murky world of the illegal arms trade. Their naivety had been immediately apparent when Colonel Luis Riaño flew to Germany, of all places, for a meeting with Admiral Wilhelm Canaris, head of German Intelligence to negotiate the purchase of aircraft from Junkers and Heinkel, who had been trying to sell aircraft to Spain earlier in the year. The Germans prevaricated and held Riaño more or less in custody for two weeks before telling him that 'with regret' they could not oblige since they were about to sign the Non-Intervention agreement.

Meanwhile the Spanish embassy in Paris, where Spanish representatives, who knew little about finance or armaments, had let it be known that they were out to do business, became a magnet for arms dealers who were 'of the most diverse nationalities and types [who] came and went at all hours of the day and far into the night, offering every class of weapon, ammunition and aeroplane'.[28]

The kind of fiasco that this promoted was exemplified by the purchase of three Fokker F.BIIb aircraft from the Belgian airline Sabena for three times the amount being paid for similar aircraft by the Nationalists. When export licences were withheld, the Spanish buyers asked for the refund of the purchase price which had been paid up front, only to be told that it was being retained pending resolution of a legal dispute over ownership. Before the Belgian courts got round to deciding the case, the hanger housing the aircraft was bombed by the Luftwaffe on 10 May 1940.

The Union Founders' Trust in the City of London, described by Special Branch as 'an ordinary commercial organisation trying to make all the money it can out of gun-running', bought twenty-nine aircraft which had the potential to be converted to operate as bombers, 'provided there were no enemy fighters in the region', with the intention of selling them to a French intermediary before flying them to Barcelona.[29] The British government publicly took a dim view since it was officially 'continuing to give full support to the French government to secure an international agreement on non-intervention in Spain', and announced a ban on exports to Spain which included civil aircraft. Only fourteen of the twenty-nine ever reached Barcelona, but that was sufficient for Union Founders Trust to turn a handsome profit.

By the beginning of October 1936, the Republican government's lamentable efforts to purchase aircraft had resulted in the acquisition, at hugely inflated prices, of sixty aircraft – only about twenty-five of which played any part in the war. When they complained to the French about the lack of armaments and spare parts they were eventually told that the private companies who manufactured them were prohibited from making any further shipments which would be against the terms of the Non-Intervention agreement.

Hitler Names His Price for Helping Franco

Hitler realised on 24 August that Franco was going to need rather more help than had already been supplied. He was fully aware that Mussolini had enthusiastically provided similar help and furthermore, was arranging for substantial numbers of ground forces to go to Spain. It was clear that any increase in the amount of German military aid could not be an extended favour and would have to be paid for. While Hitler's initial decision to help Franco was probably not motivated by economic considerations, it is clear that once the aid started to flow and increase, some in Hjalmar Schacht's German Economic Ministry were quick to make the connection between military aid and the huge quantities of mineral ores being imported into Germany from Spanish mines. Even before the military coup in 1935, Germany had brought in a little over 1 million tons of iron ore each year from the Basque provinces and Morocco. This, along with other ores such as pyrites, was urgently needed by Germany to increase its industrial output, especially in armaments, as laid out in the Four-Year Plan over which Göring exercised executive control. The Nationalists did not have access to Spain's gold reserves, nor did they have much foreign currency, so the prospect of an 'ores-for-arms' deal building on, and extending, existing trading arrangements was indeed propitious. This made good economic sense for Germany also as it, too, was short of foreign currencies to purchase raw materials. It was not lost on the Germans either that such a deal could form the basis of a longer-lasting arrangement that would be of immense benefit to them in the event of a major European war breaking out. HISMA would have a monopoly of all ores coming out of Spain and would act as the purchasing agent. The product would then be shipped and distributed to the appropriate industries in Germany by its sister company ROWAK (Rohstoffe-und-Waren-Einkaufsgessellschaft). Although both HISMA and ROWAK were nominally private companies, they were wholly financed by Nationalist Spain and Germany.[30]

The deal struck between Franco and HISMA very soon sent ripples of concern through British companies that had significant investment in the Spanish mines. The all-British Rio Tinto and Tharsis Companies accounted for three quarters of all ores output in 1935 and the British had a controlling interest in the Onconera Company also. The majority of all mines were in Republican government hands in 1936 up until late August when the Nationalists had taken possession of the Andalusian mining facilities and it was then that alarm bells starting ringing in London. Urgent meetings were held but it was agreed that after an initial shock, 'relations with the Seville authorities [Nationalists] were much improved'. This harmony did not last beyond September, however, when HISMA tried to secure first claim on all pyrites production and started manipulating the price. Very soon, the British companies began fearing that their very presence in Spain was under threat and began to obstruct the ore trade with Germany hoping that they could force a softening of terms and look forward to reinstated trading conditions when the war was over. Rio Tinto made urgent appeals to the British Foreign Office and the Board of Trade. British government ministers concluded, after hearing Rio Tinto's arguments, that Hitler was likely to support Franco militarily 'up to the hilt'.[31] When representation was made to Berlin that HISMA was 'using every means to exploit and consolidate their present situation in a manner most detrimental to Great Britain', they were told that it was a private company and no concern of the German government.[32]

The British government then turned to Franco for a hearing but could not proceed without diplomatic representation. This resulted in the exchange of 'agents' with a de facto recognition of Franco as the Spanish head of state. Göring feared that German interests might well be harmed by this and quickly appointed Bernhardt as a special representative for economic affairs in Spain to counteract the British move.

A new trade agreement between Franco and Germany would come into effect on 1 August 1937 as a result of a series of protocols signed at Burgos between 12 and 16 July, which declared that both countries would expand their mutual trade and Nationalist Spain's debt to Germany would be met by the periodic deliveries of raw materials with the result that soon half the ships in Bilbao harbour flew the German flag.

The Italians were more lenient with their demands and were happy to extend long lines of credit to Franco with no immediate pressure to repay the debt.[33] The Germans were much more successful at getting paid for their help than were the Italians. The lure of mineral ore mines in the north of Spain was no doubt an important consideration when Sperrle persuaded Franco to turn away from Madrid and concentrate on subduing the Vizcaya region in north-east Spain. The copper, iron and sulphur deposits at Minas de Almaden on the northern slopes of the Sierra Morena and the Minas del Riff in Melill were a magnet for Göring and the reason for the MONTANA project which had the ultimate goal of turning Spain into an economic colony of Germany and a source of raw materials for German industry. With precious little respect for the norms of economic practice, Rio Tinto would be deprived of any say in where the minerals from its mines were distributed.

Until such times as the mines were in Nationalist hands, any aid sent to Franco, who had no gold reserves and very little hard currency and was labouring 'under a staggering financial and economic hardships', would have to be on the basis of a 'gift'.[34] Things improved somewhat in 1937 when Franco's Junta Tecnica was established to lay down economic doctrine, the procurement of credits abroad, and the efficient revision of the tax-collection system.

The Italian counterpart of HISMA was SOFINDUS (Sociedad Financiera Industrial Ltda), which was handling trade with Italy in return for Italian military assistance. On 28 November 1936, Italy and Nationalist Spain had signed a deal that would become a template for the German agreement. While Britain retained control of sherry exports, Germany would get cotton, hides, skins, and grain. Italy got some ore and also mercury, and she took olives and olive oil for re-export to South America.

Italy had, from the start, harboured ambitions that were not conducive to seamless cooperation with either Spain or Germany. There was not, and never had been, an overall strategy for the conduct of Nationalist operations and there was no integrated chain of command set up between the three countries. Italy had joined the coalition in response to Franco's request but had gone way beyond anything he had asked for. The speed of response and the volume of aid may well have been a boost for Nationalist fortunes but the vastness of the Italian resources put at Franco's disposal meant that he could formulate no clear idea of what to do with them. Left without clear guidance from Franco, the Italian contingent chose to act in a rather independent fashion right from the start, as shown by its attack on Málaga which had no relevance at all in the context of Franco's overall strategy. While the Italian Expeditionary Force, the Corpo Trupo Volontarie (CTV) tended to pursue an agenda apparently dictated from Rome, the Condor Legion was much more attuned to Franco's strategy, although far from impressed by it.

Chapter 4

The Condor Legion

- Warlimont Arrives in Spain
- Bombing of Ibiza and Bilbao
- Vizcaya and the Fall of San Sebastian
- Warlimont Calls for More Aid
- The First Soviet Aircraft Arrive
- The Luftwaffe in Action
- The Formation of the Condor Legion

Warlimont Arrives in Spain

A second loading of the SS *Usaramo* in Hamburg, including twenty He 46C-1 tactical monoplane aircraft for Franco, and a separate agreement with General Mola to provide guns and ammunition indicated that the German mission was rapidly growing well beyond the limits originally imposed at Beyreuth. This, together with the involvement of German personnel in combat missions which would be officially authorised by Hitler on 28 August, prompted von Blomberg to review the whole structure of Operation Magic Fire. As a backdrop to all this, he was acutely aware of substantial numbers of aircraft with crews coming across the border from France to Irún and Puigcerda for the government forces, who were also operating in French territory as they manoeuvred for position in Catalonia. Clearly there was a requirement for centralised control, both of procurement and deployment. German interests were becoming significantly more involved with those of both Spain and Italy, and the risk of military or political blunder was increasing in a theatre of operations far from his immediate control. To meet this threat, he sent a General Staff officer with expertise in economics General Walter Warlimont, codenamed 'Guido', to take over from von Scheele, whose mission was rapidly expanding and transforming beyond his area of competence, and assume both diplomatic and military responsibilities.

Prior to his appointment Warlimont had no knowledge, beyond rumour, of the Spanish adventure so von Blomberg sent him, along with Canaris, to Rome to meet General Mario Roatta, Canaris's Italian counterpart, who would represent Italian interests in Spain. Warlimont's orders, under the Führer's signature, were to 'examine all possibilities and proposals for supporting the Nationalists of Spain by the German Armed Forces ... advise the Spanish Nationalist High Command ... and cooperate with the Italian forces in Spain'.[1] In Rome, it was agreed that all supplies should go to Franco's forces only, and that deployment of same would be supervised jointly by the Italian and German military who would work within a 'common plan'. It was clear that Franco was now the leading Spanish General but when Warlimont presented his credentials to the Generalissimo at his Cáceres headquarters on 5 September, it was apparent from his reception that his arrival and mission were both unheralded and unwelcome. Franco, however, was in no position to oppose the appointment given his, still urgent, need for increased German and Italian aid, but he privately bridled at the thought of foreign 'meddling' in his management of the war.

Warlimont, like all the German commanders in Spain, made every effort to form a strong working partnership with the Spanish Nationalist leadership. At no point did they carry out operations without full consultation, unlike the Italians who had entered the war for their own strategic benefit and conducted operations in ways that suited their agenda. For instance, without proper consultation, they put a lot of effort into bombing Spanish ports on the Mediterranean coastline from bases in Italy and the Balearics with a view to eventually establishing a zone of influence in southern Spain and Gibraltar. Franco, no doubt, understood this and had the difficult job of making the best use of Italian resources without allowing Mussolini to gain any geographic advantage at Spain's expense. Warlimont and his successors, while admiring Italy for its fascist politics, privately despaired of its machinations and tended to work with them in ways that did not impact on their own efficiency, which usually meant working with them in a cooperative but distant fashion.

A briefing quickly indicated to Warlimont that the Republicans were numerically and technically superior to Franco's forces, prompting him to petition Berlin for further supplies of tanks and armoured vehicles. Franco was delighted when Berlin agreed without demur but his mood was seriously darkened when he was advised that heavy Soviet tanks, much more powerful than the German Panzer Mark Is, were being unloaded in Cartagena for government use. When his appeal to Germany for something better than the machine-gun-armed Mark I was met with news that they had 'nothing like [the Soviet heavy tanks]', Franco was both disappointed and embarrassed that he had asked in the first place and never made a personal request of Warlimont for anything ever again.[2]

Bombing of Ibiza and Bilbao

The Italian Aviazione Legionaria was quickly mobilised into action, but often paying scant attention to Franco's overall strategy. In early September the island of Ibiza, largest of the southern Balearic island group, came under attack by Italian aircraft. On Sunday 13 September bombs were dropped from four raiders on a waterfront crowd at Ibiza, killing twenty-four women and young children, as well as thirteen older males. Inflamed by this attack, local Republican sympathisers machine-gunned or bayoneted all of the Franco supporters who had been made prisoners since the outbreak of the revolt in July. This reaction is cited because it repeats the experience reported from Málaga earlier in the conflict and illustrates a tendency which later became widespread in Loyalist Spain. As one writer puts it, 'Spanish governments, from the Napoleonic wars onwards, have often found it impossible to protect prisoners from the violence of a mob.'[3]

The most ferocious acts of mob violence, however, followed Nationalist air raids over Bilbao towards the end of September. Four bombing raids by German aircraft during the daytime and night of 25 September and the morning of the 26th on this important northern Spanish industrial and shipping city were described by a British journalist as a 'sheer, unmixed assault upon the civilian population, who ran in terror through the streets'. Many of the refugees who had fled to Bilbao from the coastal points further east, Irún, San Sebastian, and small villages, became so enraged by these bombings that they followed the leadership of members of the left-wing CMT (Confederaclon Nacional de Trabajadores) labour organisation and rushed to the docks where 'they massacred sixty-eight of the prisoners in the prison ships … and thought they had been merciful, for their own dead lay in hundreds'.[4] Another account in *Time Magazine* of 5 October 1936 says that the work of slaughtering the prisoners was carried-out by 'Anarchist Militiawomen'… 'Flying at these unarmed prisoners with knives, bayonets, and guns … some thirty of whom were priests, mutilating and gashing until finally stopped by the intervention of Spanish Civil Guards.'

Vizcaya and the Fall of San Sebastian

On 5 September the Basque town of Irún, through which French aid had been passing to the Republican side, was taken by the Nationalists thus closing the border with France. Large areas of the town were set on fire as Republican troops retreated in an act usually attributed to supporters of the Anarchist CNT-FAI. Nationalists would later use the example of Irún as supporting evidence when they argued that the destruction of towns such as Guernica was caused by Republican arson rather than Nationalist bombing. By the 13th San Sebastián had fallen to the Nationalists also. The Basque Republicans, who declared the formation of an autonomous Basque Country under José Antonio Aguirre on 7 October, were now cut off from the rest of Spain and could only get military aid and reinforcements by running a Nationalist naval blockade.

On 28 September, the members of the National Defence Junta convened at Salamanca and appointed Franco as Generalissimo of the Armies and Leader of the Government of the Spanish State. He assumed his new powers at Burgos on 1 October. Mola was confirmed as leader of the army in the North and Queipo de Llano leader in the South. Kindelán was elected to the Junta.

Warlimont Calls for More Aid

After Toledo had fallen to the Nationalists, Warlimont chose to rest his airmen for a few weeks to prevent them being drawn into the war too quickly and, what he feared most, having them caught up in an escalating situation over which he had only partial control. His answer was to expand the German forces to the point where they were sufficiently large to be deployed as a separate unit under Franco's ultimate command, but operationally under German control. He could see Soviet personnel coming in through Cartagena and, anticipating that much heavy Soviet aid would also come through there, was anxious to get more bombers to cut off that supply route. To press his case, Warlimont flew to Berlin. His entreaties were not well received by Göring, however, who was still not reconciled to the adventure, but Hitler had good economic and military reasons to agree.

Sonderstab W was instructed to send millions of rounds of ammunition, 2,000 hand grenades, eighty-six tons of bombs, signals equipment and field wire and forty-five trucks, together with another thirty-six He 51s. Twenty-four for the Nationalist air force and twelve as reinforcements for Eberhardt, plus three more Ju 52 bombers, a twin-engine He 59 float-equipped biplane, a single-engine He 60 floatplane for maritime patrol operations, a Heinkel He 50 bomber/reconnaissance aircraft and a pair of Henschel Hs 123s. These latter aircraft, being sent with pilots and specialist maintenance crews, were experimental types sent for testing in field conditions. Crucially, also creeping into the German plans was the decision to send three prototypes of the new Messerschmitt Bf 109, essentially for testing and evaluation also. This meant that by the end of September a total of twenty Ju 52 transport/bombers, twenty-four He 51 fighters and twenty-nine He 46 reconnaissance aircraft had been sent to Spain.[5] Hans Frank, the German Minister of Justice, however, reassured Mussolini personally that Germany was giving aid to Franco 'solely because of solidarity in the field of political ideas' and that it had 'neither interests nor aims in the Mediterranean'. According to Frank, Hitler was anxious that Mussolini should know that he regarded the Mediterranean as 'a purely Italian sea'.[6] Foreign Minister von Neurath noted, in early December 1936: 'we recognise that Italian interests in Spain go further than ours, if only for geographic reasons.' When Hitler saw the Italian Foreign Minister at Berchtesgaden on 24 October, he told him that in Spain, 'Italians and Germans have together dug the first trench against Bolshevism.'

Three of the twenty Ju 52s in the original aid package were released from transport duties to form a separate bomber unit, 'Flight Pablo', and began tactical operations against Republican ground forces on an almost continuous basis over a wide area. A few He 51s were also active as protection for the bombers but were soon made aware of the grave disparity between their aircraft and the Republican Dewoitine D.372 which outflew and outfought them at every turn. This, and the fact that now the German crews were in action they were in great demand, forced Warlimont to stand 'Flight Pablo' down, ostensibly for crew recuperation and maintenance of the aircraft, but in reality, to wrest back control of their operations from the Spanish generals.

Meanwhile the charade of non-intervention was slowly being exposed. Between 26 August and 5 October, a total of eleven German merchant ships from Stettin and Hamburg were loaded with equipment, ammunition and men and sailed to unload at the river port of Seville on the Guadalquivir. Soviet radio announced to the world what the Germans were doing and gave details of the cargoes and their likely destination. For their part, German intelligence was fully aware that a trainload of Soviet 'farm equipment' had left Marseilles on 25 August and found its way to Spanish government headquarters.

By the end of October the Germans had a bomber force of twenty-four Ju 52s and two He 70s, a fighter force of thirty He 51s and an experimental squadron in Spain. As Warlimont had feared, Soviet war matèriel continued to pour in on the SS *Campeche* which unloaded at Cartagena on 4 October. The ship also carried thirty-three Soviet airmen and on 10 September, they went into action for the first time flying combat missions in Potez 540s with mixed Soviet-Spanish crews. Ten days later, the Soviet freighter SS *Stariy Bolshevik* brought ten Katiuskas complete with spare parts, fuel and ammunition to Cartagena, having sailed from Feodosia in the Ukraine and the SS *Komsomol* brought fifty Soviet tanks and 150 Soviet air force personnel. Ten more Katiuskas arrived in Cartagena on the SS *KIM* on the 19th and another ten on the SS *Volgoleson* on the 21st. Each machine was packed into two crates, one of which contained the fuselage and engines and the other the wings and tail section. Republican pilots had received no instruction in the new Soviet aircraft so, given the Nationalist dominance of the air over Madrid, it had been clear that Soviet pilots would be required to fly them. The first few pilots had arrived in September but more arrived on this day with many more to follow during the next few weeks. Many were given a 'nom de guerre' in a vain bid to disguise their origins. Among the first to arrive were Ivan Kopets (José), Petr Pumpur (Julio) and Pavel Agafonov (Pedro). The first twenty-five Polikarpov I-15 Chatos arrived on board the SS *Lepin* from Sevastopol on the 28th.[7] The Soviet Chato aircraft bore an uncanny similarity to the American F11 Goshawk fighter and was often referred to by the Spanish as a 'Curtiss'. It had a top speed of 360km/h and carried 4 × 7.62mm machine guns as well as a 100kg bomb-load. The Katiuska was a modern high-speed bomber with an amazing top speed of 450km/h and a range of 2.300km.

The Soviet military technician Petrov wrote the following description of the docking, unloading, and assembly:

> We assembled the airplanes in daytime, as air strikes by Junkers interfered with work at night. The San Javier airfield is situated on the shore of the bay and has only four buildings, which provided good landmarks for the enemy during bombing. ...
>
> While the freighter was being unloaded I did not sleep for six nights in a row. The unloaded cargo was often left as it was, as the drivers would disappear elsewhere. On almost all Katiuskas the upper and the front stabiliser braces broke off in flight. Brackets and bafflers had to be tied down by wire. The celluloid on the navigator's canopy cracked due to the strong air stream. This also happened when enemy bombs or anti-aircraft shells exploded near the airplane.
>
> The engines are a bigger problem. They often failed. We had to replace six out of nine recently installed engines right off. I know that the factory is trying to improve the junction between the cylinder jacket and the engine block, but this joint continues to crack. The engine clatters very much. On one occasion the engine started to clatter severely. We thought that the reduction gear cogs had been displaced. I opened the cover, removed the reduction gear but did not find anything wrong, while the engine still roared even at low rpms and caused lots of shaking. On another occasion all the brackets and rods of the mixture control unit broke. One of the engines began leaking water through the junction between the cylinder jacket and the engine block, and the M-100 cylinders also leak. The magneto coupling often breaks and the ignition is often inoperable. We had to send three of our engines to the Hispano factory in Barcelona as they had a metallic-sounding clatter, the cause of which could not be detected in the field.

Oddly he concluded by saying that,

> On the whole the SB is a good aircraft and it will justify itself
> if it is used to do what it has been designed for.[8]

By now the whole rationale for German involvement had changed. Warlimont's reports and calls for more aid had resulted in a substantial increase over and above anything that he had asked for. Crucially, the inclusion of experimental He 50s, Hs123s and Bf 109s that were loaded onto the SS *Wigbert* on 8 September was a clear indication of the way German involvement in Spain was now being viewed. No longer was it a case of just sending a few items of hardware to help out a potential ally in return for shiploads of copper ore. The whole enterprise was taking on a new, more expansive, character. Soviet interference was altering the balance of power and threatening a prolonged campaign meaning that Germany was likely to be in Spain for longer than anticipated and needed to make the necessary adjustments to its plans.

Warlimont now saw the whole Spanish venture swirling out of his control. In a very short time his mission had changed beyond all recognition and the build-up of Soviet arms was elevating the war into a situation for which he was not trained or equipped to cope. He flew to Germany with Bernhardt for a meeting with Göring to whom he explained his misgivings about the direction of the war. The nature of the fighting was not something that Warlimont had anticipated and was not the one which Berlin had signed him up for. The fighting men were, especially on the Republican side, 'irregular' troops conducting what was essentially a guerrilla war, but their dominance both in the air and on the ground was worrying. Even Franco's forces, operating in small poorly coordinated units could hardly be called a modern army and it was Warlimont's view that Franco lacked the decisiveness and confidence to be an effective leader and he believed that the Spanish leader was privately reconciled to conducting a long campaign. When discussing the matter of military aid to Spain, Warlimont was clear in his advice that on no account should German ground forces become involved. Berlin, however, was gravitating towards the view that only increased German assistance could prevent total failure of the rebellion and with it not only a humiliating exit for their forces already there, but also a stunning propaganda victory for the Soviet Union. It was not lost on Berlin either that an increase in Italian aid to Franco might, in the absence of a similar German contribution, result in Italian influence in the Mediterranean becoming too dominant. As a further, though less important, consideration Berlin had decided to exploit the war for a wider purpose, namely to assess its new generation of military hardware, especially the aircraft, in real combat conditions. To evaluate their performance, they were incorporated into a new experimental squadron (Versuchskommando). Whatever the rationale for increased German aid, it was clear that Warlimont was not the man to run it and furthermore the whole mission would require a new, more comprehensive command structure to manage what was becoming a very complex military, economic and political operation.

With Spain swarming with observers and journalists, it was no secret that some quantity of German and Italian matériel, along with increased numbers of personnel, were present in Spain. The Non-Intervention Committee was embarrassed but reluctant to openly challenge these blatant breaches of the agreement, even when presented with photographic evidence, for fear of the dictators walking out of the flimsy accord leading to a break-up of the committee and escalation of the war possibly beyond Spain's borders. A measure of the desperation felt by the committee showed itself when evidence from the Spanish government of German and Italian interference was deemed inadmissible since Spain was not a signatory of the agreement. Britain, however, more for its antipathy to Germany than duty to the agreement, agreed to 'take action on these charges', but when the committee heard evidence from the German delegate to the effect that aircraft had been sent in a purely transport role and had been armed for self-defence in a war zone it concluded that 'the allegations were unsubstantiated'.[9]

The First Soviet Aircraft Arrive

To emphasise this point for Berlin, on 28 October the SS *Lepin* docked at Cartagena, having sailed from Sevastopol with fifteen pilots and twenty-five dismantled Chatos. This was timely since the government air force was rapidly disintegrating through loss and decrepitude. A few days later a further group of ten pilots and fifteen more Chatos arrived at Bilbao prompting a government spokesman to declare that they now had 'in [their] hands ... a powerful air force'.[10] The first group was quickly sent to Alcantarilla airfield near Murcia, where the fighters were assembled by Soviet technicians and then flight-tested. Spanish Republican markings of red wingtips and fuselage stripe and red, yellow and violet striped rudders were also hastily applied and a small number of Spanish pilots were allowed to crew them. Katiuska bombers that had arrived days earlier were assembled and formed into three Escuadrillas, which were assigned to Grupo No 12. All thirty Katiuskas were initially deployed in an area centred on the city of Albacete. The 1a Escuadrilla, commanded by Major Ernst Shakht, was stationed at Tomelloso airfield. The 2a Escuadrilla, commanded by Major V. Kholzunov, was stationed at Los Llanos airfield. The 3a Escuadrilla, commanded by Captain G. Nesmeyanov, was stationed at La Torrecica airfield. The airfields at San Clemente and Sisante were also used as Soviet bases. On the ground the first International Brigades (Brigadas Internacionales) were formed, their members being foreign volunteers who had travelled to Spain to fight on behalf of the Republican government.

The introduction of the Soviet aircraft was welcome given that the majority of the French-built Republican aircraft defending the Spanish capital had either been destroyed, were unserviceable or undergoing repair. Escuadrilla 3a was even forced to disband after using up the service life of all their spare engines. The situation was so bad that only one fighter was available to defend the whole of the Madrid front. A number of the newly arrived Katiuskas now operated in strategic mode when they attacked Tablada airfield near Seville some 350 km away, all three returning home without damage. Operational instructions for the Katiuskas were to carry a bomb-load of not more than 300kg, with fuel tanks filled to the brim, and always to fly to the target and back at a maximum speed.

When the Soviet Union was challenged about reports reaching the Non-Intervention Committee that Soviet aircraft were being unloaded at Republican ports it replied that the reports could not be true since the 'five-engine bombers' described in the report 'did not exist in the Soviet Air Force'.[11] The low level of intelligence reaching the committee was further illustrated by the British Admiralty reporting that two ships, the *Neva* and *Volga* (Volgoles) had unloaded '150 large Russian aircraft' at Cartagena on 24 October when, in fact, each had carried only ten Katiuskas (although completely denied by the Soviet delegate). The Soviets, however, threatened that if nothing was done about the German and Italian interference, they would consider themselves 'free to assist in defending the Spanish Republic'.

The Luftwaffe in Action

The fresh German pilots saw action at Zaragoza on 19 October; they had come up against thirteen Republican aircraft and claimed to have shot down five of them. Knüppel recalled that,

> Henrici alone had shot down three. He rammed one of them, a Breguet 19, on its wing with his undercarriage. Afterwards, he said quite simply, 'Well, after that he really "fell out of his slippers." He was able to fetch the devil out of hell.'[12]

The Nationalist aircraft continued to employ strategic methods when, on the 26th, twelve Spanish Ju 52s escorted by six Italian CR.32s claimed to have destroyed five Dewoitine D.372s on the ground at Barajas airfield. Another early example of strategic bombing doctrine emerged in an air force memo in October which pointed out that fuel depots in coastal cities such as Valencia and Barcelona should be high priority targets for the bombers. It also emphasised the importance of regular attacks on enemy airfields and called for the systematic bombardment of key railroad lines so as to cause as much disruption as possible.[13]

A further nine He 51s with ten pilots had arrived in 'a necessary and welcome strengthening', after which the Germans handed over to the Nationalists the three He 51s from the first batch that were still operationally serviceable.[14] Many of the names of these new pilots would become well known later during the Battle of Britain. Cadiz also saw the arrival of a further twelve CR.32s , accompanied by eleven pilots that were destined to form the 3a Escuadrilla de Caza del Tercio.

The He 51s flew their first close support mission for ground forces advancing along the Tagus valley, when they were called upon to conduct a low-level strafing mission against Republican infantry at Maquedas as part of Franco's drive towards Madrid. Knüppel recalled that,

> The road from Madrid to Maquedas was choked with trucks and cars, taxis and various other types of vehicles, in which enemy troops had been brought up. Some bombs dropped by our Spanish comrades into these columns caused the enemy to

panic so that that village was soon captured and enemy troops hastily driven away to the east.[15]

The Heinkels, however, were cautious whenever Republican Dewoitine D.372 fighters came on the scene and relied heavily on their own fighter escorts. The German contingent suffered its first loss in Spain on the 28th, when Oberleutnant Ekkehardt Hefter's He 51 flew into the tower of the town hall in Vitoria, crashed into the plaza and burst into flames. It is possible that he had been demonstrating his low-flying skills for the benefit of the locals.

On 23 October Ju 52s strafed the streets of Madrid and dropped leaflets over the city calling on Madrid to surrender before the 'real hell' of heavy bombing was loosed upon it. A week later the population received a foretaste of what this particular hell would be. In a raid which destroyed the Getafe hospital, approximately 150 people were killed. In his book *Freedom's Battle*, J. Alvarez del Vayo writes,

> for the first time since Spain's civil war began the capital, with its refugee swollen population of 1,500,000, cowered and shuddered beneath the impact of live bombs. So sudden was this first attack that there was no time to sound air-raid warnings, and before thousands of pedestrians and motorists on the streets could be herded indoors, the skies were raining shrapnel. Over 125 were killed, including 70 children playing in the grounds of a schoolhouse.[16]

Perhaps it was apropos of this bombing that Franco was credited with saying over the radio, 'One bomb dropped on a hospital sometimes means more than a victory.'[17]

The Formation of the Condor Legion

During October, German aircraft were constantly in action, often flying alongside Italian Fiats in support of ground troops and also to drop supplies to Nationalist enclaves under siege. All this stretched Warlimont's air strength to the limit. Cartagena was at the top of his agenda where vast supplies of Soviet equipment and personnel were pouring in and it was here that he urgently needed extra long-range reconnaissance aircraft to monitor the volumes. He had sent bombers to attack the port on the night of the 26th but had been unable to ascertain the accuracy of the bombing or the level of resulting damage. The consequences of the Soviet traffic were felt on 28 October, when unescorted Katiuskas struck at Seville, Mérida, Cácares and Salamanca airfields with impunity and Chatos beat up a battle column on the Toledo-Madrid road in 'a new phase of the air situation'.[18] At the same time, a column of Nationalist horse cavalry were catastrophically mismatched when they came up against fifteen Soviet T-26 tanks. Nationalist bombers had retaliated with strikes on Getafe and Cuatro Vientos.

On 23 October 1936, the Italo-German Protocol was signed. It included the two following clauses:

- The two governments recognise that Communism is the greatest danger threatening the peace and the security of Europe. They confirm their intention to combat Communist propaganda with all their strength and to direct their own actions in this sense.
- As the Nationalists are in occupation of the greater part of Spain and as Germany and Italy have considerable economic interests there, the two governments will recognise the Spanish National government de facto as soon as possible. They will keep in touch with one another for the purpose of announcing de jure recognition subsequently. When they announce this, the two governments will confirm the principle of non-intervention and respect for the integrity and territorial unity of Spain, her protectorates and her colonies.

When Warlimont returned to Spain, he had learned through Canaris that Hitler had gone further than what had been agreed to in his visit to Berlin and authorised the creation of a full expeditionary combat force which would mark the third phase of German involvement after Magic Fire and Operation Guido. This new manifestation would be called the Condor Legion. Primarily an air organisation, this would consist of a bomber group, a fighter group, a reconnaissance squadron, a seaplane squadron and an antiaircraft flak group with ground support personnel. Hitler's support, however, had conditions. The new force in Spain was to be placed under a German commander who would have operational control but would act under Franco's orders. German units already in Spain were to be integrated into the new Legion. German air bases in Spain would be given satisfactory protection, and operations were to be better coordinated, more regular and aimed at those ports through which Soviet aid was being routed. Not for the first or last time, Franco was taken by surprise by an important German decision taken without his consultation, but faced with evidence of massive Soviet aid going to the Republicans, swallowed his pride and agreed to all Hitler's demands 'without reservations'.[19]

Göring, who had overall responsibility for German forces in Spain, chose Major Hermann Plocher to oversee the creation of a new task force. Plocher drew up plans for an operational staff, a Kampfgruppe, K/88 comprising three squadrons, each with twelve Ju 52s, which would operate alongside the squadron already in Spain, a Jagdgruppe to be known as J/88 comprising three squadrons each with nine He 51s alongside the squadron already there, two reconnaissance squadrons, a seaplane squadron, a flak battalion and sundry support and military training units. All non-aviation units were to operate under the direct command of the Spanish ground force. Alongside the hardware would be maintenance, hospital, supply, salvage, testing and experimental, meteorological and liaison elements. By 29 November 1936, thousands of men, hundreds of tanks, guns, aircraft, weapons and many tons of equipment had been shipped out of Stettin and Swinemünde on twenty-five freighters, all bound for Cadiz and Seville. There would, however, not be a full logistical support, for economic reasons, requiring the Legion to organise maintenance facilities, vehicles and equipment from local sources.

Warlimont would be replaced by Generalmajor Hugo Sperrle (called General 'Sander' in Spain), the commander of Luftkreis-Kommando V. Hugo Sperrle was a huge 'bear of a man' with a reputation for being tough and very demanding. Although a competent military leader, his manner was crude, abrupt and impatient which made him a less than perfect fit for the diplomatic aspect of his command. He left Berlin for Spain in a Ju 52 on 31 October, travelling via Rome, together with his Chief of Staff, Major Alexander Holle.

Still governed by extreme secrecy, Wilberg and Plocher created a fictitious winter manoeuvre in the Baltic to be known as 'Winterübung

Rügen', which included flying, flak, signals and communications elements drawn from existing Luftwaffe units. Men and equipment began assembling at the port of Stettin where they boarded the ships SS *Berlin* and SS *Osorio*. Wilberg's team was assigned the code name 'Eiserne Rationen' to the air contingent bound for Spain, but this was later changed to 'Eiserne Legion'. Then Plocher was instructed by Göring to change this once more to Condor Legion, and to use the names of birds for all of its components. It would enjoy the equivalent status of a Luftwaffe Fliegerkorps.

Although German aid was initially seen as a short-term expedient, over the course of three years some 19,000 German personnel would serve in Spain, although there were never more that 5,600 at any one time. They constituted an elite force and, after a faltering start, employed state-of-the-art technology and equipment. Their main contribution would be in air power, but on the ground special mention should be made of the flak detachment with 88mm guns that played a significant role in many battles during the war. While ground units showed little enthusiasm for the adventure, flyers, especially, were eager to volunteer and put their skills and training to the test in a real war. The pilots were highly trained professionals with excellent career prospects in a modern air force mostly from a middle-class background who had prospered under National Socialism and had been imbued with its doctrines. An added incentive was the extra 'allowance for special expenditure' on offer and the chance of winning speedy promotion through combat.

It had been relatively easy to cloak the initial deployment in secrecy, building on the experience of clandestine operations at the covert joint Soviet-German training facility at Lipetsk in the Soviet Union that had been operational for a number of years. When the distinctly north-Europeans landed in the southern Spanish lands, however, their appearance made them conspicuous and their presence and purpose, although officially denied, could not be disguised. Given the ad hoc nature of early German involvement so far from home with little direction it is no surprise that, prior to Sperrle's appointment, there had been a 'low degree of military discipline' which coincided with 'the most agreeable phase of the war' for most of the personnel who had 'substantial free time'. This had led to a degree of irresponsible behaviour with a number of repatriations where behaviour had gone beyond acceptable due in no small part to 'too much alcohol' but all that would soon be changed.[20]

The presence of German personnel in Spain was an open secret, but the German government persisted with its charade of denying it. On 20 February 1937 it issued a decree forbidding German nationals from entering Spain or Spanish possessions, including Spanish Morocco, in order to take part in the Civil War. It further empowered the Minister of the Interior, Dr Wilhelm Frick, to take all necessary measures to prevent the departure or transit through Germany of volunteers, German or foreign.

Chapter 5

Franco's First Attack against Madrid

- Franco's Attack Stalls
- Strategic Bombing
- The Bombing of Cartagena and Alicante

Franco's Attack Stalls

German opinion of Franco's war leadership was confirmed when his drive on Madrid stalled. He had diverted his main offensive to take Toledo before advancing on the capital, which had allowed the Republicans time to bring in reinforcements, especially the new Soviet T-26 heavy tanks. When the drive was resumed, taking the airfield at Getafe en route, Nationalists entered the capital and occupied the Plaza de Espana but could go no further against recently recruited International Brigade forces. It was not only the tanks but the newly arrived Soviet aircraft that were making a difference. Three Katiuskas bombed Tablada airfield on 29 October and departed at a speed that no Nationalist fighter could match. This new aerial dynamic was reinforced on 4 November when Soviet Chatos and Ratas burst onto the scene and gained air superiority over the front, immediately shooting down a Ju 52 and two Fiats, while Soviet tanks dominated ground actions. An article in a Soviet journal pointed out that many bombing raids had been carried out on enemy airfields and showed that with 'a skilful exploitation of meteorological conditions and proper training of aviation personnel bombing attacks may inflict substantial damage on hostile aviation situated at airdromes'.[1] The taking of the capital had become what even Franco's own generals called a 'hopeless task'.[2]

During the last days of October, the Nationalist air force had been able to bomb Madrid at low altitude with complete impunity, but Republican forces on the ground counter-attacked with the powerful and superior Russian T-26 tanks, in use for the first time. By the second week of November, the Soviet pilots had also started to take control of the air when it became clear that the Katiuskas over Talavera, near Toledo, had higher horizontal speed than the Fiats and could escape from them. The Nationalist Savoias and Ro37s struck back with low-level attacks in 'continuous relay' which had an 'unbelievably severe' effect on the morale of Republican troops.[3] Nationalist airfields at Seville, Mérida, Cácares and Salamanca were attacked by Soviet bombers flying without fighter escort. The Soviet news service *Pravda* reported somewhat over-enthusiastically that,

> A government squadron of aircraft, after an extensive period of inactivity, appeared above the rebel airfield at Talavera (160 km from Madrid) and dropped bombs which destroyed fifteen rebel aircraft. The operation proceeded successfully, despite heavy anti-aircraft fire. The Talavera airfield was completely destroyed.[4]

The Nationalist offensive was halted on the outskirts of the city as their bombers were forced to fly at ever higher altitudes of up to 2,000m. At this point, the new Condor Legion units were still in transit and the Republican air force was much stronger. The resulting uplift of morale in the capital was palpable and prompted the Soviet Consul General Antonov Ovseyenko to call on Moscow to send more aircraft.

By 3 November, a total of sixty Fiat CR.32s had arrived in Spain, along with fifty-seven He 51s. Germany and Italy also sent 150 other military aircraft types between them too, including thirty-four transport and bomber Ju 52s and eighteen SM.81 bombers, but Soviet aircraft still were in the ascendancy. Katiuska bombers had attacked Nationalist airfields near Talavera and managed to destroy or severely damage up to six Fiat CR.32s. The next day, however, flight leaders Adriano Mantelli and Felice Sozzi of the 1a Escuadrilla de Caza del Tercio brought down a Katiuska between them, this being the first time that the actual destruction of a Tupolev bomber could be proven. Manteli recalled that,

> The monoplane was well below us and hadn't seen us. I waited, checked my speed and distance and then at the right moment

I pushed the nose of my fighter down and dived at the bomber. The slipstream whistled past and the engine roared, but I heard nothing. My eyes were fixed on the aeroplane that rapidly grew larger as we closed in at a tremendous speed. Range seemed just right so I fired the machine guns hummed.

With the first burst I could clearly see the incendiary rounds hitting the wing, sending white sparks flying. The right wing caught fire almost immediately, then a tail of flames from the left wing engulfed both the fuselage and the right wing. One wing broke off, at which point three men took to their parachutes. I saw three envelopes open, but the speed was too high and they were torn away – the three men fell like dead bodies. My CR.32 was faster and I flew past them. I was terribly excited by the victory and nearly forgot my controls, only to suddenly remember that I had to stop the aeroplane from diving. The sound of the slipstream became calmer as I pulled out, and down below me the monoplane exploded as it hit the ground.[5]

While eleven assembled and flight-tested Chatos were ferried to Madrid, the first batch of thirty-one Rata type 5s that had been shipped from the Soviet Union along with thirty-one Soviet pilots arrived aboard the transports SS *Kursk* and SS *Blagoev*. The Chatos were thrown into the battle to halt the Nationalists who had now occupied the Madrid suburb of Getafe. They each flew four missions on the day in squadron strength over Carrabanchel during which they claimed four victories in the clash that lasted barely ten minutes. In all, they claimed five enemy fighters and two Ju 52 bombers on this day without loss. It is tempting to think that more than a few Soviet and German pilots who met each other in combat over Spain might well have trained together and even flown together in the secret joint Soviet-German facility at Lipetsk between 1925 and 1933.

During the morning of the 5th came the first big aerial battle of the war when nine Fiats from Torrijones were escorting three Ro.37s. They met about fifteen Chatos and some Potez aircraft between Leganés and Madrid. Without waiting for support, the Fiats, from Talavera, attacked. The Nationalist bulletin claimed seven fighters and one Potez destroyed and admitted the loss of one Fiat. The government bulletin, on the other hand, claimed that one Fiat, and four other aircraft had been destroyed. In reality, only two Chatos were destroyed, one of which was piloted by Lieutenant Petr Aleksandrovich Mitrofanov of Escuadrilla Palancar, who became the first Russian pilot killed in Spain. Air battles became fiercer and more prolonged. The Ratas operating out of Alkalá de Henares airfield made their first appearance over the Madrid front during the day when they joined Chatos in the strafing of Moroccan troops and cavalry that had occupied the Casa de Campo on the outskirts of Western Madrid. The Soviet fighters appeared without warning at low-level over Madrid's front line and earned the nickname Ratas (Rats). In response to the appearance of the new Soviet aircraft over Madrid, the Nationalist air force officially formed the first Fiat fighter group.

Fierce engagements on the 13th saw fourteen Fiat CR.32s on bomber escort duty engage six Chatos with losses on both sides. On their return flight, the surviving Fiats met five Katiuskas, bombing Getafe and Cuatro Vientos from a height of 5,000m and damaged four of them. In the afternoon, nine He 51s took off from Ávila to provide escort for five German-flown Ju 52s and three He 46s, which were to attack the Republican positions on the west bank of the Manzanares. Twelve Ratas and the same number of Chatos intercepted them over Madrid. All Republican pilots taking part in this combat were Russians. Leutnant von Houwald, speaking of the Ratas, admitted that pilots were 'scared of them' and 'feverishly ... waited for the Bf 109s to arrive from Germany'.[6]

The Soviets, having lost four in a short time, were less than happy, but this was more to do with pilot inexperience than inadequate aircraft. Even its higher speed was poor compensation for the superior skills and experience of the Nationalist flyers. According to the report of military advisor Brigade Commander Alekseev, Grupo No 12 lost a total of eight Katiuskas within the first fifteen days to combat accidents. The Soviet pilot, Lieutenant Sharov reported that,

> In combat the enemy fighters would attack our bombers from behind and below and open fire at a range of 200m or less. The Fiats would open fire at a range even closer. Enemy fighters were deployed near the front line and usually waited for our aircraft to pass on their return leg. If they could, they tried to attack us on the way to the target. In most cases we flew to

and from the target along the same route. At the present time this procedure has been changed. I think that the enemy set ambushes 10–15 km from the front line, and the number of aircraft varied from five to twenty fighters. ...

During our first sorties we often lost our bearings and wandered around, as in the alpine terrain even landmarks such as railroads are poorly visible from an altitude of 2,000m. The enemy preferred to bomb us at night [because] they were afraid of our I-15 fighters. All of the Heinkel bombers were flown by Germans, while the Junkers were manned by German pilots and Spanish co-pilots. Most of the enemy gunners were Spaniards.[7]

The German fighters could not catch the Katiuskas which were able to undertake bombing missions without fighter escort. But even so it was a relief when the Chatos and Ratas had arrived. Maintenance was an issue for the Republicans with up to a third of their aircraft grounded for repairs at any one time. Soviet flier V.S. Goranov was not particularly happy with the situation when he said,

The SB's engines were of poor quality and the cylinder walls were too thin. The aircraft itself was very good and had sufficient speed. The fascists did not have any aircraft that could match its speed, therefore they tried to employ the tactic of placing fighters in echelons along the length of our route and waiting for our bombers.

The drawbacks of the SB included the following: the compass was placed inconveniently and the pilot could not use it in flight, the pilot's cabin was not fitted with a bomb release lever which he could use in case the navigator was killed. The SB's engines cooled down too quickly, but they also heated up fast, therefore we did not close the radiator shutters. The pilot's field of view was obscured by the engines, wings, and fuselage. The SBs were not used for what they were intended. They fought over Madrid when they should have been used to strike the enemy's rear, airfields, railroads, etc.

The pilot could look forward and upward and he could not see the ground [but] on the whole the SB is a good airplane which is easy to control in the air. The SBs were not equipped for night flying and the pilots were not trained for night missions.

There was chaos at take-offs and it was only by luck that we did not collide in mid-air. It was especially dangerous to take off at night without knowing the positions of the other aircraft, which were scattered all over the airfield. There were no orders pertaining to taxiing procedures or take-off directions. At first there were also no weather reports, a major drawback that resulted in the crash of two SBs.

At first the enemy fighters tried to catch up with the SB. They would chase the SBs at full power for about ten minutes and then drop behind and give up. Later the fighters started to attack us from ambushes on the way to the target. They usually patrolled below our aircraft, taking advantage of the poor field of view from the SB, and then delivered a surprise attack.

The personnel fight well. All pilots fly combat missions in high spirits and with great desire. The Spaniards, especially the technicians, operate our aircraft well. The lack of debriefings was one mistake by our command. The aircrew would return from their missions, have lunch, and that was it. Information was shared only informally and there were no organised discussions of our experiences.[8]

Fierce air battles continued over Madrid as German, Italian and Nationalist air units engaged in the most significant example of strategic bombing in the war to date. Franco, however, had stipulated that the wealthy areas of the city were not to be targeted. This was soon apparent to the population and the streets within the safety zone encompassed by Calle Zurbano, Paseo de Ronda, Calle Velázquez and Calle Goya were crowded at night by people who could find no safe refuge from the bombs. Leaflets were dropped warning against the killing of right-wing prisoners and threatening massive punishment when the city was taken by Yagüe's much-feared 'Army of Africa'. The bombings between 18 and 22 November were carried out by

German Ju 52s and Italian SM.81s, but because of the lack of fighter cover were very soon restricted to night-operations when targeting would have become even less accurate, especially as the capital ordered a black-out. Meanwhile in the Nationalist town of Segovia, a Republican pilot who had crash-landed was beaten to death, mutilated, dismembered, loaded into a box and dropped by parachute onto the airfield at Barajas as a 'gift [for] the red air force'.[9]

The bombing of Madrid had been encouraged by Sperrle but was eventually called off on 26 November because day bombing was too dangerous in the face of Republican superiority, and night bombing too inaccurate. Too few He 51s had been assembled in time to give the required level of protection for the bombers. Nationalist aircraft were unable to fly by day unless in large formations and under heavy fighter escort which was rarely available.[10] Italian Fiat squadrons were suffering not only at the hands of the Soviet fighters but from an internal drop in morale. The first three squadron leaders had gone: Dequal wounded and shipped home, Oliviero killed and Maccagno taken prisoner. Of their three replacements, only one remained operational.

The stalling of the ground offensive on Madrid was a blow to Nationalist morale. Franco, along with his Italian and German allies, had anticipated taking the capital thereby bringing the war to an early victorious conclusion, but Soviet intervention had blunted that ambition. Frustrated, Franco followed up with a new ground assault by Yagüe's Moroccan troops at Pozuelo on the Corunna road. At first the defenders were driven back by Ju 52 bombers but ground forces were unable to capitalise as the powerful Soviet T-26 tanks supported by Chatos and Ratas stabilised the Republican positions. Weather too was beginning to have an impact as winter clamped down, forcing Franco to pull back to Húnera-Pozuelo and hold the line until, at some time in the future, sufficient force could be brought up to launch another attack.

Strategic Bombing

Government bombers scored a morale-boosting success on 11 November when they struck at Avila airfield catching Ju 52s and He 46s on the ground while Fiats and Chatos fought fierce battles above the Pasco de Rosales.

Further attacks took place in the first weeks of November. *Time Magazine* on 23 November said,

> Choosing an early hour when Madrid's anti-aircraft guns were off their guard, three tri-motored Whites zoomed suddenly over the Capital's southeast working-class district, and plunked bomb after bomb in the streets as women and children were thronging to the market and as hundreds of men had massed in the open for a workers' meeting. Before the frenzied citizens could hurry for shelter 52 of them were killed.[11]

Geoffrey Cox, an English correspondent, referring to a night raid on 19 November, says there was,

> no panic over this attack, rather a dazed incomprehension, as if the people could not realise how such horror could come in one night, mingled with an almost childish curiosity.[12]

Describing a raid of 14 November, the *Journal of the Royal United Service Institution* reported,

> Streets were torn up, water mains burst, and general confusion reigned. Much adverse criticism has been levelled at General Franco for this and other air raids, but in fairness to the insurgents, it must be realised that he had offered to create a neutral zone for non-combatants, and cannot be held responsible if the government chose to turn Madrid into a defended locality.[13]

The International Telephone and Telegraph Corporation's fourteen-storey building, one of the most conspicuous of Madrid's twentieth-century landmarks, was a frequent target, but *Time Magazine* said,

> Scores of panic-stricken Madrid mothers decided that, even though Colonel Behn's building seemed to be a target for White bombs, it also seemed to be able to take this strafing better than any other Madrid building, and in they swarmed with their children. The Spanish moppets surprised correspondents

by not blubbering or bawling, accepted biscuits and milk from Colonel Behn after their mothers had fearfully asked 'how much will that cost?' and been reassured that the biscuits and milk were on the I.T.&T.[14]

The civilian losses in Madrid were staggering enough but the Spanish capital held out, and air raids did not seem to lessen the population's determination to resist the Franco forces, which were fighting almost within the city itself. On 25 November, a commission of six members of the British Parliament arrived in the capital to make an unofficial inspection of the effects of the war and the bombings upon the city. They toured the area in and around Madrid and 'were profoundly impressed by the calm attitude and the dignity of the people' of the besieged town and, seeing how the population stood up to the bombardment, concluded that,

> If there is an example typical of the failure of this creation of the imagination [The Douhet theory] it is certainly the action of the Nationalist aviation against Madrid ... massive bombing operations, well conducted and well supplied, could evidently do a great deal of damage; but to win the war that way alone, there is an abyss, an abyss which is far from being jumped.[15]

Another correspondent, William P. Carney, of the *New York Times*, reported that Madrid was practically defenceless against the 400 and 500 pound bombs dropped by the Insurgent aircraft, yet the city lacked neither morale nor resistance on the part of its civilian population. According to Koestler's reckoning, raids occurred on thirteen of the first nineteen days of the month, causing some 800 deaths and 2,800 injuries to civilians.

The Bombing of Cartagena and Alicante

In an effort to stem the vast flow of Soviet aid, three full squadrons of Condor Legion Ju 52 bombers of K/88 under the command of Major Fuchs struck at the ports of Cartagena and Alicante on the night of 15 November, sinking two freighters and damaging others. The flight path from their bases to Madrid, where they were now located to support Franco's attack on the city, took them on bitterly cold journeys over the high Sierra de Guadarrama and the Sierra de Gredos so some flights were rerouted to Melilla in North Africa where they were refuelled before continuing over the sea without fighter cover. Some reports suggest that Sperrle himself piloted one of the attacking bombers. Two days later they tried again to readjust the balance of air power by hitting the Soviet air base at Alcala de Henares in daylight, but all these raids were failures and did little more than to emphasise the disparity between the air forces. Very soon, Condor Legion bombers would be restricted to night bombing which, by its very nature, lacks precision and more often than not resulted in civilian casualties. Sickness and a general malaise infected German aircrew and they were forced to operate only in those sectors where Soviet aircraft were not heavily deployed.[16]

Chapter 6

Foreign Aid Increases

- Von Richthofen Arrives
- Von Faupel Calls for More German Aid
- Italy Increases Aid
- Republican Air Force Dominates
- Early Tactical and Strategic Lessons
- More Soviet Aid Arrives

Von Richthofen Arrives

Choosing to ignore the uncomfortable possibility that recent victories had been possible because of the German pilots' skill and not the quality of the obsolete He 51s, on 18 November another shipment of sixty crated He 51s, disguised as agricultural machinery, had arrived in Seville for assembly at Tablada. With these fighters had come the new designation J88 led by Major Baier, who fell ill and was replaced by Hauptmann Hubertus Merhart von Bernegg. The three Staffeln were created; 1.J/88 under Hauptmann Werner Palm, 2.J/88 under Hauptmann Siegfried Lehmann and 3.J/88 under Hauptmann Jürgen Roth. The original cadre of Heinkel pilots already in Spain were brought together into 4.J/88 under Knüppel, now promoted to Hauptman. Oberstleutnant Wolfram Freiherr von Richthofen, the former Head of Luftwaffe Testing and Development flew into Seville from Rome on 29 November. In Spain he took over command of Versuchs-Kommandos 88 to monitor the performance of the Condor Legion's aircraft in combat. The new VJ/88 (Versuchsjagdstaffel – Experimental Fighter Squadron) set up by von Richthofen at Tablada brought with them a few Bf 109 B-1 prototypes; one fitted with an

63

engine-mounted 20mm Oerlikon cannon, another with 3x 7.92mm MG 17 machine guns and a third with a variable-pitch VDM metal propeller. He was not impressed with what he found and, true to his character, was not slow to vent his spleen.

My accommodation is very bad. ... Transport and distribution, information on the arrivals of the steamers and loading lists are all completely unknown. ... The unloaded matériel is often unusable since many of the important items are often missing. Am greeted by the Chief of Staff, Holle, who is worn out and wants to be left in peace. I report to [Sperrle], who complains about the complete lack of knowledge in Berlin of local conditions here.

Our own operations [over Madrid] without fighter protection by day are considered impossible. At other locations, no Red fighters have been observed. However, if we conduct daylight raids, their surprise appearance is feared as a probability.[1]

Many pilots felt the same way about conditions in Spain. Oberleutnant Harro Harder complained that Tablada was,

a jackass station where the situation was awful. We would welcome an opportunity to sort things out. The fighters sit here and don't go anywhere. The entire operation appears increasingly like some great escapade controlled by incompetent staff officers. Are our operations justified by results? Why can't we have better aircraft?[2]

Correct German military discipline was quickly imposed with the introduction of proper uniforms and men were 'made into soldiers once again' by military discipline and exercise.[3] This did not greatly reduce the pleasant life that German personnel were leading, especially now that better lodgings and more traditional German food was provided. Billets were found in the more prosperous family homes, especially for the aircrews, and the benefits of German provisioning trickled down into local communities who had been starting to feel the effects of food shortages because of the war. Such deprivation felt by the wider communities was not, however, evident in the homes of wealthy Franco stalwarts, where Legion commanders like von Richthofen became accustomed to 'sumptuous breakfasts of lobster, champagne and caviar'.[4] The prevalence of German and Italian officers in hotels and restaurants prompted foreign journalists, in a way that would have infuriated Franco, to warn that Spain was 'well on the way to becoming some kind of German-Italian colony'. The German pilot Adolf Galland, who arrived in 1937, would testify to driving 'out to the mountain hotel of Parador de Gredos, located in stunning surroundings, where there was a magnificent view of the snow-covered peaks of the Sierra, along with brook trout and superb wine', in an area that was within easy reach of the German General Staff at Salamanca.[5] The town had grown, as a consequence of being the German headquarters, from 40,000 to 100,000 inhabitants and now 'pulsated at a rapid tempo' with many shops displaying 'Hier wird Deutsch gesprochen' signs.

Von Faupel Calls for More German Aid

Although not a member of the Nazi Party, the new German ambassador to Franco, Wilhelm von Faupel, had been appointed primarily by virtue of his connections to high party officials and upon arrival in Spain on 28 November, pompously tried to set himself up as a military adviser to Franco, which annoyed both Franco and Sperrle. Having been replaced by Sperrle, Warlimont felt superfluous in a subsidiary role and requested a transfer back to Germany but Berlin insisted that he stay as von Blomberg's personal representative until von Faupel was in place. He was surprised and appalled to find that von Faupel, upon arriving in Spain to take up a diplomatic post, immediately immersed himself in military strategy and seemed set on pointing out to Franco how the war might be brought to a rapid conclusion. Not only that, but the new man had formed links with a Spanish fascist movement, the Falange Española de las JONS, which was way outside his brief. It was, furthermore, a blow to Warlimont's self-esteem to find that he was expected to act as the military adviser to von Faupel, a man who obviously felt that he needed no such assistance, and whose solution to the stalemate in Spain was for Berlin to send more military aid. Warlimont was unwilling to be the conduit for von Faupel's requests and almost begged to be relieved. He was convinced that von Faupel would 'get into trouble with everyone [and] involve himself in military affairs ... which were strictly none of his business'. Von Faupel could see that Warlimont was going to be of no use to him and quickly granted his request for transfer back to Germany.

Upon his return to Germany, Warlimont was ushered onto Hitler's private aircraft and whisked away to Berlin for a meeting with the Führer, who wanted his views on von Faupel's requests to have three full infantry divisions sent to Spain. A high-powered meeting was convened which was attended by von Faupel, who had decided to make his case in person, von Blomberg and Göring among others, all of whom outranked Warlimont by some margin. Von Faupel was given the floor to explain how his plans would ensure that 'the war would be over in only a matter of a few weeks'.[6] Warlimont was asked to respond and proceeded to detail his objections from a purely military perspective such as the problems of supplying a large force without direct land communications and from a political and diplomatic viewpoint, in an undisguised criticism of von Faupel, emphasising the need for the war to be decided by a 'Spanish solution'. He was relieved when von Blomberg, in no way sympathetic to von Faupel's request, interrupted the proceedings to baldly state that 'we cannot possibly spare these divisions'. Hitler concluded the meeting by saying that his priority was that Franco should not be beaten, implying that he would send sufficient aid to ensure that outcome, but secondly, in a way that Warlimont found 'cruel and callous', that the war should be allowed to continue long enough to distract other European powers from his own domestic military and political agenda. Von Faupel was not daunted, however, and returned to Spain to continue aggravating Sperrle and Franco with his constant 'advice', and Berlin with his incessant requests for more military aid. Warlimont, on the other hand, continued to be Franco's spokesman in Berlin especially by opposing the deployment of German ground forces to Spain.

Italy Increases Aid

In contrast to the reticence shown in Berlin, in Rome Mussolini seemed to echo von Faupel's opinion of the Spanish as 'obviously lacking in offensive spirit and also in personal bravery'. However, they signed the Italo-Spanish Agreement on 28 November 1936 which pledged Franco to adopt an attitude of benevolent neutrality and to put at Italy's disposal 'all facilities, the use of ports, of air-lines, of railways and roads'. Il Duce sent 3,000 of his Black Shirt militiamen to 'put some backbone into the Spanish National formations', despite Franco not having asked for them.[7] It was neither the first nor the last time that the Italians would act unilaterally in apparent disregard of Franco's wishes. This did not prompt Hitler to revise his approach significantly, however. He was seriously concerned still about international repercussions of greater German involvement. The French Foreign Minister warned that if Germany sent further troop transports, in addition to the Condor Legion, such action would 'necessarily lead to war'. The attitude of France was at all times a major concern for Germany throughout the Spanish War which prompted General Keitel, Chief of the High Command to instruct German aircraft to avoid combat near the French border. The Italian ambassador in Berlin, Bernardo Attolico, was told by von Neurath that Germany was 'not prepared to [send more troops] because [it was] considered that such a step would seriously endanger the larger European situation'. He made it clear that Germany recognised 'that Italian interests in Spain go further than ours, if only for geographic reasons', but acknowledged that limiting aid at this stage could relegate Germany to second-class status behind Italy in the eyes of Spain. Mussolini, ever aware of Hitler's ambitions, greeted the news with satisfaction saying, 'If we close the door of Spain to the Russians, only to open it to the Germans, we can kiss our Latin and Mediterranean policy goodbye.'[8]

Meanwhile the war in Spain had grabbed the attention of all the major powers who were eager to learn as much as possible about the capabilities of the modern aircraft involved. US military attachés in London, Paris, Berlin, Rome, and Moscow were instructed to pay special attention, and 'utilise every appropriate opportunity to obtain data on the types, performances, and tactical use of these materials'. A US Army Air Corps officer was assigned to Spain as assistant attaché with orders to furnish the Secretary of War with information on air operations in Spain as soon as obtained.[9]

Republican Air Force Dominates

By early December, the Nationalist offensive towards Madrid was halted, allowing some Republican fighter groups to be reassigned to the Aragon front where He 51s flown by a mixed contingent of German and Spanish Nationalist pilots were operating in the Teruel area. By the end of the year, five of the six He 51s operating there had gone. One had been shot down in combat and the remaining four had been destroyed on their airfield by the Chatos. The Condor Legion was obviously finding it difficult to adjust to their new surroundings. The prospect of spending Christmas in a foreign land whose festive traditions were quite alien to them was not appealing, but conditions in the air were of more concern to the airmen.

Already Sperrle had been forced to restrict his bombers to night operations over Madrid in the face of the dangers posed by enemy fighters, and efforts to destroy enemy aircraft on the ground were proving fruitless. Reconnaissance flights had great difficulty not only in avoiding enemy aircraft but in actually locating the airfields which, in many cases, were just open fields with aircraft dispersed and hidden under trees or camouflage. Air operations at this time were not so much about achieving any tangible results, although the lack of that was certainly dispiriting enough since 'no visible results could be seen', but more about giving crews valuable experience of flying conditions. The almost total lack of meteorological services meant that the weather was of particular concern with rapidly changing conditions within a single sortie, ranging from the constant danger of icing while crossing the high Sierra to the ever-present low cloud and freezing fog 'putting a great strain on the crews'.[10] On the few occasions where bombers had been called upon to attack fortified enemy positions, they did so against fearsome fighter opposition and were dismayed when, having put themselves at such risk, ground forces failed to follow up to take advantage of their exploits and allowed the enemy troops to reoccupy the position when the bombing ceased. To ease the stress, bomber crews were restricted to no more than a single flight on any one day and the ordeal of crossing the high mountain ranges was ameliorated by Sperrle and von Richthofen deciding to relocate one of the bomber squadrons from Salamanca closer to Madrid. That turned out to be not such a good idea, however, when it came under immediate attack and was severely mauled before the aircraft had barely touched the ground.

Following the appearance of increasing numbers of Soviet fighters on the Madrid front, the Spanish Nationalist air commanders complained that the Italian airmen were under orders not to fly into enemy territory and were not sufficiently aggressive. Clearly Spanish-Italian relations were a little strained. A compromise was reached whereby a number of Fiat CR.32s were handed over to the Spanish air force to form their own unit, the Patrulla Azul. The changing circumstances of the war led, on 28 December, to dissolution of the Aviación del Tercio Extranjero and replaced by the Italian Aviazione Legionaria. The latter combined the majority of the aircraft that had been sent to Spain from Italy together with all Italian airmen participating in the mission, as well as some Spanish aviators and soldiers. A minor air component was formed as an autonomous entity, the Aviazione Legionaria delle Baleari being equipped with bombers intended for anti-maritime or coastal operations, as well as a few CR.32s for local defence. Some of the new aircraft supplied by Italy were handed over to the Aviación National for operation by Spanish crews and, occasionally, foreign volunteers.

Early Tactical and Strategic Lessons

Now that he had been in charge for about six months, Kindelán collected his thoughts and reflected on the Madrid campaign. He had issued a directive in August 1936 making a number of points concerning the proper use of various types of aircraft. For the bombers, targets should be at least thirty kilometres behind the battle front and ought to be important objectives, such as bridges, fortifications, airfields, train stations, convoys, factories, and munitions works. The big bombers should be used with care so as not to wear them out in frequent actions over objectives that smaller aircraft could take care of. Whenever enemy fighters were in the area, the bombers should have fighter protection. In October he had instructed that enemy fuel depots in coastal cities such as Valencia and Barcelona should be high priority targets for the bombers.

In December, he concluded that the Nationalist airfields had been located too far away from the battle front and units had not operated under a unified command. Furthermore, fighters had been deployed in close support operations without due regard to the threat posed by enemy fighter forces. He insisted that close support could be effective only when one's own pursuit aviation was superior to that of the enemy so that air superiority over the battle area was achieved. The greater that superiority, the more effective close support became. The importance of this observation was highlighted by the US air attaché who said that 'the only really new factor to appear in the tactical field since the First World War is the destruction and demoralising power of attack aviation', and later by German theorists who claimed that close support was of 'paramount importance', which had 'a profound effect on the future development of the Luftwaffe' and was 'the most important and significant result of the Spanish experience'. General Armengaud of the French air force would later say about the role of close support that it was like 'a general reserve artillery', and added that 'aviation's greater mobility and flexibility allowed it to be used anywhere, any time and against targets that were inaccessible to artillery fire [and that] aviation is the most potent weapon for ground offensives'. The Italians were learning their own lessons, particularly in the use of 'cadena' or chain tactics originated by the Nationalist flyer Joaquin Garcia Morata, whereby aircraft attacked in line and afterwards took their place at the back of the queue, or chain, for a second pass and so on in a continuous assault on the target, until forced to return to base. While undoubtedly effective, the ability of the 'cadena' to replace artillery as the means of blasting open a breach in the enemy lines has been hotly disputed. The dive-bomber, seen by some as the 'best type ... for this decisive function', is derided by others for its lack of precision when laying down its bombs, and also for the inherent risk to pilots which artillerymen do not face to anything like the same extent.[11]

Although modest by Second World War standards, air operations in the Spanish Civil War would provide a great deal of practical experience for those directly involved and the opportunity to learn many important lessons. Some lessons, such as Blitzkrieg tactics were learned well by the Germans but the British, observing from afar, failed to appreciate the terribly high attrition cost of daylight bombing without adequate fighter escort.

Kindelán noted that Soviet bomber forces seemed to be operating according to Douhetist theories of strategic bombing, which did not cause much damage due to lack of intensity of the bombardments and the high altitude from which they were delivered, as opposed to protection of their troops.[12] He admitted that the intensity of enemy fighter action had forced the Nationalists to reduce bombing operations and concentrate on protection of troops. Only when air superiority was re-established would they be able to resume bombing operations. He ordered that, if enemy fighters in high numbers or quality are present our aviation must always operate with fighter protection in proportion to the fighter strength of the enemy. If we lack this protection or if it is greatly inferior to the enemy strength in the sector of action, the bomber squadrons will desist from operating in the daytime until they receive the necessary reinforcements.[13]

The German analyst General Karl Drum concluded that daylight bombing missions were too costly unless escorted by substantial numbers of fighter escorts. As a consequence, the Condor Legion had developed the tactic of night bombardment. The Italian journal *Rivista Aeronautica* emphasised the need for close formation flying to maximise the concentration of defensive firepower for bomber squadrons, but it was generally accepted by all that bombers would never be fast enough to evade the most modern pursuit aircraft, the effectiveness of which would inevitably come to determine control of the air.

Soviet airmen were also impressed by the effects of close support aviation. In a series of articles by eight authors in a 1938 Soviet military journal, most argued that the Spanish experience had proved the necessity of both air superiority over the battlefield and the importance of close support in ground operations. One called close support the principal mission of the air force, another wrote that it was the decisive factor in modern combat. During the first months of the war, the Soviets had even used their Katiuskas in low-level attacks but after a number of losses to ground fire, they resorted to a more conventional high-level bombing role. The smaller Polikarpov RZs introduced in 1937 proved to be more suitable for the ground attack role, developing a very effective tactic of low-level approach in V-formation then a rapid climb to around 500ft to deliver their bombs, after which they would drop to low-level again to exit the battlefield with the rear gunner suppressing anti-aircraft fire. The RZs would often be accompanied by Chatos to ward off enemy aircraft. At this early stage, the Soviets were the only ones employing low-level ground attack tactics. The Germans would only come to recognise the effectiveness of this method of attack when they were forced to withdraw their He 51s from the fighter role, in which they had become almost sitting ducks for the Polikarpovs, and seek an alternative role for them.

The relative success they found with He 51s in the ground-attack role and the realisation that both Soviets and Italians were exploiting it to a greater extent prompted the Condor Legion to request more specialised aircraft to replace them.

The leader of Operation X reported to Moscow that for the six weeks up to 7 December the Nationalists had lost forty-seven aircraft in the air (thirty-five fighters and twelve bombers) and ninety-one on the ground, whereas the Republicans had lost a mere seventeen aircraft in the air to the enemy (three SBs, six I-15s, four I-16s, four Polikarpov R5-SSSs) and twelve on the ground. Personnel losses included eleven dead (in aerial combat), four killed in accidents, two dead of injuries, nine missing in action and five injured.[14] A Red Army air force report showed that of all Soviet bomber targets during the first year of the war 45 per cent were against enemy troops, 24 per cent against airfields, 22 per cent against rail networks and industrial objects and 8 per cent naval targets or ports. From the very first engagement the Soviets had seen its combat experience in Spain as vitally important to its ongoing military aviation programme; all airmen were ordered to submit detailed reports of their experiences and send them directly to Moscow. This information was used to bring about significant updates in design and operation of Soviet aircraft in following years.[15] The Condor Legion had been unable to gain air superiority over Madrid which had contributed to Franco's failure to capture the city. The Spanish adventure was turning sour and German morale was plummeting. Some of the German He 45 crews were so badly affected that they were sent home and their aircraft turned over to Spanish crews.[16] Their aircraft were simply unable to compete with the Chato and Rata fighters and they could not prevent the Katiuskas from operating at will.

German fighter pilots were given complete freedom to experiment with various tactical methods to both attack enemy aircraft and to defend friendly bombers. Leutnant Trautloft and Unteroffizier Erwin Kley had been chosen to test the new Bf 109s but when Kley crashed on take-off, von Richthofen rounded on Hauptmann Merhart who had recommended him, 'It was a mistake to select Kley, an unknown man, and not to have previously demonstrated the aircraft to him.' Neither was he pleased when it turned out that three more Bf 109s which should have arrived had not even been loaded in Germany. Trautloft applied his personal marking of a large green heart below the cockpit to Bf 109 6-1.

The French Air Ministry issued a report in January 1937 to summarise its views on the first months of the war. It concluded that Republican aircraft had been very successful when attacking airfields and troop positions and suggested that the French should reactivate its programme of ground-attack aircraft. The report emphasised the demoralising effect that low-level attacks had on ground forces.

More Soviet Aid Arrives

In December and January two more shipments of thirty Chatos arrived in Spain from the Soviet Union, making it possible to form a complete combat unit of four squadrons. The mix of crews is illustrated by the make-up of these units;

- Escuadrilla Zotsenko at Alcazár de San Juan had a complement of sixteen all-Soviet pilots
- Escuadrillo Kazakov at Almeria had twelve Soviet and six 'friendly' pilots
- Escuadrillo La Calle at Guadalajara had eight Spanish and four American pilots
- Escuadrillo Alonso at San Javier had thirteen Spanish and one Uruguyan pilot

It was probably through coming into contact with different nationalities that the Soviet pilots became aware of the relative paltry remuneration they were receiving in relation to other flyers. French pilots were getting five times as much, as well as bonus payments. This naturally impacted upon the lifestyle of the differing nationalities as the local economy was awash with unheard of levels of hard cash, leading inevitably to inflationary pressures.[17]

Although active in operations, Soviet pilots were increasingly employed to train local Spanish flyers, but neither the Soviet nor Spanish governments were happy about the propaganda consequences of being seen to utilise large numbers of non-domestic personnel. One solution was to send selected Spanish pilots back to the Soviet Union for specialised training. The Soviets had been doing this for many years as part of their promotion of communism throughout many parts of the world and it was also another way of eating into the 500 tonnes of gold that the Spanish government had shipped to the Soviet Union for safekeeping and as payment for Soviet military aid. The rest of the Spanish gold, which had been accumulated mostly during the First World War in which Spain had remained neutral and sold arms to both sides, had been sent to France and exchanged for hard currency to buy military supplies. The first Spanish flyers left to join a pilot school in Kirovabad on 17 January 1937 on the SS *Ciudad de Cádiz*, which sailed for Feodosia in the Crimean Peninsula.

Transfer of the gold to Moscow had been suggested by the Spanish Republican Finance Minister Dr Juan Negrín. On 14 September 1936, the gold, mostly coins, had been taken from the Bank of Spain vaults in Madrid, boxed up in 7,800 crates and taken by rail to Cartagena with a view to moving it to a location beyond the reach of the Nationalists.[18] Use of the gold which had been sent to Paris was increasingly subjected to scrutiny, restricting its utility and leaving the Soviet Union as the only destination where the rest of the bullion would be beyond theft and its uses free from public gaze. On 26 September the gold was loaded onto four ships, SS *KIM*, SS *Kursk*, SS *Neva* and SS *Volgoles*, which docked at Odessa on 2 November when the gold was taken to the State Depository for Valuables in Moscow. Stalin held a banquet and is reputed to have declared that 'the Spanish will never see their gold again'. The gold coins, some of considerable historic and numismatic value, were melted down into ingots and sold on the open market for $518 million, the Soviets retaining some 3.3 per cent commission and the rest of the cash placed on deposit with the Banque Commerciale de l'Europe du Nord (BCEN) in Paris. With each delivery of Soviet aid to Spain, the appropriate amount was taken in payment by the Soviets. Not only was matériel charged for, but also travel costs, service pay of personnel in Spain, including holiday pay and maintenance payments for their families at home, transportation of goods and personnel across the Soviet Union and at sea, and all costs associated with the training of Spanish personnel. Estimates of the total amount charged for these extra services put the bill at something in excess of $15 million.

On 27 January 1937, the Republican government were confused to receive notification of goods and services provided by the Soviet Union in 1936 with the relevant costs. Their concerns were that:

- Quantities billed did not correspond to quantities received.
- The various condition of the matériels was not specified.
- No unit prices were given; only lump sums per consignment.
- No details of spares or components were included.
- Valuations were in pesetas with no indication of what exchange rate with the rouble would apply.

This notification was not a request for payment as such, more just information pending an official invoice. When the final bill was presented, however, the price set by the Soviets in roubles was converted into US Dollars at a rate they set themselves, and then the US dollars were converted into pesetas at the open market rate. There was no indication on the bill of what the value of the goods were in roubles or what the dollar-rouble conversion rate was.

Detailed research conducted by Gerald Howson for his book *Arms for Spain* shows that as a result of Soviet manipulation of their dollar-rouble exchange rate, the prices charged were grossly inflated, as the following examples show. The official rate of exchange at the time was 5.3 roubles to the dollar but the rate applied to different categories is shown in brackets.

- An SB Katiuska bomber was billed at $110,000 (3.95) showing a hidden excess charge of $27,925
- An I-16 Chato fighter was billed at $40,000 (3.2) showing a hidden excess charge of $15,850

All the prices were said to include generous discounts, which were quite unverifiable by the Spanish given the way the bills were presented, but Howson calculates that the average overcharge over all Soviet sales to the Republicans mounted to a staggering 30 per cent. Of course, given that the Soviets were holding all the cash from the gold sales, there was never any question of the Spanish defaulting on payment. Over the course of the war the total overcharge was calculated to be $51 million, of which Howson says,

> Of all the swindles, cheatings, robberies and betrayals that the Republicans had to put up with from governments, officials and arms traffickers all over the world, this barrow-boy behaviour

by Stalin and the high officials of the Soviet *nomenklatura* is surely the most squalid, the most treacherous and the most indefensible.[19]

A special training school was set up on 1 February 1937 near Kirovabad exclusively to train Spanish pilots, taking 200 at a time. The comprehensive course lasted five months, progressing from older aircraft to the most modern. At this time, the Soviets were hopeful that the Spanish war would result in a government victory and that government would remain on friendly terms with the Soviet Union as an insurance against the future. A cadre of Soviet-trained pilots going forward, in that eventuality, would be a significant bonus for the Soviets when the explosion of the major European war, for which Hitler had already lit the fuse, occurred. Political education was very much on the agenda and all trainees were encouraged to speak Russian. Those who learned the language were paraded before Soviet audiences to promote Russo-Spanish entente. The best were taken on tours of Soviet factories and cultural centres.[20]

Such non-military use of the pilots for political ends did not play well in Madrid, where every man was 'desperately needed' to shore up the faltering government campaign as soon as possible. This was a result of the wholly unrealistic expectation that the men, already pilots in their own right, would be returned within a month, but the courses consisted of much more than how to fly. They included theory, tactics and aerodynamics. This reminded the Soviets that it was actually in their own interests to return the Spanish pilots a bit faster so as to release their own men who were operating and dying in Spain. The restricted numbers of Soviet pilots sent to Spain and the relatively low number of Spanish graduates coming back often meant that there were too few qualified men in Spain to fly all of the Chatos and Ratas that the Soviets had sent. It was also clear that the new Spanish pilots would never perform at the high levels of skill and competence of the experienced Soviets. Overall the numbers were dwarfed by the numbers of Italian and German pilots coming in on the other side. The training was not without its difficulties with accidents not infrequent and, in total, claiming the lives of ten instructors and nine Spanish trainees. Each of the first four training programmes produced about 100 flyers, but the 185 pilots in the last course were only graduated after the war had ended and many of them stayed and flew for the Soviet Union in the Second World War.

Aircraft from the US

In 1936 the United States was still struggling with the domestic repercussions of the Great Depression and had registered its insularity by passing two Neutrality Acts that imposed a general embargo on trading in arms and war matériel with all parties in a war, and forbade all loans or credits to belligerents. Crucially, however, the Acts did not cover civil wars (an omission that was rectified by the third Neutrality Act of May 1937). In September 1936, Félix Gordón Ordás, the Spanish ambassador in Mexico (the only country in the world to have supported the Spanish Republican government from the first day of the war) began to procure aircraft from the United States on their behalf. He received offers of 128 aircraft from various sources and $9 million from Spain to effect these and other purchases.

Meanwhile, shipping agent Daniel Wolf and attorney Julius Rosenbaum, on behalf of the Spanish government, had sourced nine Vultee V1-A single-engine airliners from American Airlines at $22,000 each. When Spain authorised the purchases it had great difficulty in transferring the money through various banks in Paris and London which stalled and delayed transactions for almost two months. Eventually the money went through the Soviet BCEN and ten more aircraft were bought, seven Lockheed Orions and three Northrop Deltas, through Charles Harding Babb in Los Angeles, 'the World's largest exporter of used, reconditioned airplanes and engines'.[21] In December, Wolf applied for an export licence to ship the nineteen aircraft to France. The aircraft were loaded onto three ships, the SS *Waalhaven*, SS *American Traveller* and SS *President Harding* in New York Harbour on Christmas Eve, just days before a dock strike.

As the three ships put to sea, newspapers reported that Robert Cuse, a Latvian-born 'New Jersey junk dealer' had been granted an export licence for eighteen second-hand civil aircraft to be sent to the Spanish government. His application described the aircraft as 'old civil machines unsuitable for conversion to military use', which was a bit rich considering why they were being traded, but the Spanish buyers were apparently not aware of this detail. A Spanish freighter, SS *Mar Cantábrico*, had been stalled at Pier 35 in Brooklyn due to the strike, but Cuse had sufficient influence to be allowed to load the aircraft into its empty holds, using unofficial labour, while the US Congress was debating an amendment to the Neutrality Act that would make his deal illegal. The SS *Mar Cantábrico* with only eight aircraft on board, cleared US territorial waters hours before the new Act was passed, while the other ten aircraft remained crated on the dockside. The ship sailed for Spain but was intercepted by the Nationalist cruiser SS *Canarias*, its captain and ten crew were executed and the remaining crewmen given life imprisonment. It appears that the ship had previously been used as a prison ship by the Republicans in Valencia. It is worth noting that in response to the Cuse incident, the Germans – with breath-taking cynicism – said the new US Neutrality Act 'stands in contrast to the methods of certain other countries, where [only] lip service is paid to non-intervention'. For his contribution to the charade, Franco said that Roosevelt had 'behaved like a true gentleman', while the Generalissimo was quietly taking delivery of another 250 aircraft from Italy.[22]

The passing of the 1937 Neutrality Act, meanwhile, had stifled Gordón's plan to export the twenty-eight aircraft he had managed to purchase. The Bolivian government offered to act as agent for a sizeable fee of $140,000 but their gesture was declined. In the end, only nine of the aircraft were ever sent on the SS *Ibai* (Cabo Quilates) which docked at Le Havre on 13 January 1938, by which time the France-Spain border had been closed and they got no further.

Chapter 7

The Battle of El Jarama

- Atrocities at Bilbao
- The Bombing of Málaga
- Soviet Aircraft Dominate
- The Italians Take Málaga
- El Jarama Offensive Begins
- Republicans Search for Suppliers of Aircraft

Atrocities at Bilbao

Franco eventually listened to Sperrle and admitted that his attack on Madrid was a failure, especially given the German leader's instruction to his bombers to operate only at night. Soviet aircraft acted as a fearsome deterrent by day, often landing and taking off along the wide city streets, and on the ground Soviet T-26 tanks held positions around the capital, but the city could not free itself entirely of Nationalist attention. While direct attacks ceased, the city was kept under siege while Franco looked elsewhere to progress his agenda. Sperrle had realised that sending his bombers out to find Republican airfields was a waste of time and resources, and the winter conditions both in the air and on the ground posed a serious threat to morale which Sperrle and von Richthofen were struggling to deal with, despite ensuring that crews had all the 'amenities of life that made living a little easier'.[1]

Some Condor Legion He 51s were now operating from Vitoria in the north of the country, acting as aerial artillery supporting ground forces attempting to open the road to Villareal. The region had become isolated with the Nationalist capture of Irún and San Sebastian and Bilbao became the target of Nationalist bombers. On 4 January, He 51s of 3.K/88 attacked fuel dumps in the city and one was shot down by Felipe del Rio in a Chato. The crew escaped by parachute. The pilot, Leutnant Hermann, was attacked and killed by a mob as he landed. His radio operator, 21-year-old Karl Gustav Schmidt survived a little longer. He had landed on the other side of the river and was taken alive, escorted through another angry mob and locked into Larrínaga prison which was surrounded by a crowd demanding he be handed over to them. When a battalion of Republican troops was called to restore order, they sided with the mob and attacked the prison with hand grenades and machine guns, killing sixty-one inmates there and thirty-three more at the Casa de Galera annexe. At the nearby Convent of Los Angeles Custodies, ninety-six political prisoners were dragged out and murdered also. More deaths were avoided at Carmelo Monastery by the timely arrival of Basque police who dispersed the crowds. The mob violence was particularly extreme due to starvation that was rampant because of the Nationalist blockade.[2] The feeling of hatred for the German airmen was spontaneous among all the Basques, with one graphic account by Steer being picked up by the world's press,

> the daily arrival of the planes over Bilbao and the incessant bombardment of fourteen kilometres of riverside and port meant that they were suffering the same cruel fate as their fighting menfolk. The riverside and the port, and Las Arenas were precisely the parts of Bilbao where the poorer classes lived and the refugees were quartered. I neither desire nor intend to make any claim that the German aircraft which made its daily mess of industrial Bilbao were out to kill civilians. They wanted to hit factories; and more often than not, they missed. They did, however, break the Air Warfare Rules drawn up at The Hague in 1923, which expressly forbid the bombardment of military establishments or depots, or factories constituting important and well-known centres engaged in the manufacture of arms, ammunition, or distinctively military supplies, where such localities cannot be bombarded without the indiscriminate bombardment of the civil population.
>
> The sirens changed to a most melancholy song of two notes, one high and the other low, signifying peril. The women of Bilbao had already seized up their children and gone below

with streaming hair into the refuges; the men followed them hotfoot. Bilbao became a city where only police lived, and Red Cross men stood ready at their cars; in a few minutes all noise of circulation had gone, except the flutter of old paper along the streets. With appalling deliberation, the foreign fleet passed over the cringing city of Bilbao.[3]

The raids on Bilbao in April were more severe than those of January, but the behaviour of the population was better. A particularly heavy raid on 18 April would kill sixty-seven and wound 110, with bombs penetrating to underground shelters where the people had sought refuge.[4] By then *Time Magazine* reported that the city had had '980 buildings completely or partially destroyed by aerial attack, 1,490 persons killed, and 3,488 wounded, according to reasonably trustworthy figures'.[5]

The Bombing of Málaga

Málaga, on the Mediterranean coast, was also a target of Italian bombers in the early months of 1937. They ranged over the city singly or in pairs and dropped a small number of bombs, but the psychological effects were devastating and widely reported internationally as a vindication of Douhet's prophesies. Arthur Koestler, the Hungarian author, arrived in Málaga the day following the destructive raids of 27 January 1937 and noted in his diary that,

> Madrid after the great air attack and artillery bombardment was a health resort compared with this town in its death throes.

And, when the bombers came again on the 29th he recorded that,

> Everyone runs hither and thither in feckless confusion; the panic is much worse than it was in Madrid ... the population is obviously demoralised. Since yesterday the physiognomy of the town has changed; no more trams, all shops closed, groups at every corner and every face shrouded in the grey cobweb of fear ... I feel the contagion of fear getting me too. Rebel planes strafed the refugees who fled along the coastal roads to escape capture.[6]

Soviet Aircraft Dominate

The Condor Legion continued to suffer mounting losses of its He 51s. Oberleutnant Harder commented:

> We were all convinced that it was madness to continue sending the He 51 s on escort missions over Madrid. The Ratas played cat and mouse with us. Even the 'Martin' [SB] bombers were at least 50 km/h faster than us. The morale of the pilots was excellent, but all the guts in the world were useless with such technical inferiority. So once again we were to be employed in low-level attacks. Apparently, several more of us would have to be shot down before they became convinced of the stupidity of these orders.[7]

The commander of of J/88, Hauptmann Hubertus Merhart von Bernegg, brought the German dilemma sharply into focus when he informed Sperrle that his open-cockpit biplanes were technically incapable of matching the Fiats for speed, manoeuvrability or firepower and he would no longer send his men on suicide missions to engage the enemy. This was received with something less than equanimity by Sperrle, a huge man with fierce demeanour, who furiously confronted von Bernegg. Neither would give ground and von Bernegg threatened to resign which, had he done so, would have placed Sperrle in a very embarrassing position so early in his command. After a tense silence in which Sperrle managed to control his anger, he turned without another word and strode back to his aircraft. To his credit, Sperrle then petitioned Berlin to alter the tactical deployment of the He 51s, which Wilberg agreed would now concentrate on low-level attacks against enemy frontlines. The whole battle tactics of Condor Legion aircraft underwent a seismic shift as a result of Soviet dominance of the skies. The ground support role was a new departure for the pilots very few of whom had any training for it and heralded the start of a tactic that was to become of increasing importance in Spain and later during the Second World War. With the initiative firmly on the Republican side, German morale was sinking fast. The need for better aircraft was acquiring critical dimensions. Those pilots who were familiar with it wanted the new Messerschmitt Bf 109, but although it had been operational for more than a year it was still not far beyond its experimental stage and was untried in combat. Even if it was sent, it would take some time for pilots to get used to this 'delicate' and 'unforgiving' aircraft. Crews, especially those of the long-range reconnaissance unit, were exhausted to the point where they were 'becoming a danger to themselves' and were released to return to Germany while their aircraft were turned over to Spanish crews.[8] Reconnaissance itself suffered a blow to its importance with so little usable intelligence flowing back to inform operations. Too often, commanders would divert reconnaissance crews to bombing and ground-support missions.

Lehmann's 2.J/88 with ten He 51s was now moved to Vitoria, in northern Spain, while another Staffel was sent to León. The other units remained on the Madrid Front at Escalona and Ávila. From Vitoria, the Heinkels engaged in regular ground-attack missions, dropping fragmentation bombs on Basque positions and strafing road transport where enemy forces had launched an attack at Villarreal de Alava. Holle had, by now, become totally exhausted and it was no surprise when he was replaced by von Richthofen as Chief of Staff of the Condor Legion. von Richthofen was well received by Franco, given their mutual contempt for communism, and he became a valuable liaison tool. It was a bonus, too, that von Richthofen was fluent in both Spanish and Italian. Sperrle was ever mindful of the importance of his 'eyes in the skies', and was able to persuade Berlin to send a few of the new Dornier Do 17s to replace the He 70s for long-range reconnaissance, but it was soon apparent that the Do 17 was just as vulnerable as the He 70 whenever the Soviet fighters were around. The Ju 52 bombing fleet had seen its activities greatly reduced as a result of Soviet fighter activity but Berlin had little in the way of ready-made replacements. Its only option was the Heinkel He 111, which was only just starting to come off the production lines. The first thirty He 111 B-1s arrived in Spain in February and conducted their first bombing run over Alcaláde Henares and Barajas in March.

Alongside the realisation that Berlin had seriously underestimated the combat effectiveness of the Soviet fighters came the sobering awareness of the inadequacy of their operational command structure and practices. Sperrle was paying the price for the ad hoc approach that Berlin had allowed to proliferate as the 'helping hand' gesture of July 1936 had uneasily morphed into embroilment in a serious war with the prospect of even deeper entanglement. So much of what they had gone through since July 1936 was quite new to them and mistakes had been made. The battlefronts varied considerably and each required a different approach. Whole units with ground crews had been forced to relocate at short notice and while it was not so much of a problem for the air crews, ground support vehicles were of such a wide assortment that maintenance was a nightmare and accidents, many fatal, along narrow mountain roads were frequent. The constant movement of battle command posts however, while problematical at the time, gave important experience that was to stand the Wehrmacht in good stead in the fast-moving campaigns of the Second World War.

Modifying aerial tactics and operational procedures took up much of the Condor Legion General Staff's time. Logistics was a challenge and one which, in the case of transportation, often defeated them. Staff had to be rotated in line with the instruction that as many active servicemen as possible should gain experience of war while it lasted and still the façade of non-intervention had to be maintained even though it was, by now, quite transparent to all observers.

Perhaps the section that benefited the most in terms of developing a structure and operational procedures, at least in the short-to medium-term, was communications and liaison. The Group, of necessity, had been split between Condor Legion headquarters, Spanish command, Italian command, weather reporting and all working under the burden of constant movement from one theatre to another and sometimes back again. Faced with these difficulties and the antiquated Spanish communications network, the group was forced to innovate and experiment which, although tiresome and exhausting, was to provide experience that would prove invaluable over the coming years.

A close second to communications in the area of reassessment and redevelopment was logistics. The awkward presence of France straddling the continent from the English Channel to the Swiss border was a stubborn block on any overland supply routes. As a result, almost everything including men, machines, ammunition, fuel and spare parts had to shipped 1,200 miles by sea.

The Italians Take Málaga

The worsening winter weather was now a constant threat to the Legion's morale. It's not that they were unused to cold weather, but in Spain they lacked proper winter clothing and were without suitable maintenance facilities for their aircraft. They were often grounded for days on end up until the early part of February. Meanwhile, Italian morale received a boost when, against minimal opposition, Italian forces under the Duke of Seville won an easy victory at the port of Málaga which opened up a new, more convenient supply channel.

El Jarama Offensive Begins

While the Italians were concentrating on Málaga and the Condor Legion aircraft were grounded, Franco launched a pincer movement designed to encircle Madrid but the Nationalists in the capital with their armoured brigade of heavy Soviet tanks had anticipated it and were preparing a counter-offensive. A Nationalist ground offensive was launched on 6 February to create a bridgehead over the El Jarama river and sever Republican communications along the Valencia-Madrid road. In appalling weather conditions, a brutal hand-to-hand battle ensued along the river. Soviet aircraft dominated the skies and were generally successful in preventing Legion bombers from intervening. Again and again the bombers would be driven back from the front lines and they concentrated instead on disrupting communications on the roads leading to Madrid. On the 7th the 1a Escuadrilla moved to the old Hispano-Suiza aerodrome in Guadalajara and began operations at El Jarama, and although the river crossing was successful there were heavy losses. Torrential rain caused the river to flood and Republican T-26 tanks threatened to retake the Pidonque bridge and blunt the attack. The lack of air superiority made it impossible for Nationalist forces to make any further advance. Ground forces suffered heavy casualties in a stalemate situation but Franco stubbornly insisted on continuing the offensive. Condor Legion Ju 52s had halted the Soviet T-26 tanks on the Pindoque bridge but the Republicans had overall aerial advantage. On the 14th, the appearance of forty Soviet fighters was enough to deter the Spanish crews of six Ju 52s from completing their bombing mission on Arganda del Rey, despite being escorted by fifteen CR.32s and eighteen He 51s. Two days later, twenty-four CR.32s flew close escort to Ju 52s out to bomb Arganda del Rey and were set upon by Chatos coming from behind and above. The Republican drive was halted short of their objective, Alcalá de Henares, but they dug in and held what ground they had won. As the weather lifted on the 24th, two dozen Condor Legion bombers struck at the Republican supply base of Albacete and followed up with repeated attacks. The battle descended into a bloody stalemate with neither side able to break the deadlock.

The Italians, now disengaging from Málaga and intent on operating according to their own agenda, infuriated Franco by planning an attack against Sagunto and Valencia. The Generalissimo was embarrassed by the large numbers of Italian troops in Spain which he had not asked for and could barely control in a relationship characterised by 'hostile cooperation'.[9] He was adamant that when the time was right, Valencia would be taken by Spanish troops as part of his own overall strategy and he flatly refused to authorise the attack. Instead, to divert them, Franco considered giving the Italians troops who 'have been sent [to Spain] without [his] authorisation' an alternative objective by relieving the pressure on the Jarama front with an attack through Gaudalajara.[10]

On 7 March, some 30,000 Italian troops led by General Mario Roatta, were in position to advance from Algora along the road to Guadalajara but, again, the weather turned foul. The four divisions of men, with tanks and artillery, were, however, poorly trained and low on morale due to their lack of winter clothing. Temperatures plummeted and bitterly cold rain and sleet swirled all around. Despite the lack of protection from the air, with aircraft unable to take off from waterlogged airfields, Roatta ordered the advance on the morning of the 8th and the Italian 'Black Flames' battalion made nine miles towards Brihuega. On the following day, the Black Flames and Black Arrows pushed on free of any interference from the air taking Brihuega on the 10th and Trijueque on the 11th. The first Republican reconnaissance aircraft were now able to brave the weather and make a pass over the columns and report that extreme wet weather was making all off-road areas impassable and, more importantly, they had received no anti-aircraft fire from the ground. This was a signal for the Republican air force to come out on the 12th with 140 aircraft including Chatos and Ratas to bomb and strafe the columns that found it impossible to disperse. Soviet tanks followed up the air strike and smashed into the Italians retaking Trijueque in one of the first and best examples of air-ground coordination seen in the war, but Spanish infantry would not be so eager to advance. On the 13th the weather lifted sufficiently for Republican aircraft to begin operations from their hard-surface airstrips, but when Nationalist aircraft tried to intervene they were driven off and the Italian columns continued to take severe punishment. The Italian armoured columns were unable to move across open country which had been turned to mud, and were confined to the hard surface of the road. By the next day, the air battles were a little more even with the Soviet fighters drawn more and more into an air combat, but the reticence of the Republican infantry to engage allowed Roatta, faced with 'a complete rout with no discipline whatsoever', to effect some regrouping of his men, but essentially only to carry out a more efficient retreat and avoid encirclement. An observer, Sandro Sandri, reported,

> The flight of entire units was provoked by the machine gunning and bombing of communist planes … Everyone ran, and among the first many officers. This naturally led to heavy losses that would not have been suffered if the officers had kept the troops calmly in the lines.[11]

Brihuega was hammered by twenty-five Katiuskas with thirty Chatos for protection and retaken by ground forces on the 16th. The weather closed in again to save the Italians further punishment as they made it back to Algora, but the Nationalists were unable or unwilling to pursue them and the battle cooled with the weather clamping down on all air activity. The Republicans had saved Madrid but in the end it was the weather that had saved the Italians from further punishment.

The defeat was a shattering blow for Italian morale and it did little to improve the levels of confidence placed in them by Sperrle and Franco, but questions persisted over the level of support given to them especially the failure of Franco to ease the pressure by diversionary attacks at Jarama. It is not inconceivable that he, to some extent, orchestrated the Italian defeat to clip their wings and bring them more under his control, which is exactly what happened. Roatta deflected criticism by claiming that 'the essential cause of the failure to reach our objective was the lack of support by the Spanish troops on the Jarama'.[12] For their part, the German leaders had been 'appalled at the rapid collapse of the Italian forces'.[13]

Mussolini, in particular, would be highly critical of Franco's failure to support the CTV at Guadalajara, in what critics had dubbed 'the Spanish

Caporetto', and lamented that 'Spaniards show us no great affection'. He told von Neurath during his visit to Rome on 3 May that both Italy and Germany had made enough sacrifices for Franco and that he intended to inform Franco at the beginning of June that he would withdraw the Italian militia if the war were not being prosecuted more energetically by that time.[14] The Spanish, he claimed 'had no idea of modern warfare'. Clearly Italian-Spanish relations, never strong at the best of times, were on a downward spiral. The Italians had, deservedly or not, acquired a reputation for what von Richthofen called 'blithe incompetence', which clung to them throughout the rest of the war and the Germans in particular were loath to carry out joint missions with them.

Kindelán changed his tactics and now ordered his fighter commander Joaquín García-Morato y Castaño to engage even when outnumbered. He felt that Aviatzione Legionaria units were being too cautious and that the Republicans were close to securing air superiority over the front line. The Condor Legion also realised that they could no longer avoid the obvious fact that the He 51 was completely outclassed by the Soviet fighters. The need for Bf 109s was becoming urgent. Nevertheless, they felt they had to once again attempt daylight bombing as a more effective use of air power, but in a matter of a few days they were forced to abandon it in the face of unsustainable losses. Sperrle petitioned Berlin for more modern aircraft, which started trickling in ostensibly as part of von Richthofen's experimental unit, but which did not see combat until the pilots had been given sufficient time to become familiar with them.

Republicans Search for Suppliers of Aircraft

The Nationalists were boosted by the SS *Aniene* delivering twelve more Fiat CR.32s and eleven more pilots after docking from La Spezia. With the arrival of these new fighters there were now sufficient aircraft to organise the CR.32 *stormo* into two *gruppi* of three *squadriglie* each.

Military aid continued to pour into the Republican side with the first Polikarpov R-Z Natacha biplane reconnaissance bombers arriving in Spain in late February. In March further fighters arrived by sea when eight Czech Letov Š.231 biplane fighters were delivered aboard the SS *Sarkani*, sailing out of Estonia for cover, to strengthen the Republican air force. These were

Above: The Condor
Legion marches
through the Spanish
city of Gijon, 1937.
(Alamy)

Right: Condor
Legion Commanders:
Hermann Göring
(Nov 1936 – Oct
1937) and Wolfram
Freiherr von
Richthofen (Oct
1938 – Apr 1939).
(Alamy)

Tetouan on the Mediterranean coast of Spanish Morocco. In the background, the foothills of the Atlas Mountains. This was the place from where German Junkers Ju 52 transport aircraft, with the paintwork of the German Condor Legion, started their flight loaded with Moroccan soldiers to the Spanish mainland. (Alamy)

Four Italian bombers, type Fiat BR.20 'Cicogna' on a Feindflug over a mountain chain in the Spanish Civil War. The cockades of the Italian Aviazione Legionaria, which resembled those of the German Condor Legion, are easily recognizable. There is a white letter M in the black cockade on the hull, which stands for the M in the signature of Benito Mussolini. (Alamy)

Right: Spanish women sewing Spanish, Italian and German flags for the Condor Legion in a workshop. In the foreground two women are sewing a swastika onto a flag. On the table, two banderas are being sewn. (Alamy)

Below: An Italian armoured car (L3/33, Carro veloce 33) in the streets of Santander on 27 August 1937. A man and a woman are standing on the tank with a rosette decorated with national colours. Behind, a tank commander of the Italian Corpo Truppe Volontarie (CTV) leans out of his vehicle. In the background on the right, a German officer of the Condor Legion. (Alamy)

A captain of the Condor Legion (seated), who is in a conversation with a Spanish officer (right) on a command post of the Spanish national troops at Llanes, Asturias. Behind, there are scissors telescopes, as well as other Spanish officers. (Alamy)

Photo of the rear of an Italian two-man tank (L3/33, Carro Veloce 33) of the Corpo Truppe Volontarie (CTV), passing through the centre of Villaverde del Rio, north of Seville. The crew wears leather helmets. (Alamy)

A commander's (First General Staff Officer) office in the Wohnzug (special train that was used as home) of the commandant Chief of Staff of the Condor Legion, Major General Wolfram Freiherr von Richthofen at Toledo railway station, Castilla-La Mancha, 1939. (Alamy)

A first lieutenant of the Condor Legion inspects the bomb stock of 250kg aerial bombs piled up on an airfield in Spain. (Alamy)

A Messerschmitt Bf 109 of the Fighter Squadron 88 of the Condor Legion during a take-off on a Spanish airfield. At the rear there is the saltire of the Spanish Air Force. In the background there are buildings and other aircraft: Junkers Ju 52, Fieseler Storch. In the foreground are aerial bombs. (Alamy)

A German Junkers Ju 52 of the Deutsche Lufthansa AG 1939 at Salamanca airport, Castile and Leon, Spain. The aircraft bears the name 'Bruno Rodschinka'. It is just being loaded. In the foreground, two policemen of the Guardia Civil. (Alamy)

A Messerschmitt Me 109 of the Condor Legion in Spain undergoing maintenance. (Alamy)

A Messerschmitt Me 109 of the Condor Legion in Spain being fuelled-up. (Alamy)

An almost completely destroyed suburban area in Asturian Oviedo after a Spanish national bombardment by the Condor Legion in 1938. In the attacks that lasted for months, 125,000 artillery shells were fired and 15,000 aerial bombs were dropped on Oviedo. (Alamy)

The aftermath of the bombing of Guernica on 26 April 1937. (Historic Military Press)

part of about a hundred Czech aircraft offered to Spain, most of which were rejected on the grounds that 'to send valuable airmen in them against an enemy would be an act of murder'.[15] In the end, a mixture of forty-three 'fairly useless' military aircraft were bought at a cost of £120,000, but most were held up at Gdynia docks during which time the Nationalists tried to hijack them. A number of murky deals were struck and the freight piled up massive storage fees on the dockside. Eventually the Republicans were deemed the rightful owners and the aircraft were shipped out on the SS *Hordena* on 8 April. Eight days later, however, the ship was intercepted in the Bay of Biscay by the Nationalist cruiser *Almirante Cervera* and taken into El Ferrol. The aircraft eventually flew with Franco's air force. As payment for their part in the subterfuge, the Estonians demanded that Spain buy eight of their old Bristol Bulldog fighters and eight of their antiquated Potez 25s at extortionate prices. These were shipped to Gijón on the SS *Viiu* in June. British non-intervention observers turned a blind eye on the understanding that the Estonians would use the proceeds of the sale to buy twelve British Spitfires which, in the end, were never actually delivered. It was also a blow to Republican morale when pilots were asked to fly the antiquated Gourdou-Leseurre GL.32 parasol fighters which had recently been bought from France having arrived without armament and hastily modified for combat.

The Soviet intelligence agent Walter Germanovich Krivitsky was tasked by the Kremlin with procuring arms on the open market on behalf of the Spanish Republicans. One company he established was the Societé Française des Transports Aériens (SFTA) that negotiated a deal with the Fokker company to buy the new G.1 fighter about to undergo trials in Amsterdam. To circumvent the prolonged testing of the aircraft, required due to its revolutionary design, it was agreed that Spanish pilots, including Colonel Riaño would have special secret access to try it out. Their approval led the SFTA to place an order, payment in advance, for twenty-six and plough funds into establishing a production line. When the first aircraft were produced, however, the Dutch government were given priority and only six were ever allocated to Spain, none of which were delivered before the war ended. Fokker also sold licences to Republican Spain for the manufacture of D.XXI fighters in Alicante but only one was ever built.

Chapter 8

Franco's Drive into Vizcaya

- Franco Turns to the Basque Country
- Germans Frustrated with Franco
- The Bombing of Guernica
- More Soviet Aid Arrives
- The Bombing of Valencia
- Bilbao Falls
- Kindelán and von Faupel Fall Out

Franco Turns to the Basque Country

The attacks on Madrid had illuminated the poor fighting capabilities of both Spanish and Italian ground forces and their vulnerability to the superior Soviet arms on the Republican side. Only Yagüe's Moroccan and Foreign Legion troops, notable for their ferocity and ruthlessness, could be considered an effective fighting force. After failing to take Madrid, Franco eventually abandoned his obsession with taking the capital and, frustrated by the Italians' independent mindset, began to listen a little more to his German allies who advocated a concerted campaign to attack the most vulnerable Republican territories. The Condor Legion was revitalised by the introduction of new, more modern, aircraft and encouraged by Franco's willingness to give von Richthofen a more prominent say in the organisation and execution of combined air-ground operations. The Republicans held the advantage in the central regions so it was decided that the most inviting target was the industrial Basque region and Asturias along the coast of Biscay and its capital Bilbao, which held a half of all bank deposits in Spain.[1] German enthusiasm for this operation was underpinned by the prospect of gaining access to, and control of, the mineral-rich mining industries and heavy steel-making plants whose products could be diverted to augment German military production. Vizcaya, already under blockade forcing some starving inhabitants to resort to eating cats and seagulls, became isolated, making it almost impossible to reinforce even if Madrid had wanted to divert resources to defend what, for them, had always been an independent and troublesome region. The entire Condor Legion, with up to 5,000 personnel, now began to deploy to airfields in northern Spain with 1,000 tons of bombs to coordinate the air war in that region. Franco agreed to place all Spanish and Italian air forces in the area under German control. This gave Sperrle, who had moved his headquarters to Vitoria, about 150 aircraft at Burgos, including six He 111s, seven Bf 109s and three Hs123s, which would come up against a mere handful of Republican aircraft.

In a bid not so much to intervene but more as an act of humanitarian aid, British warships were stationed off the mouth of the river Nervion as British cargo vessels ran the blockade to deliver food to Bilbao. The SS *Seven Seas Spray* brought 3,600 tons of supplies on 20 April, while SS *Macgregor*, SS *Hamsterley* and SS *Stanbrook* followed under the guns of HMS *Hood* and the baleful gaze of the German pocket battleship *Graf Spee*. SS *Stesso* and SS *Turston* docked on the 25th and *Sheaf Garth* landed 2,000 tons of coal on the 26th.

The Nationalist 'Vizcaya' offensive against the prosperous industrial region around Bilbao began at the end of March with ground forces under the control of General Mola now boosted by the support of the whole Condor Legion. It was generally understood by the Nationalist leaders that the war would not be ultimately won in the North and one major concern was that the campaign there should not be too costly in manpower. Immediately all three Staffeln of J/88 at Vitoria, now deploying sixteen Bf 109s, fitted out and tested, went into action with three squadrons of He 51s, obsolete as attack aircraft but able to operate as such supporting the Nationalist infantry of the 4th Navarre Brigade with bombing and strafing attacks in the almost total absence of Republican aircraft. von Richthofen, operational commander of the strike force, noted with satisfaction that 'J/88 appeared and pinned the enemy down'. The three squadrons of Condor Legion Ju 52 bombers, based at Burgos, were employed essentially in a tactical role as support for ground forces even though the overall military commander in the North, General Mola, had wanted them to bomb armament factories in

Bilbao. He had leaflets dropped on the besieged towns with the message, 'If submission is not immediate I will raze all Vizcaya to the ground.'[2] Sperrle managed to persuade Franco that industrial facilities would be of immense value after the area was secured and Mola's idea was quietly dropped.

Germans Frustrated with Franco

The ground forces of both sides at this point were generally inexperienced and poorly led allowing the Condor Legion aircraft to play a decisive role in support of Nationalist troops by acting as mobile artillery but the German leadership was becoming increasingly frustrated by the lack of coordination between their aircraft and Spanish troops who were slow to follow up after air strikes had created opportunities for advance. It was only as a result of the intense effort of Sperrle and his commanders to improve communications with the Spanish ground forces and to undertake meticulous pre-planning of attacks that any progress was made in this regard, but it was a struggle. Neither did Sperrle have much confidence in the Italian air force whose aircraft, he conceded, were equal to the task but whose crews were, in his opinion 'very poorly trained and … inclined to bomb the wrong targets'.[3] His gloomy outlook was not improved by a sense that Franco had allocated insufficient forces to Mola to complete a double-fronted attack.

In truth, very few Spanish generals on either side had much experience of combat and lacked an extensive military education. Sperrle and von Richthofen privately thought many of them simply 'incompetent', but officers in the second tier of command, such as Mola's Chief of Staff, General Juan Suero diaz Vigón, were found to be much more professional and it was through these that most communication and effective cooperation flowed.[4]

During this phase the Germans picked up on the Italian idea of 'shuttle attacks', whereby bombers sometimes flew three or more sorties each day to make repeated attacks on the same target to maintain constant pressure on a position, a tactic that was to have resounding consequences after it was employed at Guernica.[5] This placed immense pressure on both air and ground crews. There would, however, be no rapid Blitzkrieg breakthroughs against Basque forces well dug-in behind their 'iron ring' of strong fortifications. Success would depend very much on how well aircraft were able to coordinate with ground forces in a series of set-piece battles. The Condor Legion had some experience of this but nothing on the scale of what was required now. Theory, however, did not always translate into practice and so German liaison officers were ordered to stay very close to Spanish ground commanders to ensure that air attacks were speedily followed up with ground assault. Careful planning of each move saw air and army staffs working together to exploit every situation from the initial reconnaissance to the aerial bombardment prior to the ground attack right through, where appropriate, to harassment of retreating forces, not giving them time to regroup. Republican forces in retreat would try to stabilise by occupying towns and villages where supplies and reserves could be held and these became prime targets for the bombers. Despite his best efforts to galvanise Mola into swifter action, von Richthofen was so infuriated by the slow speed of follow-up to his air strikes that he urged Sperrle to confront the Spanish general, but Sperrle decided that von Richthofen's command of the language and his obvious anger would bring better results. Never slow to express his opinions, von Richthofen accused Mola of a 'want of energy [and] lack of leadership'. Mola argued that his troops were not trained to carry out rapid manoeuvre and that Condor Legion aircraft should instead concentrate on strategic targets behind the lines which, under the circumstances, von Richthofen privately called 'nonsense'.[6] It seems that the confrontation cleared the air somewhat and galvanised Mola into a response because on 5 April, an artillery and air attack by German and Italian bombers at Ochandiano and Mount Monchetegui was better supported by ground forces, taking the Basque positions against little resistance with the He 51s strafing fleeing civilians and preventing reinforcements from moving to the front.[7]

Sperrle and von Richthofen regularly observed the effects of air strikes from forward command posts. von Richthofen described the attack on Mount Monchetegui in his diary,

> I ordered new attacks by the Ju 52s, VJ/88 and the Italians on this mountain stronghold. I was lucky in the timing, as the air formations struck simultaneously at the targets. The stronghold turned into a gruesome spectacle of flames and smoke from about sixty tonnes of bombs that fell within two

minutes. With the first bombs, the Reds again began to run in thick droves into a forest situated towards their rear, where most of the bombs fell, effecting a horrible slaughter.[8]

Overall, however, there was little improvement which caused von Richthofen time and again to complain. Sperrle took up the case by complaining personally to Franco that in his opinion, there were too few ground forces allocated to the North and the slow pace of progress was giving the defenders too much time to reinforce their positions. Franco was no more receptive to German advice than he was to Italian criticism but did, after several days, thank Sperrle for his views. Little changed, however and Sperrle's argument was not helped when reports reached Franco of German and Italian aircraft bombing their own lines. Mola was quick to capitalise and return von Richthofen's earlier criticism with some of his own.

During the attack on Ochandiano, von Richthofen had been very impressed by the Italian bombing patterns which were much more concentrated than those of the Condor Legion. This was the result of 'relay' bombing attack which von Richthofen now employed against the Basque town of Durango. Despite dogged defence in the steep hills surrounding the city, the fall of Bilbao could not be forestalled and the intensified efforts of the Franco forces to encircle and capture the city led to repeated attacks upon all the area surrounding it. Durango, a town of some 10,000 inhabitants on the main road between San Sebastian and Bilbao, was bombed on 31 March and 1 and 2 April. On the first raid, four heavy bombers and nine fighters appeared in the early morning. George Steer reported that, in his estimation,

> The objective of this bombardment ... was to terrify civilians, and to knock so many houses across the roads that they would be impassable to motor transport.... The Germans wanted to strike terror into everyone who lived in Durango, everyone who passed through it, and everyone who heard of it.[9]

The first recorded use by Nationalists of incendiary bombs was on Durango on 25 April 1937.[10] Mola had reported that Republican troops were consolidating their position in the town but by the time the Germans struck there were only civilians left to face the bombs. Some 250 were killed and 500 injured, which prompted Sperrle to call the bombing 'a waste of resources'.[11] Four days after the bombing of Durango, Franco met the Italian ambassador and explained that when he bombed cities he was not, as some might think, 'making a war like any other', but carrying out the 'slow task of redemption and pacification'.[12]

The *Times* reporter George Steer called the half-hour long bombing of Durango with its scores of civilian casualties 'the most terrible bombardment of a civil population'.[13] Other witnesses reported that on 2 April, at Durango, fighter aircraft dived and machine-gunned people fleeing for shelter. A third day of bombing by Escuadrilla de Chatos del Norte on the 18th killed 67 and wounded 110 in the Old Town of Bilbao.

The Bombing of Guernica

The attack on Durango was followed by a radio transmission from Salamanca which threatened 'a mighty blow against which all resistance is useless'.[14] The next morning, the 26th, *London Daily Express* journalist Noel Monks left Bilbao and passed through the busy market town of Guernica, whose population had been swelled by as many as 3,000 refugees who had fled from Durango. It was Monday and market day. Food was scarce and local farmers had brought what little produce they had. The local mayor, José de Labauria, fearing the worst after Durango, had instructed the inhabitants to make what bomb shelters they could and had ordered the construction of a number of pine municipal shelters in the centre of the town. About eighteen miles beyond Guernica, Monks saw a fleet of about a dozen bombers with an equal number of fighters heading for the market town. He reported that

> The bombers flew on towards Guernica but the Heinkels, out for random plunder, spotted our car, and, wheeling like a flock of homing pigeons, they lined up the road – and our car.... Machine-gun bullets plopped into the mud ahead, behind, all around us.

Meanwhile, at Bolibar Steer had been strafed by He 51 fighters spreading 'terror and noise'.[15] These actions were on the fringes of what proved to be an event that reverberated around the world. Condor Legion records state that the main attack of the day was to be against the Puenta de Renteria (Rentria bridge) about 250 metres north of the market square in Guernica and the Astra gun factory, just outside the town, but Steer claimed that the real target was Guernica itself, the 'symbol of Basque nationalism' and that it was bombed 'as a warning to the people of [Bilbao] of their fate if they did not surrender'.[16] As early as December 1936, when trying to stem the flow of supplies along the Valencia–Madrid road, Condor Legion flyers had known how difficult it was to score a direct hit on the small stone bridges of Spain, and how resistant they were to damage even when the bombs hit the target. Antony Beevor says that everything 'points to [the bombing of Guernica as] a major experiment in the effects of aerial terrorism'. Neither the bridge nor the arms factory was hit and neither justified the use of anti-personnel bombs. It is also doubtful if the bomb-aiming techniques of the Condor Legion at this time were anywhere near accurate enough to suggest that they would ever attempt such precision bombing.[17] James Corum, however, believes that 'There is no evidence to indicate that the German attack on Guernica was a "terror bombing" [designed] to break the morale of the Basque populace.'[18] The Council of the League of Nations, a few weeks later, passed a unanimous resolution condemning attacks on open cities in Spain.

Whatever the opinion, the events are not disputed. A lone He 111, piloted by Major Rudolf von Moreau, passed over the town at 4.30 in the afternoon; having attracted no flak, it came in again and dropped six bombs around the railway station. Fifteen minutes later, forty-three bombers and fighters of 1. and 2.J/88 and 3 SM.79s of Aviazione Legionaria dropped about fifty tons of high explosive, shrapnel and incendiary bombs on the town. The aircraft attacked from the north, unloaded their bombs and went back to Vitoria to reload and refuel before repeating the process. The raid lasted a total of three hours during which time no Republican aircraft intervened, nor did an anti-aircraft gun fire. A survivor told Monks, who went to the town in the evening, 'At four, before the market closed, many aeroplanes came. They dropped bombs. Some came low and shot bullets into the streets.' Both Monks and Steer sent first-hand graphic accounts of the carnage – 'flames, smoke and the smell of burning human flesh. Houses were collapsing in the inferno' – back to their newspapers and the world began to take note of scenes that would soon become catastrophically common from Warsaw,

Rotterdam and London through Berlin and Dresden to Hiroshima and Nagasaki.[19]

The bombing of Durango and Guernica was condemned by local Catholic priests: 'nothing justifies, nothing excuses, the bombing of open towns'. An eye witness, Catholic priest Father Alberto de Onaindia, wrote,

> bombs fell in the area around the Convent de las Madres Mercedarias ... heavy planes ... dropped large numbers of bombs, and behind them followed a veritable rain of incendiary bombs. Single machines ... came down to a height of 200m to machine gun the poor people who were fleeing in terror.... At a quarter to eight on that glorious April evening the systematic destruction of our sacred town had ended.[20]

A vital line had been crossed and the age of 'total war' was born with Guernica as midwife. The German flyer, Adolf Galland, said 'the bombing of Guernica was a brilliant success for the Condor Legion.' Corum believes that there is no evidence that von Richthofen, admittedly a ruthless operator, had any idea of the symbolic significance of Guernica for the Basque people and had chosen to attack it because of its geographical location as an intersection of two major roads and because it housed two major Basque battalions, the 18th Loyola and the Saseta.[21] It seems clear that Guernica was bombed with a view to complete destruction of the town, but probably for military reasons, albeit 'without regard for the civilian population', to prevent it becoming a defensive stronghold against Mola's ground advance.[22] Despite describing the raid (Operation Rügen) as a 'technical success' demonstrating the effect of explosives and incendiary bombs on a town where the buildings were primarily of wood, von Richthofen was again frustrated by the slow advance of the ground troops who only entered the town three days later. In his diary he recorded the use of incendiary bombs as approximately one third of all ordnance dropped causing dense smoke everywhere. 'Nobody could make out streets, bridge or targets on the edge of town so they just dropped everything wherever they could,' he wrote.[23]

A colonel on Mola's staff told a journalist that, 'This [bombing of Guernica] had to be done with all of Vizcaya and with all of Catalonia.'[24]

Over the next few days, von Richthofen gave his fighters 'a free rein to attack the roads around Guernica'. The He 51s flew constantly during the battle for the heights near Amorebieta and the Vizcargui, which dominated the surrounding area. Oberleutnant Harder described the action,

> bad weather again. The clouds hang low over the mountains. I manage to make it past Udala with my Kette and find good targets on the Durango–Bilbao road. The Reds had apparently not bargained on the famous 'motor-vehicle hunters' coming out in this awful weather. They have assembled their vehicles without camouflage. Flying low, we shoot up about twenty…. Again and again, we dive beneath the low clouds. The next day we're back at it again…. Once again we come across a vehicle column. Bombs on target. A few bursts at the church tower in Durango, where there are reported to be machine gun posts, then I roll over the town at low-level as usual and then head back home over Udala.[25]

More Soviet Aid Arrives

The Republican forces in the north had very little air cover, but further south Soviet aid continued to come in. A second batch of thirty-one improved Katiuskas was delivered on 1 May. These aircraft were fitted with ShKAS machine guns and were powered by M-100 engines with an extended service life but the engine cooling system still remained inadequate and the engines overheated in summer. This allowed Grupo No 12 to equip four Escuadrillas two of which had Spanish crews and leaders. It was clear now to all involved that the war was not going to end soon and to disrupt the Republican supply lines the Nationalists reviewed their plans for a blockade of the Mediterranean ports. Kindelán suggested that all the forces involved in the blockade should come under a unified command.[26]

The International Non-Intervention Committee was unable to come up with agreement between all signatories of the Agreement on how to effect a blockade of arms going into Spain and only a vague system of naval patrols and frontier posts were agreed on by 6 March 1937. The Italian and

German navies withdrew after the 'inadvertent' bombing by two Katiuskas of the pocket-battleship *Deutschland* off Ibiza on 29 May and the French, who had never been interested in the first place, soon followed suit leaving the Royal Navy to do the job alone. Only ships registered in countries of the signatories of the Agreement could be legally boarded and searched but even so, Italian vessels were often accompanied by their own warships and refused to stop. The British Foreign Office was painfully aware of the level of military aid going into Spain but publicly denied having 'reliable information on the matter' and was still trying to maintain the pretence that there were no German aircraft in Spain.[27]

The British were now also growing frustrated with rumours that Cot, variously described by the Foreign Office as a 'young crook' and 'a proper little ruffian' was attempting to supply a number of Potez 54 bombers to the Republicans.[28] When an official complaint was made the company supplying the aircraft was forced into bankruptcy and the Spanish government lost another $300,000 deposit. Cot, however, survived as Air Minister when Blum's government fell in June 1937.

A second group of Soviet volunteers also arrived in Spain having travelled through France with Dutch passports. Arriving with them were Spanish Republican pilots who had been undergoing fighter training at the Soviet flight school near Kirovabad. At the same time sixty-two new I-16 Type 5s were delivered from the Soviet Union to bolster the Republican air force, but these new fighters quickly proved to be far from combat-ready. Their M-25A engines demonstrated poor quality control and their wings lacked proper strengthening. A series of fatal accidents ensued, causing a loss of confidence in the aircraft. Soviet representatives in Spain even went as far as to label the new batch of fighters the 'sabotaged aircraft' in the reports they sent back to Moscow. Konstantin Kolesnikov of the 1a/21 was killed when the wings of his I-16 folded up in mid-air and Dmitriy Lesnikov was killed when his Rata suffered a critical wing failure during flight. All remaining Ratas from this batch were subjected to improvements in the field, including the strengthening and replacement of the fabric skin on the outer wing panels. An escuadrilla of Rata fighters, designated 1a Escuadrilla of Grupo de Caza No 21 (1a/21), was organised to perform defensive duties from Cartagena and Elche to Alicante, protecting Republican warships and cargo vessels from insurgent air raids. The level of Soviet investment in Spain spawns numerous questions of motivation. The lure of Spanish gold was undoubtedly one, but why the Soviets would sacrifice so many of the most advanced modern front-line aircraft and tanks in the world, especially considering its expectation of an imminent major European war, demands scrutiny. A feasible explanation is that Stalin was searching for common ground with Britain and France, in particular, against the threat of fascism. His fear was that, when the inevitable clash of ideologies plunged the Soviet Union into war with Germany, the Western powers would stand by and watch the two belligerent nations destroy each other on the Eastern Europe plains. Nothing that happened in Spain gave Stalin any reason to suppose that if the West had to take sides, it would either obfuscate and prevaricate until it was too late to make a difference or it would come down, albeit reluctantly, on the side of the fascists – either overtly or clandestinely. In that sense it was a clarification that informed Soviet policy over the next few years and persuaded it to avoid precipitating an open conflict with Germany, preferring instead to maintain a low profile until the West could no longer tolerate the threat posed by Germany and found itself inexorably drawn into war against the forces of fascism.

The Bombing of Valencia

In May, after repeated calls for assistance from their compatriots in the Basque region, the Republican leadership made desultory efforts to comply. On 8 May, nine Chatos and six Natachas flew from Reus, on the Mediterranean coast to try and reach Bilbao. A direct route over Zaragoza would have meant flying through Nationalist air space, so they took advantage of an unofficial agreement with the French for refuelling facilities and chose an indirect route via Toulouse. The French, however, were acutely embarrassed and, under the watchful gaze of international observers, disarmed the aircraft and ordered them to fly south again to Valencia. Another flight of Chatos, led by a DC-2 pathfinder, tried the same tactic on the 17th, this time flying to Pont Long airfield at Pau through a snowstorm hoping to avoid scrutiny, but only four made it to Santander; the others either ran out of fuel or returned to Reus with engine trouble. Another flight of Chatos also made it to La Albericia airfield at Santander on a perilous direct route from Madrid. There appeared to be no enthusiasm in Madrid to risk sending more aircraft into a region that was now so comprehensively dominated by Condor Legion air power. The result was that the Republican air units in the North at San Juan de Somorrostro and Sondica were destroyed both in the air and on the ground, after which Condor Legion bombers had free rein to pound Republican defences along the 'Iron Belt' with saturation bombing.

Further south, the bombing of Valencia had started on 1 May when eight Savoia SM. 79s flew from Palma and struck in a surprise low-level attack killing thirty-two people. Malcolm Cowley, an American writer in the town wrote, 'All the victims were civilians; most of them women and babies. It was a new kind of warfare, without reason, without honor, a blind malice.'[29] The city was bombed repeatedly and suffered its worst air raid of the war, killing at least 200 with about fifty buildings destroyed on 28 May. The American Socialist Norman Thomas was present upon this occasion and, 'uninjured but considerably ruffled', is reported as saying, 'It was diabolical. I shall take a first-hand report of this to President Roosevelt.' At almost the same time Barcelona was subjected to an attack, apparently by Italian planes, with resultant casualties of between sixty and seventy dead with over 100 wounded.

That the Loyalist forces were not entirely idle during this period is revealed in a statement by a member of the British Parliament relative to the bombing of Merida, a city in Badajoz province forty miles east of the Portuguese frontier. He reported that three 'Russian' planes had raided the town just before he arrived there, killing twenty and injuring fifty-seven civilians. 'It is very difficult to see what military purpose, or what purpose at all, is gained by such attacks. If the idea is to overawe the population it seemed to us to have quite the opposite effect.'

Bilbao Falls

Sperrle and von Richthofen both commented on the 'backbone and courage' of the Basque defenders and never failed to comment on the Spanish ground forces who were 'always late in arriving'. Neither were they impressed by an Italian force, which Mola had allowed to join the battle 'as a favour', that had got into trouble north of Guernica because of what von Richthofen called 'their own stupidity', and were only extricated by the intervention of German aircraft flying perilously through thick cloud.[30]

On the approaches to Bilbao, Condor Legion bombed Republican positions and roads north of Miravalles but were now, possibly as a reaction to the outcry from the Guernica bombings that had hit headlines all over the world, ordered not to bomb, under any circumstances, villages or populated areas. Concerned by the appearance of some Chatos and Ratas over Bilbao, Sperrle again voiced concern over the slow advance of ground forces calling it a consequence of 'no command leadership ... inefficient coordination ... poor shooting [and troops who] do not move forward under air protection'.[31]

A setback for the Nationalists was the death of General Mola on 3 June when his Airspeed Envoy aircraft flew into Mount Alcocer in thick fog but their advance through northern Spain continued under Major General Fidel Dávila Arrondo. With strong and effective air support, Dávila's forces advanced steadily towards Bilbao. Saturation bombing of positions was followed up with ground assault in increasingly well-coordinated operations in which Condor Legion tactics of air support were honed and modified, albeit in a theatre of almost absolute air supremacy. The new Condor Legion Dornier Do 17-F reconnaissance aircraft photographed the whole of the Basque defences searching for weak points while the He 46s concentrated on monitoring movement on the front. The German success in the air was founded on careful reconnaissance, planning and execution. Having detailed information allowed them to concentrate resources against the most vulnerable defences. A forward command post gave commanders first-hand intelligence when the attack started. With no air defences to speak of, the Republicans were blasted out of well-prepared defensive positions by German bombers, and harassed and prevented from bringing up reserves by the new Bf 109 fighters which were operating regularly over the front.

Doctors sent to Bilbao by British and French charitable organisations to examine Basque children prior to evacuating them to points of safety outside Spain found that the air raids were so constant that children could only be examined by night; a final raid carried out during their embarkation killed eleven, and prevented over one hundred others from joining the ship.

After massive bombing on the 12th, 13th and 14th south of Fica, the road was opened and Bilbao was taken on 19 June in a significant move that deprived the Nationalists of a major industrial and commercial base, as well as the loss of large numbers of fighters who fled to France or were captured. It is estimated that 200,000 people fled Bilbao and, by whatever means available both on land and at sea, tried to reach Santander. Condor Legion aircraft bombed and strafed the crowded roads even though it was clear that the mass of fleeing humanity was made up primarily of civilians. The taking of Bilbao had seen the largest concentration of air power in the war to date. The victory, after eighty days of fighting, was the cause of some softening of feeling and building of bridges between the Nationalist allies. Sperrle praised the 'proven comradeship of the Italian and Spanish air forces' while Franco, for his part expressed his 'appreciation' of the German air force which had operated 'effectively and brilliantly under [Sperrle's] command' pointing out also his appreciation of von Richthofen who had 'worked with such great skill'.[32]

The primary Republican aim was now to capture the region's principal town and port, Santander, and both the CTV and the Aviazione Legionaria played a key part in achieving this. Fighter units initially assigned to this operation were 31a and 32a Squadriglie of VI Gruppo, at Villarcayo. The Republicans, however, had sent forty-five Chatos and eight Ratas to establish the Escuadrilla de Chatos del Norte, under the command of Capitán Ramón Puparelli Francia, in the defence of Santander.

With the taking of Bilbao, the Germans had demonstrated just how important they were to the Nationalist campaign and saw an opportunity to take advantage of the contribution made by their Condor Legion. German engineers moved into the factories and steel-making facilities that Sperrle had previously persuaded Mola to spare from destruction. Most of the industrial production from the area now went to Germany to meet the bill for their military aid. Santander was overwhelmed by the volume of refugees pouring in from Bilbao and the surrounding country. Food became scarce and bombing was relentless. The city was taken on 26 August.

The Republicans had not made a determined effort to get reinforcements to help the beleaguered defenders of Bilbao, given the difficulty in getting them there, and preferred to rebuild their military structure and mount an offensive that would help it reclaim international credibility and draw Nationalist forces, especially aircraft away from the battle for Santander. An attack on the Nationalist forces massed in a salient close to Madrid seemed to be their best chance to do so. They built up a large force, including some their best troops, to the north and south of Madrid, with a view towards closing a pincer to the west of the capital at Brunete and cutting off the Nationalist forces.

Kindelán and von Faupel Fall Out

In June, the Nationalist air force chief, Kindelán, wrote a long memo to Franco expressing his frustration at the large number of cargo ships still entering the Mediterranean ports and supplying the Republican forces with military aid, especially aircraft, from the Soviet Union. Kindelán wanted all Spanish, Italian and German air units assigned to supporting naval units in the area to operate under a single command on Mallorca and undertake aggressive action against the enemy vessels both at sea and in port and against dockside facilities but the navy bluntly refused to give up control of its aviation.[33]

Kindelán's main arguments were finally accepted however, and Franco's headquarters ordered an intensification of aggressive action from the air against the enemy fleet, maritime communications, and ports with the air units being based on Mallorca under a unified command with only one small unit of seaplanes under direct tactical command of the navy. All this resulted in a sustained strategic air offensive against government-held ports and seaborne traffic that lasted for the rest of the war and had a strong influence on the level of Soviet aid getting in.

Meanwhile there was discord in the German ranks. Von Faupel's continuous interference in military matters was a constant thorn in Sperrle's flesh and Franco was no more impressed by his meddling in political affairs. Von Faupel had continued to lobby for greater German involvement but Sperrle and von Richthofen both understood that it would be politically damaging for Franco to be seen as relying too much on external assistance and restricted themselves to providing the best strategic advice in a professional and confidential manner. The matter came to a head when von Faupel sent a memo to Berlin denouncing Sperrle in the strongest possible terms. He accused the Condor Legion chief of sowing discord between the Germans and Spanish quoting Kindelán's criticism of Sperrle's derogatory comments about the Spanish leadership. The accusations became ever more personal when von Faupel told the German Foreign Ministry that he could no longer work with Sperrle who had refused to speak to him. In Berlin, Hitler decided to replace both men with von Faupel being the first to go and replaced by Dr Baron Eberhard von Stöhrer. So as not to draw too much attention to the spat, Sperrle would stay on a while longer but plans were put in place to find his successor.

Chapter 9

The Battle of Brunete

- The Battle of Brunete
- Soviet Morale in Jeopardy

The Battle of Brunete

Since May 1937 the Republicans had been trying to break the Nationalist stranglehold around Madrid, especially at Segovia, but had been unable to make progress owing primarily to Nationalist domination of the air which the Republican ground forces attributed to their own aircraft that 'arrived late, remained for a very short time … and bombed from too high an altitude'.[1] They now expected Franco to turn once again to Madrid and tried to pre-empt it by staging an attack on the thinly defended Nationalist salient at Brunete just to the west of the city. For the Soviet forces in Madrid, defence of the capital was of the utmost importance given its political significance and the fact that it was the centrepiece of their international propaganda campaign. It was the Soviets, who were now exerting more and more control of Republican operations, who devised the plan to attack from the north towards Brunete, and simultaneously break out from the southern suburbs of Madrid towards Alcorcón to close the pincer at Móstoles and surround the Nationalists at Casa de Campo. To do this they had brought together the largest concentration of men and arms so far seen in the war, but this strength was also a weakness as supply lines became overstretched and command structures struggled to cope.

At the start of the Brunete offensive, the Republican air commander was the Soviet General Yakov Smushkevitch, known in Spain as 'General Douglas'. He was initially successful in defending air space over the battlefield by day, but the ground forces were punished by night-time bombing, which continued unabated. To counter this, Soviet pilots Serov and Yakushin began organising a night-fighter group which was called the Patrulla de Noche. This was difficult because their airfields were not equipped with lighting and they had to improvise by using car headlights and bonfires to guide the aircraft back in to land at Alcalá de Henares. Only one Spanish fighter unit, the 2a Escuadrilla of the Grupo No 26, was committed to the campaign.

On 6 July the Republicans launched a three-hour air assault destroying the Nationalist front-line positions. The Nationalists responded by sending in He 51s at low-level to supress ground fire allowing Ju 52 bombers to follow up in relative safety, but Brunete was taken by nightfall. Gravely worried by the sudden Republican surge around Madrid and the fall of Brunete, Franco sent a telegram to Sperrle at Vitoria:

> It is urgent that the Bf 109 fighter is put into action tomorrow at the front from Ávila. I request that you order the transfer from the said airfield.

Sperrle replied that a transfer of individual or specific units of the Legion would not be possible and he would prefer to transfer a large proportion of the force to Ávila. Subsequently, the Bf 109 'Verfolgungsjäger' of J/88, A/88 and the He 70s of VB/88 were moved to the Brunete sector and 1. and 2.J/88 hurriedly relocated from Burgos to Escalona del Prado and Ávila. When he arrived and set up his command post at San Martín de Valdeiglesias, Sperrle was given total command of all Spanish and Italian aircraft in the region. He assigned his He 51s to neutralising Republican flak batteries and command posts, especially those at Villaneuva del Pardillo, that were preventing his Ju 52s from operating over the lines. This, for the newly arrived Adolph Galland, was a 'terrific baptism of fire', but it opened the way for the bombers to operate on 8 July over what was becoming a chaotic, often hand-to-hand battle fought in staggering heat. Messerschmitt Bf-109B fighters flew above to maintain air superiority, while He-111s attacked both strategic and tactical targets. At the same time, He 51s came in below 500ft, strafing and bombing troops and anti-aircraft batteries. The biplanes came in waves of nine-across formations, wingtip to wingtip, each carrying six 22-pound fragmentation bombs and dropping them simultaneously. Sperrle initially directed all his bombers to strike at Republican airfields then at areas just behind enemy lines. This was followed up by bombing strikes at ten-minute intervals over the front lines, immediately followed by strafing attacks which were notable for their 'ferocity'.[2] The attacks on the lines continued for several days and sometimes into the early night. The new Bf 109s that had joined the Fiat fighters were starting to contest air superiority and alter the balance of air power which was a crucial factor in halting the Republican advance on the river Guadamara. By 24 July, waves of Nationalist bombers with 'devastating [air strikes] the likes of which had never been seen before' were forcing them to fall back in a disorganised panic.[3]

The fierce Spanish heat was a shock to the system of flyers coming down from the rain and fog of the northern mountains. Both personnel and machines suffered. Aircraft cooling systems were unable to function below an altitude of about 6,000ft. The J/88 commander, Hauptmann Handrick, found conditions almost unbearable,

an insane heat raged, between 40–45° C in the shade ... mechanics worked exclusively in their swimming trunks and protected their heads from the scorching heat of the sun with wide-brimmed sombreros. During flight our aircraft just could not be kept cool at all.

The Staffeln of the Gruppe were located some 50km away from each other. This made communication between the units quite difficult. In this summer of 1937, our activity was made even more difficult by the scorching heat. We normally woke at 06.00 hrs, and our nightly sleep was never especially refreshing. During the night, the temperature was 'only' around 30° C, and flies and mosquitoes buzzed. We isolated ourselves with mosquito nets and often took to sleeping out in the open, but the nights were never refreshing in and around Escalona.

On the other hand, the evenings were a little more pleasant. We refreshed ourselves as far as it was possible, by bathing in the river, but unfortunately the water was almost constantly 25–30° C. We ate, but in a careful way, we drank wine, or sometimes the expensive local and highly regarded beer, when we would plant ourselves in deckchairs in the tolerably cool courtyard of our 'castle'... In the distance lay burning villages.[4]

The fighting in the air was as fierce as the blazing heat. Oberleutnant Lützow recalled that,

> We constantly had to fight against a three- or four-fold enemy superiority. That meant that one never had the time to 'hang on' to an opponent in the air for a long period of time. One had to see to it that, during the time that our own bombers or reconnaissance aircraft were operating, one kept the enemy at bay and at a distance.
>
> From the break of dawn until dusk, two pilots had to always sit strapped into their aircraft. When the air raid warning service or the forward flak batteries reported enemy aircraft, the Alarmrotte had to take off immediately, for otherwise, with our proximity to the front, the enemy could not be prevented from reaching the bombing zone. Everywhere, the extremely bitter fighting carried out by both sides naturally resulted in a certain amount of wariness, and it thus often happened that the warning service reported our own aircraft as those of the enemy, so that our Alarmrotte took off in vain. Such fruitless take-offs didn't do anything to comfort the state of our nerves. A state of over-excited nervousness very soon set in. Everyone grumbled at the slightest excuse and even took it out on his comrades when something didn't go right.[5]

The Soviet flyer Leitenant Mikhail Yakushin's described his experience on the Brunete front,

> 24 aircraft fought over the small space in the sky. All around, grey biplanes with black crosses and green ones with Republican insignia. Burning aircraft and parachutes appeared … gradually, ours became all more numerous and only our I-15s remained in the air by the end of this battle.[6]

When the Republicans failed to follow up on their initial breakthrough, the Nationalists were given time to respond and this included daily bombing and strafing by small numbers of aircraft in relays. While the new Do 17s and He 111s pounded Republican troop columns by day, the older Ju 52s carpet-bombed their front lines by night. Throughout the offensive, the Condor Legion aircraft daily bombed Republican supply stores behind the lines at El Escorial, Collado Villabla, Manzares el Real, Colemar Veieijo, Matallana and San Augustin de Guidalix while He 51s strafed road traffic. On the 25th bombers pounded the Republican positions at Brunete with repeated low-level attacks allowing the Nationalist infantry to make swift progress and drive the Republican forces from the town.

The Nationalist counterattack resumed when the Condor Legion aircraft caught a large Republican ground force in the open and inflicted heavy casualties. The early Republican impetus dissipated as a result of José Miaja Menant's prevarication as commander of the Central Zone and when the advance slowed, his troops became sitting targets for the Condor Legion aircraft which were based only thirty minutes flying time from the front and could operate shuttle attacks all through the day. Nationalist leaders, under German influence, gave their field commanders a modicum of freedom to use their initiative during the fighting which would become a distinctive feature of German operations during the Second World War. The Brunete campaign would prove to be a significant victory for the Condor Legion against the Republican air force in a prolonged campaign that saw Republican losses some seven times greater than those of the Nationalists. Air superiority would allow the Condor Legion to continue their close air strikes in support of ground troops. Republican fighters were rapidly shedding morale as their commanders failed time and again to provide the required level of leadership, precipitating a number of revolts and mutinies in what was starting to look like a futile campaign against a backdrop of heavy casualties.

The tide of war started to turn at Brunete as Condor Legion air power began to dominate, and slowly the last great opportunity for the Republicans to regain the initiative slipped away. The introduction of high-flying Dornier Do 17 bombers had helped to transform the aerial battle. After their quiet, glided approach to target gave little warning, they were able to pull away and be well out of range when Republican fighters responded. New aircraft and a more adventurous attitude to experimenting with new tactics was putting the Condor Legion aircraft very much on the front foot. No longer were engagements limited to a few aircraft, when air battles took place; now they took on a different character involving many dozens on both sides that swarmed all across the sky in chaotic frenzy. Nationalist air-ground coordination had also been extensively modified in the light of experience and was now reaching a level of some sophistication. In the field of administration, the speed with which German air units had relocated to the Madrid sector showed a markedly higher level of efficiency. Fierce air battles raged for days over Brunete as Republican dominance was increasingly challenged. For the first time Bf 109s came up against the Ratas on 12 July and the initial outcome favoured the Soviet aircraft as Unteroffizier Guido Höness was shot down, but later in the day both Leutnant Rolf Pingel and Feldwebel Peter Boddem in Bf 109s each claimed a Rata in reply. The next day the American pilot Frank Tinkler also claimed to have shot down a Bf 109 and another on the 17th over Navalcarnero-Escorial.

On the 18th, Nationalist counter-attacks were described by Hauptmann Handrick:

> The success of our low-level attacks was quite considerable. Spanish observers reported that on one occasion following our low-level attacks on a 150 m-long stretch of foxholes, 100 Red Spaniards had been taken care of by our machine guns. It was possible to make this determination because immediately after our attack the foxholes were taken by Nationalist Spanish infantry.[7]

Sergente Maggiore Brunetto di Montegnacco of 6a Squadriglia recalled,

> The battles on the Brunete Front had reached their zenith. Despite our air superiority, the Red bombers attacked again and again.

Oberleutnant Harder of 1.J/88 described being greeted by

> a real display of fireworks. Shells burst beside, above and below us, sometimes almost right in our machines. We went over to a low-level attack and were met by intense 20 mm fire from every direction. Everywhere one looked there were

He 51s dancing and attacking through the flak. The battle lasted about eight minutes, until we had dropped all our bombs. Although we had almost no ammunition or bombs, we so shook the Red infantry that they left their positions and ran in headlong flight. We flew in close formation very low up the valleys, approaching the enemy position from the rear. At a sign, the bombs were simultaneously released and our load went down in a cluster. We called this 'the little man's bomb-carpet'.[8]

On the ground, Cyril Sexton, who fought with the British Battalion on the Republican side gives a sense of what it was like to be caught on the wrong end of a bombing raid,

I saw bombers and it looked as if they were coming our way ... I went into a house and there was a big metal oven so I crawled into it and waited. Seconds later there was a whistle of bombs and then explosions and inside the oven I was bouncing up and down. When the explosions had finished I pushed open the oven door with difficulty since most of the house had collapsed on it and crawled out ... the enemy air force was having a field day what with enemy bombers coming over dropping their bombs on the vehicular traffic and the enemy fighters strafing anything that moved.[9]

During the night of 25 July, Starshiy Leytenant Anatoly Serov and Leytenant Mikhail Yakushin of 1a Escuadrilla headed for Escorial where bombers were hitting the Republican lines. Yakushin later described the first Republican night victory during the Spanish Civil War when he shot down the Ju 52 of K/88 over Valdemorillo:

At midnight we received a telephone report of an enemy bombing raid on Republican troops near El Escorial. It was the first time that we had approached the front after dark. The search area was outlined by the fire started by the bombing. Serov remained at our initial altitude of 6500ft, while I climbed 3250ft higher. My luck was in, for ten minutes later I spotted an enemy bomber heading towards me. He would not get away. Having let him pass, I turned and began to approach him at the same height from his right and behind. We had learned by then that the Junker's fuel tank was positioned near the right wing root. Having approached the target and slowed down, I fired at that area. Flame appeared along the right side of the bomber's fuselage. Almost at once the enemy gunner responded, but he was too late. His bomber was already going down in flames. I followed him down almost to the ground. After that we left our patrol area a few minutes early and rushed home to spread the news of our victory. Once out of my cockpit and back on the ground I was immediately grabbed by Serov. He looked as triumphant as I was because our vertical split formation was his idea![10]

Later an Escuadrilla de Bombardeo Nocturno (night bombing squadron) was established to harass the Nationalists by operating single-aircraft sorties behind enemy lines at fifteen to twenty minute intervals. Equipped with twelve R-5 Rasantes, the unit was led by Teniente Walter Katz from Bujaraloz airfield, in Aragon. In August, with the resumption of operations in the north, the three Staffeln of J/88 moved to Herrera and Alar del Rey, which was declared 'Arbeitsfähig' (ready for work) for Bf 109s during the first few days of the month.

By 26 July, the battle for Brunete was over as Republican forces were thrown back to a position only five kilometres from where they had started the offensive and the Condor Legion had come of age as a superb close air-support outfit. von Richthofen, however, was a stickler for correctness and was not overly impressed with discipline. His diary records: 'Was at the airfield, where disobedience reigns. Half of J/88 have already relocated themselves against orders. The rest … are only half-ready for operations.'[11] Sperrle used the performance of the new aircraft to back up his requests for more to be sent out from Germany, but his status had been undermined by the dispute with von Faupel and he only narrowly avoided being recalled. His days in Spain were numbered however, with von Blomberg looking around for a replacement. Albert Kesselring was briefly considered but the most likely candidate seemed to be Generalleutnant Hellmuth Volkmann. Meanwhile, Republican air units had been reinforced by the first five Spanish-built Chatos to be completed at the SAF-3 factory at Reus and another sixty Ratas were delivered from the Soviet Union.

Soviet Morale in Jeopardy

Republican air power had been reduced by nearly half from its peak of January with only 222 aircraft now operational. Furthermore, the introduction of the Bf 109 had started to make a significant impact. It was hoped that local aircraft construction might fill the gap but while fuselages were built, engine and armament production could not keep up. The leader of the International Brigade, Manfred Stern, sent an urgent request to Moscow for increased shipments.

> It is precisely the enemy's air force ... that appears to be the main factor behind their success during this period.... The aviation question has been transformed into the Republic's greatest problem of the war.... At a minimum [we] require 110–120 SBs and 200–250 fighters, in addition to what [we] now have.[12]

Even though Soviet flyers often completed six to eight sorties per day, three or four of which would likely involve combat, morale of the Soviet pilots seems, to have held up, at least in an official report that may well have been simply stating what Moscow wanted to hear which said: 'Enormous moral and physical endurance are expected from the comrades, but I did not encounter any complaints about fatigue.'

One of the biggest problems for later-serving Soviet airmen was the low level of training received prior to arriving in Spain. The Russian historian Novikov found that after two years of preparation in Red Army flying schools, some Soviet pilots had logged only 30–40 hours of flight time. This contrasted with the Italian and German pilots who, in many cases, had 300–400 hours of experience. Critically, Soviet pilots had no experience of high-altitude flight or night flying and had to learn how to negotiate uneven or makeshift airfields with fully laden bombers. Crashes on take-off and landing were also common. In December 1936 alone, fourteen Soviet aircraft were lost in accidents due to pilot error – six were completely destroyed, and eight required extensive repairs.

Between 25 October 1936 and 1 July 1938, the Soviets were to register less than half the total losses of the Nationalists and performed very favourably in aerial battles: 163 losses for the Republic to 572 for the rebels, but the most striking difference is in the number of aircraft lost through accidents and landings in enemy territory: 147 by the Republic, of which almost 90 per cent were attributable to pilot error, compared to just thirteen by the Nationalists.

Chapter 10

Santander Falls

- The Montana Project
- Franco Targets Santander

The Montana Project

The protocols signed at Burgos on 16 July 1937 came into effect on 1 August and had opened the door for Germany to secure total control of Spanish mineral deposits. Only a few weeks later on 9 October, however, Franco issued a decree which suspended all transactions involving the transfer of mining property and declared null and void all titles to such property acquired after 18 July 1936, pointing out that a provisional government had not the right to make permanent dispositions of the national heritage. It was a direct attempt to curb German investment in Spain by HISMA who, since 18 July through the Montana project, had issued seventy-three new contracts for mining rights. This was a dispute that would rumble on for months until March 1938, when it was clear that in order to reach a conclusion to the war before the Germans pulled out, Franco urgently needed more German military aid and so was forced to allow German investment once again, but only to the extent of 40 per cent in any particular enterprise. The Germans were having none of this and seeing that Franco was desperate, pushed for full control of all subsequent mining exploration companies. It was starting to look as though Franco had decided to treat the Germans a little more disdainfully now that the tide of war was very much in the Nationalists' favour. This became further apparent after the Sudetenland crisis, when any hope that Franco would be a German ally were dashed after he declared that Spain would remain neutral in the event of a major European war breaking

115

out. Spain would be in desperate need of a period of relative calm, if not to heal then at least to put an end to its self-mutilation. For its part, Germany was now rehearsing its lines for a starring role on a bigger stage and started looking for ways to extricate itself militarily from the Spanish theatre.

Although there were undoubtedly political and military aspects of Hitler's intervention in Spain, the Montana project constituted the whole aim and purpose of German assistance to Franco in the economic field. Bernhardt voiced the Third Reich's determination when he said,

> The object of our economic interest in Spain must be the deep penetration into the main sources of Spanish wealth, namely, agriculture and mining. Whereas the products of agriculture fall to the share of the German Reich more or less without effort, since the Spaniards are forced to find a market, the mining problem is of tremendous importance in every respect. We must be clear about the fact and must make it evident to the leading figures in Nationalist Spain that Germany is engaged in an economic war and thus has a claim to immediate deliveries by Spain for her own economic war.[1]

A day of reckoning was to come later when Germany's expenditure in Spain approached 500 million marks, with another twenty million marks in interest and compound interest. Italy's commitment had leaped from an original twelve transport planes to more than 1,000 aircraft, 6,000 men killed in combat, and 14 billion lire expenditure.[2] After discounting the payments made through HISMA and SAFNI, Franco's indebtedness has been variously estimated at 100 million dollars to Germany and 263 million to Italy. While Germany was assiduous in raking in the benefits of its involvement by maximising exports, Mussolini had been content to let the Spanish run up an enormous bill but then complained to the German Ambassador in August 1939 that the Spanish had 'bled him white'.

Franco Targets Santander

Republican failure at Brunete, coming after the loss of Bilbao, especially with growing evidence of the surge in Condor Legion air power, put the

Republicans firmly on the defensive but Franco chose not to continue his counter-offensive. Given that the Condor Legion was now superfluous to requirements there, Dávila called for them to return to Vizcaya for a renewed attack towards Santander, but Sperrle's forces had taken losses at Brunete and many of his seventy or so aircraft were undergoing extensive maintenance and repair. Despite this, he was keen to see the northern campaign concluded but feared that Franco might be content to rest on his laurels when what was required, in his opinion, was an immediate intensification of effort on the Vizcaya front. Franco, however, confounded everyone by agreeing to the redeployment of not only the Condor Legion, but also aircraft of the Italian Aviazione Legionaria and the Nationalist Air Brigade to ensure complete aerial domination in the North. It was probably of less comfort to Sperrle to discover that the ground offensive would rely heavily on the Italian CTV ground forces.

With the resumption of operations in the North, the three Staffeln of J/88 moved to Herrera and Alar del Rey, which was declared 'Arbeitsfähig' (ready for work) for Bf 109s during the first few days of August. The Bf 109s of J/88 moved to airfields close to Gijón from where they operated over Santander, but after the Republican attack in Aragon, the He 51s from 3.J/88 were rushed to the area and heavily committed. Galland recalled that the frequent relocations endured by J/88 at this time seemed 'quite without plan or purpose'.

For their part, the Republicans hoped that if they could hold out in Santander and Asturias until the end of the year, the winter weather would give them respite as the mountain passes filled with snow. The plan was then to consolidate their position in Catalonia and Aragon, centring their headquarters in Barcelona. They were, however, given no respite. The Nationalist advance on Santander began on 8 August, with air operations focused on the Reinosa sector to the southwest. In a well-used pattern, Nationalist artillery and Navarrese troops, backed up by low-level attacks from the air, struck the enemy line, while German bombers, escorted by Bf 109s, flew deep into Republican territory. He 51s again flew continuous attacks on road and rail targets. Aircraft in waves of forty or fifty aircraft would pound defences for up to an hour at a time. Desperate counter attacks were quickly subdued.

Reinosa, with its small-arms factory, was taken on 16 August and now began providing weapons for the Nationalist side, indicative of a further slow deterioration of Republican strength. On 17 August, a nine-strong Rata escuadrilla (1a/21) led by future ace, and Hero of the Soviet Union, Starshiy Leytenant Boris Smirnov arrived at La Albericia airfield, in Santander. The unit was comprised of Russian and Spanish pilots who were the first of that nation to fly the Rata. This was timely because during the next night, K/88 with some twenty He 111s carried out a large-scale night bombing mission on airfields around Santander and claimed the destruction of a dozen aircraft on the ground. During the night of the 24th, in an attempt to slow down Nationalist advances and take the military initiative in this area, the Republicans launched an offensive between Quinto and Belchite in Aragon, but their air units were taking a terrible beating. While twenty CR.32s from XXIII Gruppo were escorting Ju 52s, which were bombing enemy troops around Belchite they suddenly spotted eleven American-made Martin B10 bombers flying below them, above Fuente del Ebro. They attacked them and ten were claimed shot down. Two of the Heinkels, however, were claimed destroyed over the bridge El Musél by the last few Rata based in the Asturias.

Hauptmann Gotthard Handrick recalled:

> Around the middle of August the Nationalist Spaniards pushed ahead in three columns with a considerable amount of artillery, munitions and armoured cars west of Santander to the coast of the Bay of Biscay. The Rojos defended themselves desperately, and in this hilly and occasionally mountainous region, there resulted continuous and fierce fighting for roads and high-lying features. For us 'low-flyers', an extensive field of activity offered itself. We were deployed to attack the enemy positions, which commanded the heights and the roads, and naturally the roads themselves, which ran along beneath these heights. The mountain positions were strongly and very well laid out, making them very difficult to attack with machine guns and bombs. It was at times, therefore, impossible for us to ease the work of the ground troops in the way we would have wished. Nevertheless, we were successful, even if in the end only slow progress was made.
>
> The Nationalist advance had to deal not only with the natural hindrances of the terrain, but also the fact that many of the roads passed over numerous bridges. The Rojos had not neglected to blow up every bridge that they were unable to hold. We therefore

often received the special task of hindering the blowing up of some bridge or other, forcing the Reds to call a halt to proceedings until the Nationalist infantry had been brought up. We would loiter over these previously selected bridges and allow nobody to approach them. Our bombs and machine guns could, when the defences were not too strong, mostly isolate them.

From the air, we could then observe how our infantry worked their way towards them. When we saw the forward infantry patrols advance and take possession of the bridges during the course of the day, we knew we had thus fulfilled our task. If, however, nightfall came before Nationalist troops arrived, the bridge usually had to be given up as it then became impossible for us to recognise enemy demolition patrols from the air and attack them.[3]

In the Condor Legion fighter force, No. 1 Staffel was supplied with Bf-109B-2 fighters in late August 1937, resulting in a reorganisation of J/88. Hauptmann Gotthard Handrick became the group commander, and Oberleutnant Adolf Galland was given command of 3./J88. Oberleutnant Douglas Pitcairn was reassigned as capitän of the reconstituted No. 4 Staffel. Numbers 1 and 2 Staffeln were flying Messerschmitts, while Nos. 3 and 4 Staffeln were ground attack units flying Heinkel biplanes.

Santander fell to the Nationalists on 26 August. By early September, the whole of J/88 had assembled at Pontejos. From here, the Bf 109s escorted bombers striking at Gijón, while 3.J/88 flew more freelance patrols, operating directly in front of the advancing ground troops, as well as engaging in the art of 'Kochenjagd' ('hunting to eat') – a nickname given to vehicle-hunting missions, often at dusk, of which a leading exponent was Oberfeldwebel Ignaz 'Igel' Prestele. Oberleutnant Adolf Galland remembered that during such intensive operations in the He 51,

reloading the machine guns you usually cut your knuckles open on one of the many obstacles in the unbelievably confined space of the overheated cockpit. On hot days we flew in bathing trunks, and on returning from a sortie looked more like coalminers, dripping with sweat, smeared with oil and blackened by gunpowder smoke.[4]

Hauptmann Handrick recalled the combats over Gijón:

> Our raids on Gijón did not always go quite so smoothly and
> without problems. The Rojos also put up enormous resistance
> against us in the air, and their Ratas and Curtisses were by no
> means easy prey.

The Condor Legion bombers, escorted by Bf 109s from 1. and 2.J/88,
attacked ships in Gijón harbour setting three freighters on fire. It was from
here that the defeated Republican forces, including many Soviets, were
attempting to flee. In the panic, eight of the most modern Soviet Chato and
Rata aircraft had been left behind intact. They were dismantled, crated and
sent back to Germany to be examined and studied by the Luftwaffe technical
staff. Air battles raged over the port during the whole of September. On
21 September, 3.J/88 moved to the airfield at Llanes, on the Asturian coast,
which had only recently been captured. From here it harried the Republican
troops as they retreated west. Galland recalled:

> Llanes was the funniest aerodrome I have ever taken off from.
> Situated on a plateau whose northern side fell sheer into the sea,
> with the three remaining sides almost as steep, it was like taking
> off from the roof of a skyscraper situated on the seashore.[5]

During the campaigns in Santander and Asturias the Republicans lost
forty-three Chatos and Ratas with many of their Spanish pilots killed,
wounded or reported missing. They had been fighting under conditions of
clear inferiority due to their lower numbers and the vulnerability of their
airfields to attack from German bombers, but exhibited what German pilots
acknowledged to be 'outstanding aerial skills [and] heroic determination'.[6]
The campaign in the North drew to a close with the remaining units of
Escuadrilla de Caza del Norte fleeing to France. On 21 October, after a
series of fierce aerial battles, the Nationalists entered Gijón to complete
the occupation of formerly Republican territories in northern Spain in
what had been a surprisingly short latter part of the campaign. With the
seizure of this region, Nationalist troops, naval vessels and aircraft now
could be transferred to other operational areas. The Republican government
abandoned Valencia for Barcelona.

Chapter 11

Condor Legion at the Crossroads

- Adolf Galland
- Volkmann Replaces Sperrle
- The Condor Legion Considers its Options
- Italian Independence of Action
- Soviet Air Power is Overcome

Adolf Galland

While centres such as Salamanca had thrived economically as a result of the German presence, not everywhere was so welcoming. In outlying regions where the benefits were perhaps less in evidence, there was resentment towards the Germans who seemed to control everything subjecting the Spanish population to 'permanent threat and strict supervision'. The inevitable culture clash between northern European and southern temperaments and sensibilities at a time when few on either side had been exposed to the other led to a certain arrogance on one part and simmering hostility on the other. In restaurants, even the most respected civic leaders were not seated until all late-arriving Germans had been accommodated. The casual disregard for traditional sensibilities was clear when German personnel would stroll through the town in shorts on a Sunday causing 'quite a sensation'.[1] Throughout the whole of nationalist Spain, the reluctance of the majority of the Spanish population to warm to the Germans began to dilute the pleasures of climate, in summer at least, and scenery. It was perhaps the recognition of the homesickness that was quite evident in many that played into the policy of personnel rotation exercised by the Condor Legion.

Adolf Galland, who became one of the Luftwaffe top aces during the Second World War and who was feted by the Allies afterwards, has the unenviable reputation of having invented the precursor of napalm. He felt that the small 22-pound bombs carried by the He-51s lacked the destructive power to destroy anti-aircraft and machine gun installations and so, with his ground crews, developed the 'Devil's Egg', a drop-tank with a 25-gallon mixture of gasoline and used engine oil was attached to the bomb and when it hit the ground, the tank burst open and the bombs detonated, igniting the mixture into a sticky, flaming mass. This was first used during the attack on Santander.

Another innovation credited to Galland was a specially modified train to transport his entire squadron to sectors where it was needed, which often demanded long journeys with little warning. Packing, transporting squadron personnel, and unpacking was a time-consuming operation, so at Galland's request Franco had the Nationalist army provide twelve railroad passenger coaches that were converted to accommodate sleeping quarters, dining rooms, kitchen, workshop, briefing room, office, toilets and a bathroom in a few days. Thereafter, Galland's Staffel never travelled without its train. 'No more war without an apartment' ran the slogan above the canteen dining car.[2] This also was an innovation that gained favour in the Second World War. During his time in Spain, Galland prepared many reports on the development and theory of tactical air power that were eagerly read by Luftwaffe officials in Berlin and he would later be recognised as one of the greatest Bf 109 pilots of the Second World War but when he returned to Germany from Spain in 1938 he had still never flown a Bf 109 in combat.

Volkmann Replaces Sperrle

On 30 October Sperrle handed over command of the Condor Legion to Volkmann who was supported by von Richthofen, as his Chief-of-Staff at the Legion's new base at Burgos. Sperrle and von Richthofen had worked well together professionally but there was no love lost between them on a personal level. Sperrle thought von Richthofen an insufferable snob, while the latter deplored Sperrle's 'uncouth' manners. Volkmann was rather more refined than Sperrle but von Richthofen still found fault with him and, ominously for Volkmann, the 'Red Baron's' cousin was held in very high esteem in Berlin. There ensued a serious clash of personalities graphically illustrated by von Richthofen who wrote, 'I request my release from business immediately, vacation here and then a return trip home. Volkmann beams with agreement.' Two days later, he wrote to his wife, 'Volkmann and I must part company at the soonest possible date.'[3]

One of Volkmann's first measures as commander of the Condor Legion was to restructure J/88 by enlarging it into four Staffeln under the command of Hauptmann Gotthardt Handrick as follows:

1. Staffel with Bf 109s under Oberleutnant Harro Harder
2. Staffel with Bf 109s under the newly arrived Oberleutnant Joachim Schlichting
3. Staffel with He 51s under Oberleutnant Adolf Galland
4. (Pik As) Staffel with He 51s under Oberleutnant Eberhard d'Elsa.

The men and aircraft to form the latter unit had arrived at Vigo by sea in early November 1937 and had formed up at León.

The Condor Legion Considers its Options

At the end of October 1937 the Condor Legion found itself at a crossroads. Its mission had expanded to an extent that would have horrified Berlin had they known what was to come when the first aircraft had been assigned. Its purpose had ostensibly been to give Franco a small level of aid to help him quickly crush a Republican force, but the introduction of Soviet aircraft and armour and the failure of the Italian forces at Guadalajara soon disabused them of the notion that there would be a swift resolution. There had been little option but to stay and make the most of it. Göring took advantage of this to use Spain as a testing ground for the new generation of high-powered aircraft coming out of German factories. This would have the dual benefit of boosting Nationalist air power and simultaneously allowing the evaluation of the performance of the new aircraft in combat, and how they might contribute to the development of revolutionary ideas of air-ground cooperation that heralded the age of Blitzkrieg. After von Richthofen had established himself as the dominant German commander, albeit one that was not yet ready to lead the Legion, he took the opposing view that further involvement in a war without a clear end in sight, in support of an ally who was clearly not up to the required level of military efficiency, was pointless. Much had been learned, but he felt further involvement would not greatly expand the volume of experience and analysis and was certainly not worth more German lives and the loss of more of the precious new aircraft. Many in Berlin agreed with him, but Hitler, ever mindful of the diplomatic and political ramifications of abandoning their allies while the war raged on, chose to increase the level of aid and make a renewed commitment to the Nationalist cause. By 30 January it was time for von Richthofen to take a break and he was replaced by Major Hermann Plocher, an administrator from the Luftwaffe General Staff.

This gesture of support for the Legion was welcomed by many such as Oberleutnant Pitcairn who 'had the feeling that [the Legion] had been sent to Spain and then deserted'.[4] Ground crews struggled to find spare parts to keep aircraft flying. When he arrived, Volkmann, known in Spain as General Veith, had a reputation as a 'good, honest and hard-working commander [who was] highly respected by his officers and men'.[5] In his first meeting with both Spanish and Italian General Staff it was agreed that the next logical step was for Franco to push on through Aragon to the Mediterranean coast. It was a rude introduction to the realities of the war in Spain when, to Volkmann's great surprise, Franco ignored that advice and chose, once again, to try and take Madrid. Either Volkmann thought he could change Franco's mind, or he was just hedging his bets, but either way he settled the Condor Legion bombers at El Burgo de Osma and the fighters at Torresaviñan from where they could operate either in Aragon or over Madrid, but the distances from base to targets were such that auxiliary fuel tanks had to be fitted to many aircraft.

Italian Independence of Action

Meannwhile the Italians, who had become increasingly detached from Condor Legion operations, brought in more CR.32s allowing 33a Squadriglia to be formed on 1 October and assigned to VI Gruppo to bring the unit up to full strength of three squadriglie. The Nationalist aerial defence of the Aragon front was reinforced by sending XXIII Gruppo

Caccia to Zaragoza-Sanjurjo. These units were joined by the CR.32s of XVI Gruppo. VI Gruppo was also transferred from Villarcayo to Alfamèn. This was virtually all the CR.32s on mainland Spain, with both the Spanish CR.32 Grupo and the whole 3o Stormo Caccia dell'Aviazione Legionaria. K/88 under Major Mehnert could field three Staffeln of He 111s, the last Ju 52/3ms by then being confined only to specific night missions on relatively quiet fronts. Nine of the trimotors had already been passed on to the Spaniards. In late November, thirty newly built CR.32s were shipped from La Spezia to Seville aboard the steamer *Aniene*. They were delivered to the Aviación Nacional, who in turn passed twenty-five examples on to the newly formed Grupo de Caza 3-G-3's Escuadrillas 3-E-3 and 4-E-3 in December. The remaining five fighters were given to the 3o Stormo Caccia of the Aviazione Legionaria. The Italians had spent huge sums of money on their expeditionary force in Spain and, still with ambitions of gaining a permanent presence on Spain's Mediterranean coast, seemingly had no intention of putting any sort of brake on expenditure at this stage.[6]

Soviet Air Power is Overcome

Soviet control of the air was lost at some time between September and December 1937, in part because of the Nationalist blockade of Republican ports which, coupled with the closing of the French frontier, slowly cut off Soviet aid to the Republic. Alongside this, the inexorable rise in numbers of available Italian and German aircraft altered the balance of air power. The introduction of the Bf 109 was a turning point at which technical advantage passed to the Nationalists. The Soviets now restricted operations to tactical support of ground forces at which they were quite proficient and, German claims notwithstanding, pioneered the dive-bombing technique with their Chatos.[7]

Chapter 12

The Battle of Teruel

- The Condor Legion at Soria
- The Battle for Teruel
- Richthofen Leaves
- Air Battles over the Alfambra
- Germans and Italians Contemplate Leaving
- Soviet Aircraft Manufactured in Spain

Volkmann kept his crews busy with attacks on Republican airfields during December, on those days when the winter weather allowed. This led to the loss of a Bf 109 and a He 111, both of which were sufficiently intact to be sent to France and then the Soviet Union for examination. The attacks on Republican airfields east of Zaragoza were less than satisfactory, even though eighty-eight bombers and fifty-six fighters were deployed. The slower SM.81s and Ju 52s were to attack the nearby airfields in the Barbastro zone while the faster SM.79s, Breguet 20s, He 111s and Do 17s the airfields at Sariñena, Bujaraloz, Candasnos, Puebla de Híjar, Selgua, Pomar, Lérida and Balaguer. The Republican air force was not yet beaten, however. Nationalist attacks failed to achieve the desired result having found the airfields empty with Republican fighters airborne and waiting for them. The Republicans had constructed a large number of airfields and at each was based at most a single squadron, its aircraft widely dispersed around the airfield perimeter. In addition, they had built a number of decoy airfields with mock-up aircraft.

Oberleutnant Harder recounted:

> Another major action on December 10. The Fiats patrolled the front, we flew deep into enemy territory with fifteen Bf 109s. Fifteen Curtisses and fifteen Ratas climbed up in

close formation. There was nothing else to do, we attacked repeatedly, but so many aircraft immediately dived on us that we were happy just to escape in one piece.[1]

The whole Nationalist air force now reorganised itself into the 'Brigada Aerea Espana', and in the process incorporated the new tactical and strategic concepts that had been developed as the result of operations to date. Air units were created, each with its own command structure, giving them a high level of flexibility to move and operate as situations demanded. This gave rise to an increase in the number of strategic bombing missions against airfields, fuel dumps, bridges, railways, electricity generation plants, and arms factories which was noted by the US attaché. In particular, he reported on the great amount of damage inflicted on the port of Valencia, which had suffered grievously from air attacks. Practically all the storage sheds and dock installations had been hit and the constant bombing of shipping was seriously disrupting incoming supplies. At the same time, the French naval attaché noted that Nationalist fuel supplies would be gravely damaged as two British fuel tankers were set ablaze in Alicante and oil storage was fired in Barcelona by bombing.

The Battle for Teruel

On 15 December while Franco was planning his attack on Madrid, the Republicans launched a surprise assault in a snowstorm on the Nationalist salient at Teruel in the Aragon region east of the capital and initially won air superiority. Franco, in his usual fashion, eschewed complicated flanking or diversionary operations and launched all his troops into a 'head-on' collision in what many of his allies saw as a hubristic and macho fashion. Against strong German advice, he abandoned his attack against Madrid and rushed to confront the Republicans at Teruel. Volkmann hesitated to throw all his weight behind Franco as the bitterly cold winter weather started to cast the region under an icy grip, but when it was clear that Franco had committed himself, there was little option. The winter conditions were brutal and prompted ground crews to improvise new methods of remaining operational. Many Germans must have started asking just what they were doing in Spain. With temperatures down to -18° C aircraft engines were insulated and warmed up with special blankets before starting them. Leutnant Eckehart Priebe was the Technical Officer with the new 4.J/88, and he recalled:

> At León we received Spanish uniforms, put our Heinkels together and off we went to the Guadalajara Mountains for another of those 'final assaults on Madrid' which never took place. Instead, on Christmas Eve 1937, we had to hurry to a field called Calamocha, south of Zaragoza, to help the beleaguered garrison at the city of Teruel which the Reds had surrounded in a surprise offensive. For more than two months we were engaged in a most bitter battle in ice-cold Aragon. We flew three to four ground-support missions a day at very low level, strafing trenches or dropping our six 10 kg bombs on gun positions or military transport. Aerial combat was left to the Bf 109s, as the Heinkels were no match for the Soviet-made Ratas.[2]

Hauptmann Gotthardt Handrick, CO of J/88 recalled:

> The struggle for Teruel – a projecting tongue of the Front that lay far to the east in enemy territory – was particularly difficult for us. At the beginning of this battle, I was located in Calamocha, a tiny 'nest' that was about 80 km away from Teruel. Whereas in the summer just passed we had enjoyed much more of the well-known Spanish sun than was good for us, we thus came to know in dreary Calamocha that there was indeed a Spanish winter which also spoke for itself. None of us had believed it to be possible that in Spain it could become really cold. The scorching heat of the summer had, in fact, helped to give us the notion that we would also experience a warm and pleasant winter. Shockingly, when I made my first reconnaissance flight to the Teruel Front on Christmas Eve, the thermometer showed -18°C. It was especially difficult for our groundcrews at Calamocha. Night after night and hour after hour, a special Kommando had to rev up the aircraft in order to keep them warm.[3]

On the Republican side, the pilots were equally stressed. Aleksandr Gusev reported that 'We fought the Fiats at the limit of our abilities throughout 1937.'

The battle of Teruel was a decisive moment for aerial reconnaissance in the Spanish Civil War when its contribution to Nationalist victory proved to be of paramount importance. Up until this point, photographic reconnaissance on both sides had been used mainly to keep track of troop movements and to report on the result of bombing although with significantly greater purpose by the Nationalists. Of special concern for them was the flow of Soviet aid through ports, especially Cartagena which was closely monitored and regularly bombed throughout the war, but after December 1937 their reconnaissance aircraft contributed more and more to informing the planning process before ground assaults. Battle commanders were becoming much more aware of how intelligence could be used as a 'force multiplier' and showed skill and imagination to interpret aerial photographs in ways that allowed them to focus artillery bombardment and deploy ground forces to gain a tactical advantage. It required allocation of resources to train personnel and provide equipment and facilities for rapid evaluation of the images while they were still pertinent, something that their Republican counterparts signally failed to do.

At the beginning of the war, both sides had about equal numbers of Breguet XIX aircraft many of which were used in the reconnaissance role, but these aircraft had been in production for over ten years and it was immediately clear that they would not survive for long in a hostile environment. When the Condor Legion arrived they brought Heinkel He 70 (Rayo) light bombers which were quickly modified to carry cameras. They would later use Dornier Do 17Fs equipped with powerful radio transmitters to send intelligence back to ground commanders giving them real-time data on which to base their decisions. The Germans had developed a comprehensive doctrine for the acquisition and exploitation of aerial intelligence (Truppenführung) and had two specialist units in Spain: A88 (Aufklärungsgruppe 88) and the maritime equivalent, AS88 (Aufklärungsgruppe See 88). Both visual and photographic reconnaissance was carried out depending on the circumstances; each had advantages and drawbacks. Visual reconnaissance was preferred when urgency was the main motivator, or when light levels were low but photographs were more precise. The technical aspects of the latter meant that many hours lapsed between taking a photograph, returning to base, developing the images, analysing them and making use of the intelligence; many hours in which the position of targets in a dynamic battlefield could move some distance. In order to minimise the delay, the Condor Legion even had a mobile laboratory built into a truck which was available for rapid deployment.[4]

The reconnaissance capability development to a high level of sophistication by the Condor Legion was never at any stage matched by the Republican air force whose attempts to develop a doctrine were 'chaotic' and characterised by a 'scarcity of resources and a lack of coordination'.[5] In November 1936, a member of the Republican General Staff, Ángel Riaño, was tasked with meeting the 'essential and urgent need to organise the [aerial intelligence]'; however, his facilities were constantly moved from place to place, and he found everything needed to be 'redone again and again'. The flow of intelligence was sporadic since 'fighter and bomber planes [did] nothing more than complete their missions without saying what they have seen [and] don't give any information'. Riaño dedicated himself 'with body and soul … living only for that service', but was forced to concede that in the end, he had 'no mission to complete … because nobody is in charge'. His frustration, which further impacted on his already precarious state of health, was manifest when he wrote: 'This information section is useless … I haven't managed to make [the pilots] take even a single photograph in spite of my continuous efforts. It can almost be said that we do not have reconnaissance aviation.'

Republican troops commanded by generals Hernández Sarabia and Leopoldo Menéndez captured Teruel on 8 January, taking the surrender of Colonel Rey d'Harcourt. The harsh winter conditions prevented the timely arrival of troops sent by Franco under the command of Generals Varela and Aranda, but despite the bitter cold, air battles continued all around the town during January when the weather permitted. On 20 January, XVI Gruppo went into action between Teruel and Aldehuela. Italian pilots were credited with shooting down five 'Curtiss fighters' and two Ratas, while on the other side, 1a/21 with its Ratas had a field day claiming eight victories when the escuadrilla claimed one He 111 and one Bf 109. Eighteen SBs attacked Salamanca with both Spanish and Soviet crews flying from their base at San Clemente but the Nationalists slowly regained the initiative. Hauptmann Torsten Christ of the General Staff of the Legion Condor noted that it was 'only on account of the attacks by the Legion Condor, especially those by the He 51s, that the Red advance was brought to a stop'.

A report sent to Kindelán in February shows how important aerial reconnaissance was at Teruel by emphasising how it was used as the basis for planning, especially in identifying the location of enemy fortifications. Vertical 'itineraries', a series of photographs taken from the same height over a strip of land, were combined into larger 'mosaics', allowing commanders to 'see other fortifications that nobody had any idea existed and others that had a different size than [we] had thought'. The report, however, also noted that 'mosaics' were often passed on to ground commanders 'with little or no interpretation', owing to 'a lack of time and of qualified personnel'.[6]

Richthofen Leaves

The Condor Legion, with all available Nationalist air strength, including Ju 87 dive-bombers deployed for the first time in the war, led the counterattack at Teruel, the battle being fought mainly along the River Alfambra, north of the city. Ironically, von Richthofen was not on hand to witness the Ju 87s in action. He had vehemently opposed their development when the idea was mooted by Luftwaffe Chief Technical Officer Ernst Udet in 1934, but would later become one of its staunchest advocates and went on to command the dive-bomber VIII Fliegerkorps during the Battle of Britain. Early in the war, he had brought from Germany a small number of Henschel Hs123 biplane dive-bombers but had preferred to utilise them as ground support in which role it excelled. He did not abandon the dive-bombing concept, however, and had arranged instead for a number of Ju 87s to be sent out to Spain for evaluation.

Richthofen was recalled to Germany, possibly as the result of his opposition to continued German involvement in the war, and was replaced by Plocher as second-in-command to Volkmann, on 11 January. He would, however, return to command the Legion as the war drew to a close. Saturation bombing of Republican front lines allowed the infantry to break through, at which point air power was switched, as was now customary, to interdicting reinforcement movements behind the lines. This proved to be successful until snowstorms grounded all aircraft and allowed the Nationalist troops to regain some ground. When the weather allowed, Katiuskas bombed

Calamocha railroad station near Teruel, but Bf 109s were now in the ascendant. Hauptmann Harder recalled:

> None of us would have had good memories of Calamocha had it not been for 7 February 1938. This was the date of a quite special triumph for my Gruppe, for we were successful in shooting down no fewer than 12 enemy aircraft – ten Martin bombers and two Ratas within five minutes. We had participated eagerly in the fighting over Teruel, and day-by-day we had carpeted the enemy positions with bombs ... up to now we had never seen so many Red bombers – there were 22 of them – and we got them under our guns. Not only that, but it appeared as if the bombers were not accompanied by any fighters at all.
>
> When the Reds recognised us, they turned away, but it was too late. As they turned our 2. Staffel caught them, and two Red machines dived into the depths, leaving enormous trails of smoke behind them. Their crews saved themselves by parachute. The remaining twenty attempted to slip away, but they were already near enough to be held under our fire. In a wink of an eye, eight Reds began to burn and crashed like flaming torches. Meanwhile, the enemy fighter protection also showed up on the scene. Three or four squadrons of Ratas suddenly came down on us like a warm rain, and there resulted a wild and lurching twisting and turning dogfight, which ended up with two enemy fighters sharing the same fate as the Martin bombers. For us, it was now high time to protect our own bombers from the fighters. The enemy had, however, obviously lost his appetite. He withdrew in the direction of Valencia and our Kampfgruppe was able to accomplish its task unmolested.[7]

Air Battles over the Alfambra

Volkmann met his Spanish counterparts on 9 February and tried to convince them of the 'stupidity of further attacks on Teruel', favouring instead a drive through Aragon to the Mediterranean coast leaving Madrid for later. The

Spanish, however, appeared to see the relief of Teruel as a 'moral necessity' and flatly rejected Volkmann's idea.[8] They were none too happy with the German even before this, having become convinced that he was secretly negotiating with Berlin to have the Condor Legion withdrawn from Spain altogether. Neither was his earlier reluctance to commit fully to the attack on Teruel in December forgotten. Volkmann defended himself against such accusations by saying that he was merely concerned that at some point in the near future, the Legion's position might be compromised by the impending Austrian crisis. Rather than continue with a frontal attack, Yagüe attempted a flanking manoeuvre down the valley of the Alfambra. Meanwhile, Condor Legion aircraft pounded the Republican lines incessantly and, as the Republican flanks came under attack, the three experimental Junkers Ju 87 'Stuka' dive-bombers came into action for the first time. The accuracy and effectiveness of their precision bombing attacks was remarkable and contributed significantly to the collapse of resistance on 22 February as Teruel was retaken. It was another disastrous defeat for the Republicans who were stripped of men and equipment under skies now imperiously ruled by German aircraft.

Germans and Italians Contemplate Leaving

The relationship between Franco and his allies, never cordial at the best of times, was sorely tried at this point. Franco's pride had never allowed him to become reconciled to the fact that, while much of his success on the ground was due to Yagüe's 'Army of Africa', his battles would have been immeasurably harder had it not been for outside help in the form of Italian and German air power. From the perspective of his allies, Franco's poor decision-making with regard to where, when and in what strength the Nationalists should strike was a constant bone of contention, but they could not agree a strategy to improve matters. Mussolini was not satisfied with the way things were going. His ambitions for a glorious campaign with swift victories had been thwarted, and rather than examine too closely the Italian failures, he blamed Franco for timidity. He sent a personal message to him urging a more robust effort, but Franco – despite the crushing victory at Teruel – was cautious, perhaps still feeling the after-effects of his failure to take Madrid. Or maybe he now felt that the tide of war was running in his favour and did not want to lose the initiative by taking too many risks. The Germans, too, had urged a more aggressive approach, telling Franco that he could 'not to take German material assistance for granted', but at the Hossbach Conference of November 1937, Hitler had indicated to his military, economic and foreign policy leaders that Germany was still interested in a continuation of the war in Spain to distract France and maintain tensions between Italy and France in the Mediterranean.

In late December 1937, Mussolini, in a blatant attempt to gain greater influence over strategic decisions, had urged that a unified high command be created to control all Spanish, Italian and German troops in the hope and expectation that Italian voices would be given more attention, but the German would have none of that and vetoed the idea. von Blomberg and Keitel believed that there already was a unified high command in the person of Franco whose place could not be taken by anyone else. The Italians were tiring of being the 'poor relation' in the Nationalist family and threw another minor tantrum. Ciano expressed Italian exasperation with Franco's military leadership by accusing him of missing 'the most opportune moments [at Teruel]', and of giving 'the Reds the opportunity to rally again', and made veiled threats to begin Italian withdrawal. An urgent conference of military personnel including General Mario Berti, Commander of the CTV in Spain decided, however, that it was vital for national prestige to maintain solidarity with Franco and remain in Spain until a complete victory had been achieved.[9]

By now the Republican air force was well below strength, mainly owing to the reduced number of aircraft arriving from the Soviet Union. Apart from the limited supply of Ratas, such aircraft as did arrive were little improved from those delivered right at the start, whereas the Germans had significantly boosted their effectiveness by the introduction of the Bf 109s and He 111s. At the start, the Italian Fiat CR-32s and the German Heinkel He 51s had performed poorly against the Soviet Chatos and Ratas, and the Junkers Ju 52 bomber could not match the Katiuska, but by early 1937, all that had changed. Antonov-Ovseenko called for urgent supplies of more modern aircraft to bolster morale among the Republican troops. The air force advisor Iakushin understood that neither a tactical redeployment of the available machines nor heroic efforts by his men could offset the disadvantage caused by the lack of effective aircraft.[10]

Soviet Aircraft Manufactured in Spain

Right from the start it had been an integral part of Soviet plans to begin the manufacture of military aircraft in Spain itself, rather than have each machine dismantled, crated, shipped and reassembled, often having to run the gauntlet of Republican bombs in the process. Only airframes were built however, the engines were still shipped in from the Soviet Union. The first three Spanish-built Chatos flew in August 1937 but production was increasingly hampered by Nationalist bombing of the factories. Overall, more than 200 were built during the course of the war but because of the shortage of engines, many of them never flew.

Chapter 13

Franco's Drive into Aragon

- Aragon
- The Germans Increase Aid
- The Bombing of Barcelona
- The Soviets Send More Aid
- The Messerschmitt Bf 109-C-1 Arrives
- Condor Legion Strategic Bombing

Aragon

After Teruel, Volkmann gloomily expected Franco to dust off his plans for Madrid, but German and Italian pressure seems to have had some effect when, much to their relief, in the spring of 1938, Franco 'amazingly' abandoned his plans for a renewed attack on Madrid and turned instead to the east with a plan to drive through central Aragon to the Mediterranean coast and split the Republican forces, leaving their troops in the south cut off from their main supply routes from France.[1]

A day before the three-pronged attack was launched towards Belchite. Volkmann ordered first Ju 87 Stukas, then two full squadrons of He 111s coming in at low level to destroy the bridge over the Ebro at Sástago but, once again demonstrating how difficult it was to hit a small target with any sort of accuracy, all the raids were complete failures.

The Spanish air crews had now been well trained by their German and Italian allies and constituted a significant proportion of flyers in action at this time. During this offensive the Italian air force would support their own ground troops while the Condor Legion would cooperate with the Moroccan and Naverese divisions, but first it carried out an extensive campaign against Republican airfields in the area destroying many aircraft on the ground in an attempt to claim air superiority from the start. The advance began on 9 March.

The Republican lines were quickly breached and Condor Legion transferred its main effort to interdiction of Republican reserves, preventing them reaching the front line. The war had now become one of rapid manoeuvre to which the Condor Legion adapted quickly by employing its reconnaissance squadrons to good effect to keep abreast of the situation on the ground. It was on the Aragon front that the first embryonic 'Blitzkrieg' tactics were employed.[2]

The Bf 109Bs of J/88 were moved to Estracón and the Condor Legion started with saturation bombing of the Republican front lines at Huerva, but at the same time struck at the Amposta bridge across the river Ebro to cut off the movement of supplies and the munitions factory at La Puebla de Hijar. Volkmann repeatedly sent his bombers, heroically serviced between sorties by ground crews, to pound enemy lines and strafe infantry movements. When the Republicans tried to establish a new line west of Belchite, Volkmann was on hand to order all his bombers, in their fourth mission of the day, to launch an immediate saturation strike to prevent it. The rapid Nationalist advance was causing serious problems for them however, given that it was often difficult to know which positions were in enemy hands and which had been taken. The combat zones were migrating ever further from Volkmann's command post and while telephone lines were quickly rolled out, communications were stretched to breaking point. On the plus side, the early strikes on enemy airfields had almost completely cleared the skies of Republican aircraft.

On 10 March, K/88 made three missions from Alfaro to attack Candasnos. The Do 17s of A/88 took off from Bunuel and all four staffeln of the Jagdgruppe took off from Sanjuro. Conditions were hazy at Caspe, Sarinena and Candasnos but five enemy aircraft were claimed destroyed on the ground. The airfield of Bujaraloz was bombed by the Do 17 Staffel and soon afterwards was forced to endure a low-level strafing attack by several He 111s. On the 12th, Nationalist ground forces advanced up to thirty-six kilometres in a single day.

During the night, ground crews frantically worked to service the aircraft and Volkmann's command post was moved closer to the front. By the next morning, reconnaissance was reporting that the enemy lines were so chaotic that it was hard to determine where the air strikes should go so, at first light, the bombers were sent out to hit enemy airfields, having a great deal of success and maintaining supremacy in the air. Later in the morning Belchite was bombed and strafed. Reserves of the International Brigade, containing at least one German battalion, were spotted and 'completely destroyed' by an He 51 strike.[3]

Volkmann again moved his command post further east to keep up with the action. The town of Belchite was taken when tanks appeared in the narrow streets and brought the defenders under direct fire. Fleeing enemy were continually strafed by Condor Legion aircraft. By the time Franco arrived at Belchite it was completely destroyed. The Legion relocated again on the 13th and prepared an attack on Caspe with the customary bombing and strafing to soften the enemy positions but Yagüe hesitated, giving the defenders time to regroup; when the Spaniard eventually made his attack in the afternoon, he failed to dislodge them. Hard fighting ensued and even with tanks and airpower, the town could not be taken. Yagüe's prevarication had cost many lives, even as his men pushed beyond the town and came under repeated guerrilla counterattack.

On 22 March Volkmann set up his forward headquarters overlooking Huesca but when the attack started, the weather clamped down and grounded all aircraft for twenty-four hours. After a short pause, the attack to the north of the River Ebro was resumed with eighteen Fiats from 2-G-3 supporting the Navarre Army Corps as they entered the Huesca sector. All the time, refugees were flooding back towards the coast trying desperately to keep ahead of the bombers, but on 26 March as many as fifty were killed in the small town of Fraga, and Lleida felt the weight of Condor Legion bombs on the following day. Lleida was already carrying the scars of bombing that had occurred on 2 November the previous year, when almost 300 had been killed. As towns and villages were occupied by Yagüe's forces the customary gruesome summary executions of captured Republicans and public officials were swiftly carried out.[4]

The stress that Condor Legion pilots were experiencing was evident on 2 April when two He 111s returning to Alfaro airfield collided in mid-air as they circled to land, with one of them going down in flames. Two days later there was a similar incident when two Bf 109s flying from Zaragoza to Lanaja were also in a mid-air collision with both aircraft going down. Canaris was in Spain at the time and witnessed the distress that rippled through the leadership of the Legion at these losses, obviously caused by pilot fatigue. Another aircraft was lost on the 7th to anti-aircraft fire over Artesa de Segre, and all this against a backdrop of increased supplies coming into the Republicans through the Cartagena and Almería channels that no amount of effort seemed to prevent, and the worrying news from home that Hitler had marched his troops into Austria. Two He 51s went down on a strafing attack on the 12th. Another only just survived a similar fate on the 13th. News that Nationalist troops had reached the Mediterranean coast at Vinaroz suggested that soon the Spanish nightmare would be over, but events were to prove that the war was far from over and it would be another brutal winter before many of the Germans would see their home again.

The Germans Increase Aid

The German Foreign Minister von Ribbentrop was insistent that the withdrawal of Italian and German forces from Spain would be interpreted by Franco and the wider world as a political retreat, and Wehrmacht chief Field Marshal Wilhelm Keitel agreed. It was actually proposed to increase Condor Legion strength to bring the war to a quicker conclusion, but while Hitler accepted that they would have to stay in Spain, he was not willing to authorise any escalation.

The Bombing of Barcelona

General Kindelán was ready with his own excuses for the failure to bring the war to a swift conclusion. His argument was that the Nationalist air force had been prevented by Franco from applying what he believed to be the most effective strategies, which in his mind were the pure Douhetist 'terror bombing' of urban centres. Had they not had their 'wings clipped' by Franco's timorous half-way measures, he claimed, both Madrid and Barcelona would long since have fallen, Franco's action in easing the aerial bombardment, however, had probably stemmed, at least partially, from his unwillingness to wreck important industrial and transportation centres beyond the point where they would be useful to him when captured.

Kindelán's ambitions for application of Douhetist strategy found expression through the Aviazione Legonaria, which had been based on

Mallorca and given free rein to bomb the Catalonian coastal region. The Italian chain of command rarely bothered to consult its own CTV leadership in the peninsula and usually operated under direct orders from Rome. The attacks could be interpreted as preparing the ground for subsequent land occupations by the CTV considering which places were bombed most severely. It is no coincidence that the actions of the Aviazione Legionaria focused on the places where the Frecce Nere acted in 1938: locations between the Maestrazgo and the Mediterranean Sea. The Italo-Spanish occupation of Tortosa on 19 April, which divided Republican territory, was facilitated by an intense bombardment that broke bridges and the defensive lines of the Republican Army. The Aviazione was following orders from Rome, in support of the conquering troops, with the aim of avoiding a repetition of the disaster of Guadalajara.[5]

On 15 March, the French had reopened their border with Spain to allow transfer of military supplies, and Mussolini took it upon himself to interdict this by bombing the Catalonian capital, Barcelona. For months the city had been subjected to sporadic bombardment which had seen some escalation since the beginning of the year. Ciano was pleased to call the resulting destruction 'so realistically horrifying'. After a pause in the bombing during which the British had tried to curb Italian enthusiasm for the operation but failed to do anything constructive, the raids started up again with greater intensity. Again, Ciano stepped in to laud his father-in-law by declaring that 'Mussolini believes that these air raids are an admirable way of weakening the morale of the Reds.'[6]

On 16 March the 8th Stormo Bombardamento Veloce ('the Falcons of the Balearics') started an intensive all-day bombing campaign which was followed up by the XXV Gruppo Autonomo Bombardamento Notturno during the night. These raids came without warning, giving the population mere minutes to take shelter in the many makeshift air-raid shelters that had been hastily constructed using rubble from previous raids. The Italians experimented with high-explosive, penetrating explosive and incendiary bombs but they also dropped anti-personnel mines marked 'chocolati' to attract children, with the inevitable horrific consequences.[7] The bombardment continued for three days unabated. Ciano was clearly confident that the reputation of the Italian air force would be enhanced when he said, 'This will send our stock up in Germany too, where they love total and ruthless war.'[8] Trueta's hospital received 2,200 casualties during this period; a single bombardment brought 300 casualties to another hospital in the space of fifteen minutes.

Here at last was the most egregious implementation of Douhetist theory of strategic bombing designed to break the will of a population, carried out by the air force which he had implored to adopt it. The results, however, were not those he had predicted. Dr E.B. Strauss, who delivered a lecture on the subject to the Royal United Service Institution in London in January 1939, spoke of the experiences of the Spanish people under bombardment. The war, he said, had

> shown that the civilian population can become accustomed to air-raids with all their attendant horrors and danger to life, with the result that the number of acute psychiatric casualties is greatly reduced in the course of time.

It was evident that the most chronic anxiety was engendered not by the bombing so much, as from the population not knowing from one hour to the next whether a raid was to be expected. Strauss noted that one of the most remarkable effects of the bombing of open towns was the welding together into a formidable fighting force of groups of political factions who were previously at each other's throats.

If the object of bombardment was solely to terrorise the civil population into submission, it had been abundantly proved that no matter how intense the bombardment, the morale of the whole of the population of a city cannot be broken, provided, of course, that passive defence measures have been properly organised. It takes a lot to crush the morale of a great city where men and women must still go on living.

The Soviets Send More Aid

The Soviets, meanwhile, had sent thirty-one more I-16 Type 10s powered by new M-25V engines to Cartagena, which were unloaded amid a massive air strike by all the available Condor Legion He 111s. A report from the US Assistant Chief of Staff noted that the Nationalists were carrying out systematic, daily attacks on the Mediterranean ports and shipping in the harbours to create a blockade of material coming in. Over fifty commercial vessels had been sunk or damaged in the two previous months which severely curtailed the importation of oil, and food shortages were having a significant debilitating effect on the Nationalist effort.[9] With the Mediterranean all but closed to Soviet ships by the predation of Italian submarines, all aid now had to come from Murmansk and through the Atlantic if it was to avoid passing through the English Channel.

The Soviet pilots who flight-tested the new aircraft reported several alarming faults in the construction of the engines, as well as unsafe armament, resulting in a general reluctance among them to fly combat missions in the new fighters. The Republicans would go on to lose sixty aircraft through enemy action during the offensive in Aragon – mainly Chatos and Ratas, half of which were destroyed on the ground or abandoned during the retreat, while several others were lost through accidents.

The Messerschmitt Bf 109-C-1 Arrives

The introduction of the Bf 109 to the Spanish Civil War was one of the most significant developments, and one which helped to tip the balance of air power in the Nationalists' favour. The experimental prototypes were sent at first, to be tested under combat conditions, but as new variants came off the production lines over the course of a couple of years, they were also sent. The Bf 109 types used in Spain were:

> **Bf 109 V-3**: This machine was quite distinctive and had, in addition to the two Mg 17 above the engine cowling that would become standard on all Bf 109s, an engine-mounted Mg 17 (or possibly an Mg FF 20 mm cannon) firing through a cut-down propeller boss. The wheels were also larger than on subsequent aircraft, necessitating bulges on the upper surface of the wing to house the retracted landing gear.

> **Bf 109 V-4, V-5 and V-6**: Much less is known about these aircraft, and few photographs seem to exist, but they are all thought to have had the same general arrangement, with armament confined to two Mg 17s mounted above the engine. These aircraft served as the pre-production versions of the

Bf 109 B. All lacked the under-wing oil cooler found on later prototypes and production aircraft.

Bf 109 A: Fitted with Junkers Jumo 210 D engine. Armament was initially planned to be just two cowl-mounted 7.92 mm machine guns but experiments were carried out with a third machine gun firing through the propeller shaft. Fitted with a 2-blade fixed-pitch wooden propeller and an oil cooler mounted under the port wing. The first aircraft had spinners that were slightly smaller than the forward cowling which exposed small annular air intakes around the propeller. The seams between fuselage panels may have been taped, since they are not clearly visible on photographs. Wing slats were full-length. Many of these Bf 109 A-0 served with the Condor Legion and were often misidentified as B-series aircraft, and probably served in Spain with the tactical markings **6-1** to **6–16**. **6–15**, ran out of fuel and was forced to land behind enemy lines where it was captured by Republican troops on 11 November 1937 and later transferred to the Soviet Union for a closer inspection.

Bf 109 B: The Bf 109 B-1 was fitted with the 670 PS Jumo 210D engine driving a two-bladed fixed-pitch propeller. During the production run a variable-pitch Hamilton propeller was introduced and often retrofitted to older aircraft; these were then unofficially known as **B-2**s. Several aircraft were produced with an engine-mounted machine gun but it was very unreliable, most likely because of engine vibrations and overheating.

Bf 109 C: The 109C was powered by a 700 PS Jumo 210Ga engine with direct fuel injection. Another important change was a strengthened wing, now carrying two more machine guns, giving four 7.92 mm (.312 in) MG 17s in total.

Bf 109 D: Reverted to the Junkers Jumo 210 D engine, but had the additional wing guns. It was the standard version of the Bf 109 in service with the Luftwaffe just before the start of the Second World War.

Bf 109 E-1: Powered by the Daimler-Benz DB 601 engine, driving a three-blade propeller. An entirely new nose shape resulted from the installation of this engine, as well as new under-wing radiators. A much bigger cooling area was needed to disperse the extra heat generated by the DB 601, and this led to the first major redesign of the basic airframe. To incorporate the new radiators, the wings were almost completely redesigned and reinforced. There were numerous other minor alterations which mean that Bf 109 Es are quite distinctive from most angles. It had two 7.92 mm (.312 in) MG 17s above the engine and two more in the wings.

Bf 109 E-3: As the Bf 109 E-1, but with the wing guns replaced with 20mm Mg FF canon, which had muzzles that projected beyond the leading edge of the wing.

During this time, the major international allies on both sides had continued to send in supplies, but the wider political picture was changing and this had repercussions in Spain. Following the Anschluss of 12 March 1938, Hitler had become anxious about the amount of war matériel being sent to Spain, especially the new generation of aircraft, and looked at the possibility of starting to withdraw from the arena. In his view, it was only a matter of time before the Nationalists were able to crush the Republicans completely and stabilise the situation, but he also knew that a precipitate German exit could revitalise the Republicans and prolong the war. The key for him was whether the Soviet Union was also losing interest in the war and what the Italian reaction to a German withdrawal might be. Another twenty-four Bf 109s had already been promised and arrived in Spain in April and included five new Augsburg-built Bf 109C-1s, into which it had been planned to fit a 700hp Jumo 210G engine with fuel-injection and a two-stage compressor. This configuration was to be augmented by a pair of wing-mounted MG 17s to provide more firepower and a cockpit radio. Unfortunately, the engine was simply not ready, so most models were still powered by the Jumo 210D. A couple of months later, five Bf 109Ds arrived out of an eventual total of thirty-five. The E-series (Emil) was the first of many redesigns, with the 1085hp Daimler-Benz DB 601 engine, forty-five of which would burst onto the scene in the final days of December 1938, just in time for Franco's final push in Catalonia.

The Bf 109 had been the subject of much scrutiny by many observers ever since the arrival in Spain of the first prototypes. On the rare occasions that one of them fell into enemy hands there was a desperate attempt to salvage it for examination. On 14 June, Oberleutnant Helmut Henz's Bf 109 was hit over Castellón and he crash-landed his machine north of the Mijares River. He tried to set his fighter alight but was subsequently taken prisoner and his assailant, Sergento Tarazona, later recorded his vain attempt to save the aircraft:

> A plane, leaving a trail of white smoke, was turning towards the north. I pointed this out to Claudín. We dived. We discovered that it was an Me 109. It had been hit. We swooped over it, without firing, where it had landed on the beach, on the right bank of the River Mijares…
>
> … On reaching Sagunto I received orders to go out and bring back the Me 109. We went in a lorry, various mechanics, armourers and myself…
>
> …'There is the ugly bird', said one of them. 'The pilot is nearby, in a gully at Villareal. He has been detained; he is only a lad of about 18 years.'
>
> I am enthralled with the beauty of this fine piece of German aeronautical engineering. I admire it from the outside for a long time. Then, with aplomb, I sit in the cockpit. The oxygen, the radiotelephone, the fuel tank which serves as the pilot's seat…
>
> … We need to fly it; to study its characteristics, to compare it more closely with our own fighters. It is intact. As we are talking, the rattle of friendly machine-guns and the hollow sound of cannons from both sides serve as a background. The enemy is barely fifteen kilometres from us; within sight of Castellón…
>
> … The rumble of aeroplane engines makes us look up. The noise increases; it seems as if they are coming along the road, but they are not yet visible.
>
> There they are!

Six Me 109s appear over the sea, skimming the water. When they reach the Mijares estuary they make a gentle bank to starboard.

They are coming towards us…

Get out quickly!

The monoplanes form a circle around the Me 109 on the ground. They fire at it. At their second attack it bursts into flames…[10]

Condor Legion Strategic Bombing

The prolonged exposure of Condor Legion aircrews to almost daily combat, notwithstanding the policy of personnel rotation, continued to exercise Plocher's mind. On 16 April, forty He 111s were ordered up to Seville in preparation for air strikes. On the way, one aircraft flew into a mountainside near Badajoz in the mist. Another was badly damaged when its landing gear collapsed and four more were grounded after being found unfit to fly. When the raid over Cartagena took place it encountered heavy anti-aircraft fire as usual and when the aircraft returned to their bases in Grenada, only twenty-seven remained. This sort of attrition was having a serious effect on morale. Plocher and Volkmann, who had moved their base up to Benicarló on the coast, however, were keen to pursue the Republicans who were 'completely disorganised [and] fleeing in all directions', but Franco paused and looked again to the South, which gave the Catalonians time to regroup and continue getting aid across the border from France.[11] The Condor Legion was instructed instead to support an attack south along the coastal plain towards Valencia but became embroiled in bitter air battles in stormy weather that slowed the Nationalist advance as the ground turned to mud. Losses of men and equipment mounted in what Plocher saw as entirely the wrong strategy which encountered enormous problems for the taking of 'such a small stretch of territory'. Condor Legion fighters were fully committed in bomber escort missions, leaving Republican bombers many options for attacking even as far as Condor Legion headquarters at Benicarló.

Despite reluctance to destroy major infrastructure, smaller targets – especially those that played a vital part in the Republican supply chains – were not spared. Alicante suffered a series of raids on 25 May, most of them, according to a Report of the British Commission of Investigation, 'deliberate attacks on a civilian area of a town killing 290 and injuring 295'. Sagunto, another coastal town just north of Valencia, boasted that it had withstood Nationalist bombings better than most Mediterranean cities. In almost two years of war, up to June 1938 it was reported, Sagunto had undergone 138 attacks, but it had not wilted and the town's industries had continued to be productive. One of the worst raids of the late spring took place at Granollers, a small town just north of Barcelona, on 31 May with reportedly 200 dead and 300 injured. There were almost daily raids through June, the deadliest of which was against Alicante on the 25th, when as many as 100 civilians were killed.

Volkmann flew to Berlin on 10 June to assess the European situation and ascertain what impact it was likely to have on the Condor Legion in Spain. He saw a major European war as inevitable and called for extra aid to expedite an end to involvement in Spain. The combat status of the Legion, he said, was at an all-time low with half of his fighters out of service. The He 51s, almost worn out by combat, could not operate in the face of overwhelming Republican air power. If the situation was not remedied the Legion would simply cease to function. He offered two solutions: resupply the Legion to bring it up to its former strength, or get out of Spain as quickly as possible. The consequences of a complete withdrawal, however, would give the Republicans and their Soviet allies a major propaganda victory and the French might be tempted to become more involved. Von Ribbentrop dissembled the German decision by suggesting that they were obliged to remain in support of the Italians. Hitler, reluctantly, took the only decision he could by agreeing to reinforce the Legion 'to the extent necessary for maintaining its fighting strength'. Back in Spain, Volkmann tried to boost morale by organising sporting events and showing films brought in from Germany. The Mediterranean beaches were a bonus for crews given precious time off and they were encouraged to join in local fiestas.

The general state of the Condor Legion bomber group, K/88, was beginning to suffer from flying four to six missions daily. However, a new batch of He 111s, of the latest 'E' model, arrived at the start of July, in time for the Ebro offensive. Faster, and capable of carrying a larger weapons payload, the He 111Es assured the superiority of the Nationalist camp in the months that followed. The group set itself up at Zaragoza, where the aircraft had to land carrying their bomb-loads, ready to bomb the port and the station of Sagunto. On 10 July, thirty-nine aircraft bombed the enemy lines at Sierra de Espadán and Vall de Uxo and then operated in company with A/88 over the sector of Adzaneta. The next day they attacked the roads to the south of Castellrón, where big aerial battles took place during which six He 111s from K/88 were hit, two of which had to carry out forced landings in the countryside.

The Bf 109s of J/88 were in action during the 15th claiming nine Chatos shot down. Oberleutnant Mölders claimed his first victory flying a Bf 109C over Villamalur. It proved a tough challenge for him to manoeuvre his Messerschmitt in an engagement in which his formation of six fighters were outnumbered by twenty-five to thirty Republican machines, and he found himself 'sweating like a bull'. The Bf 109s of J/88 claimed six more shot down on the 17th. Bombers of K/88 continued relentlessly bombing the stations of Segorbe and Soñeja, then, during a second sortie, attacked the road from Segorbe to Sagunto.

Italian flyers were feeling the heat too. The CR.32 pilot, Maggiore Zotti described the action in his report:

> The Ratas tried to fragment our compactness into a widespread battle, reduce our operational height and bring the broken formation down into the 'Curtiss fighters' engagement zone – a restricted combat zone that would have put us in a disadvantageous position.
>
> Having seen off the Ratas, which suddenly vanished, our CR.32s turned their attention to the 'Curtiss fighters' that had dived down low in order to engage us in close combat. This tactic left us with no room for a diving attack. In the second action, which lasted a good twenty minutes, we resisted the temptation to make individual attacks. Instead, we remained in formation, thus forcing the Republicans to fight us as a unified mass that dominated the battle from a higher altitude. During this second combat five 'Curtiss fighters' were shot down.[12]

Despite the Republican tactic, most Italian pilots stayed in formation and manoeuvred without losing height. The Ratas were tackled first in an engagement that lasted ten minutes, with Republican documents showing that three Polikarpovs were lost and two pilots killed. However, it appears that these aircraft were shot down by Legion Condor Bf 109s that had independently joined the battle at a higher altitude. At least one of the Ratas that force-landed at Utiel airfield was one of the new four-gun I-16-10s recently delivered to Spain.

On a visit to Valencia in August 1938, the US attaché noted that the port area had sustained greatly increased damage since his last visit three months previously and was now virtually unusable. Mains services were cut and the entire port had been evacuated. The whole appearance of the port was one of devastation, he said, and the civilian population showed war-weariness and low morale. In Barcelona the impact of the bombing was equally obvious. The food supply was bad and getting worse. Electricity supplies and transport were almost eliminated. The bombing campaign against the port cities was widely condemned in many foreign capitals, which depicted them as examples of indiscriminate terror bombing. Spanish Republicans were eager to provide evidence of 'open' cities with casualties invariably being women and children. The Nationalists and their allies countered by insisting that the bombed cities were vital military and economic centres and therefore legitimate targets. The cumulative effects of the first sustained strategic bombing campaign ever attempted, was a significant factor in weakening the Republican effort and destroying, what the US attaché called the 'heart that fed all of government Spain'.[13]

Chapter 14

The Ebro Offensive

- The Ebro Offensive
- The Soviets Send More Aircraft
- The Germans and Italians Start to Pull Out
- The Battle on the Ebro Plays Out
- The End

The Ebro Offensive

Volkmann, in his headquarters at Burgos, was becoming increasingly disturbed by reports from his reconnaissance aircraft of Republican activity north of the river Ebro. He was quite correct to be concerned. The enemy was reputedly on the verge of total collapse, but intelligence was reporting a great deal of activity in their front lines. Volkmann's aircraft, fitted out with the most up-to-date cameras had obtained a complete map of the Catalonian front which, in itself, was an enormous improvement on the obsolete road maps in use at the start of the war. As early as July, General Yagüe had been made fully aware that a concentration of up to 500 small boats, big enough to carry six or seven men, and transport vehicles had been observed on the east bank of the river near Cherta. Intelligence put the Republican 11th International Brigade between Ginestar and Benifallet and the 12th massing just to the north of that. The level of troop movements was a clear indication of an impending attack.

By 23 July it was noted that 'traffic continues without interruption [so that the Republicans] are able to realign their forces quickly' to be in a position to launch a frontal attack across the Ebro on the vital Nationalist-held road junction at Gandesa.[1] The Nationalists front along the Ebro on the southern front, and its tributary the Segre, extended almost as far

150

south as Valencia. Fearing that the fall of Valencia would signal the end, the Republicans hoped to draw off the attackers with an offensive in the north which they opened with successful night river crossings between Mequinenza and Cherta against minimal opposition. At the start of the offensive the Republicans could muster 176 serviceable Chatos and Ratas and Grumman G-23 Delfins while the Nationalists had 168 CR.32s and Bf 109s (ninety-six Italian and thirty-six Spanish CR.32s, and thirty-six German Bf 109s).

Initially it was Aviazione Legionaria Savoie 79s and Ro 37s in action but as the build-up continued, the Condor Legion Do 17s, escorted by Bf 109s, did most of the work. They were redeployed from the south of the Nationalist Aragon salient to meet the threat along the Ebro where they were able to halt the Republican advance, but both sides became bogged down while aircraft tried to destroy the Ebro bridges to prevent supplies and reinforcements moving up to the front. Bf 109s and Ratas battled for air superiority as the Germans introduced new battle tactics with their Rotte and Schwarm system replacing the V-formation with spectacular results. Sonderstab W issued a situation report stating that, 'In the five days since the delivery of twenty-two new Bf 109s, the German Jagdgruppe has shot down twenty-two Red fighters without loss.' With a clear advantage over the Soviets, the Germans brought up their Ju 87 dive-bombers to tackle the bridges and the new Henschel Hs123 to act as effective ground support. The Ju 87s in particular were used extensively at this point and proved to be well able to avoid the Republican flak.

From the very first Republican attack on 25 July, Volkmann had placed the entire Condor Legion at Yagüe's disposal, but it was two days before the Republican air force was able to muster a response. On 27 July, K/88 flew six missions. Firstly, nine aircraft attacked the crossing points on the Ebro between Mora la Nueva and Rivarroja, while twelve others bombed the enemy positions between Pinell and Corbera. Next, another formation of nine He 111s smashed the sector between Fatarella, Corbera and Venta de Camposines, against an intense flak barrage. Another Staffel bombed the roads on the axis Flix-Camposincs, and a third the pontoon bridges on the Ebro to the north of Ginestar. Finally, twelve He 111s operated against the roads between Gandesa and Pinell and concentrations of troops to the north of Ginestar and to the west of Asco.

The Republicans failed to reach their objective, Gandesa, in time to prevent it being reinforced and they suffered in the open under repeated aerial attack by Condor Legion bombers and Stukas. When the Republican attack inevitably stalled, Franco launched a counterattack using aircraft to blast their positions incessantly before advancing with ground troops. Repetition of this strategy continued over several weeks as different sections of the front between Cherta and Fayón were targeted and the Republican line was inexorably pushed further and further back.

On the 29th, thirty aircraft from K/88 attacked the crossings of the Ebro between Asco and Miravet, destroying fuel reserves. The operation was repeated a little while afterwards with the same number of aircraft against the bridges between Vinebre and Ginestar, hitting at least one bridge and a flak battery. Later, the same formation succeeded in breaching one of the bridges at Flix.

The bridge at Mora de Ebro was attacked thirty-four times between 25 and 18 September, receiving a total of more than 600 tonnes of bombs causing it to be damaged and rebuilt five times. The bridge situated to the north of Ginestar was the next most seriously damaged with thirty-two attacks between 26 July and 6 September, receiving over 500 tonnes of bombs and damaged eight times. The infantry foot bridge at Miravet was attacked six times but Republican engineers and bridge-builders worked quickly, using the nights to repair the damage made during the days.

Hauptmann Harder recalled:

> There come the Red fighters, first several Curtisses, then swarms of Ratas, spiralling upwards. By turning tightly we are able three times to keep them from attacking the bombers. Suddenly the Reds are gone. There are still two Curtisses south of Sagunto at 4,000 metres. I attack one of them. In the instant I begin to fire he pulls up and opens fire at me while on his back. I pull up and at the same instant I am attacked by four Ratas. One is already on my tail in firing position. I dive away but can't shake him off. I try everything to lose him: full throttle, shallow dive, radiator flap up, propeller pitch set for diving flight. The Rata sits somewhat off to my left and tries to get below me by diving steeply. There are machines in front of me, many Red fighters! The way is blocked!

I try to count them. Ten, twenty then a new swarm approaches, I can only estimate their numbers. I try to slip past them at the coast but that fat radial engine is still behind me. The Reds fail to notice me until I'm at their altitude, too late for them. Not far from Castellon, at an altitude of 1,000 meters, my pursuer gives up. How would things have turned out if I hadn't had the fastest machine in the Gruppe?[3]

The Republican attack had been blunted but it had taken the pressure off Valencia, the loss of which would have been a hammer-blow. On the Ebro, however the front became stationary and descended into a battle of attrition reminiscent of the First World War trenches. Volkmann suggested a diversionary attack from the north, but Franco would not be persuaded. His judgement was clouded by the prospect of a major European war erupting in which he expected France would invade Catalonia. Republican resistance along the Ebro infuriated Mussolini, who complained to Ciano about Franco's 'serene optimism [and] flabby conduct of the war'.

The Soviets Send More Aircraft

Early in August, the Republicans received ninety improved I-16 Type 10 fighters, some of which had been fitted with the more powerful Wright-Cyclone R-1820-F4 engines to improve performance at higher altitudes. Higher ceilings meant that pilots now had to wear oxygen masks, and the latter led to the 4a Escuadrilla being given a new nickname – la del chupete (dummy). This enabled additional escuadrillas to be formed, but this was the last shipment of Ratas the Republicans were to get.

The total number of Ratas shipped to Spain in 1936–38 amounted to 276 I-16s and four UTI-4 trainers. Monthly shipments were thirty-one in October 1936, sixty-two (and four UTI-4s) in May 1937, sixty-two in August 1937, thirty-one in March 1938 and ninety in August of that same year. Within three months of the last Ratas having been delivered to the Republicans, all Soviet pilots had been withdrawn from Spain on direct orders from the Kremlin and returned to the USSR. The Soviets had seen enough and wanted only to go home. They handed over all their Chato and Ratas to the Spanish and withdrew 10,000 troops. It begs the question of why the Soviets abandoned the war so soon after they had sent the final shipment of ninety Ratas and why the Ratas were even sent, given that a crisis was brewing in the far east of the Soviet Union with the Japanese. On 9 August the Republicans collected twelve brand new Type 10 Moscas from Celrá and took them to Vendrell airfield, where the unit was based for Ebro operations. Two weeks later they received four more and these were ordered to fly to the Central-South area, where its pilots operated from Liria airfield before moving to Almodóvar del Campo.

The German flyers were being withdrawn also. On 6 August K/88 began using Spanish crews, nine men taking their places in aircraft two and three of the Kette of the Staff formation. On 25 August, to contain the government counter-offensive in the bend of the Zújar, Nationalist fighter groups returned to Mérida, where they remained until 18 September. The Nationalists could field 180 fighters in total (including the Aviazione Legionaria and the Condor Legion).

All the frontline fighter units fielded by the Nationalists in continental Spain were now gathered together close to the Ebro theatre of operations. These included eighteen CR.32 squadriglie and escuadrillas and three Messerschmitt staffeln, with serviceable totals of about 180 CR.32s and thirty Bf 109s, respectively. At the beginning of September, the Nationalists successfully embarked upon a local counteroffensive along the Gandesa-Corbera-La Venta de los Camposines route, which was well supported from the air. Among the aircraft involved were fighters from the Aviazione Legionaria's XVI Gruppo, based at Caspe, and XXIII Gruppo at Sariñena. On 2 September, in line with the German policy of rotating personnel in Spain, Hauptmann Siebelt Reents took over from Schellmann in 1.J/88. Hauptmann Handrick was relieved as commander of J/88 on the 10th and replaced by Hauptmann Walter Grabmann. On the same day Major Mehnert passed command of Gruppe K/88 to Major Haerle. Simultaneously a number of other experienced pilots returned to Germany due to the looming Sudeten crisis.

The last twenty-four Spanish-built Chatos were completed in January 1939 to take the total number of airframes produced to 237 units. Of this total, some ninety-six, built between November 1938 and January 1939, stood incomplete for lack of engines and other equipment. As a result, the total number of Soviet-made and locally built Chatos said to have participated in the Spanish Civil War varies between 272 and 368.

By 1 January 1939, a total of 197 Chatos had reportedly been lost, including eighty-eight shot down, twenty-seven destroyed on the ground, sixty-seven written off in accidents, nine downed by anti-aircraft artillery and six captured after force-landing in enemy territory yet Nationalist pilots (Spanish, Italian and German) reportedly claimed that about 500 Chatos had been shot down in air combat! Actual Chato losses were probably comparable to those of its principal rival, the CR.32. By January, all Soviet pilots had been withdrawn back to the Soviet Union (orders for withdrawal were sent in late October 1938). A total of around 160 Soviet fighter pilots had seen action in the conflict, with thirty-five being created Heroes of the Soviet Union.

The Germans and Italians Start to Pull Out

The wider European situation continued to impact events in Spain as the Czechoslovakian crisis intensified. Volkmann was instructed to return to Germany a sizeable portion of his aircrews and a quarter of his reconnaissance fleet and Spanish pilots were expected to take a more active role. Volkmann furiously complained to Berlin at the depletion of his forces and offered scathing opinions about the quality of Spanish military leadership. This persuaded the German General Staff that it was time for another change and so they looked for a new leader of the Legion to steer it through what were clearly the final stages of the war where diplomacy might prove more important than military might. Hitler was becoming increasingly distracted by the Czechoslovakian issue but the Munich agreement on 30 September cooled the tensions a little. He was, however, more anxious than ever that the Spanish war would come to a conclusion and agreed, with Mussolini, to withhold any more aid until Franco showed that he had a plan of action that all could agree to. None of the three wanted to lose face by falling out publicly and none certainly wanted to see the war peter out without a clear victory so perhaps it was inevitable that German and Italian help would continue, although Hitler flatly rejected von Richthofen's suggestion that aid should be significantly increased. It was a surprise to some, therefore, that von Richthofen was chosen to replace Volkmann, but his previous close rapport with Franco was clearly the deciding factor. Plocher, who had replaced von Richthofen at the beginning of the year, briefly would be in command of the Legion between Volkmann's departure on 13 November and von Richthofen's arrival but he, too, was replaced when Oberstleutnant Hans Seidemann became the new leader's Chief of Staff.

The Italian VI Gruppo was ordered to disband, along with other units of the Aviazione Legionaria, in accordance with wider commitments made by the major powers that signed up to the Münich agreement. This document, which was meant to avert the growing crisis in Europe, called for the removal of all foreign soldiers from Spanish soil. VI Gruppo's CR.32s were duly handed over to the Spanish Nationalist air force at the end of September.

The Battle on the Ebro Plays Out

Although events were going very much against the Republicans on the ground, air battles over the Ebro were intense. In the morning of 5 September, CR.32s from both Aviazione Legionaria gruppi, as well as the Comando di Stormo, escorted SM.81 bombers sent to attack Republican targets on the Gandesa front. A large-scale engagement ensued involving more than 100 fighters. For over thirty minutes, this swirling mass of aircraft drifted east over Republican territory beyond Falset. The Republicans lost five Chatos and four Ratas, including a Type 10 from 2a Escuadrilla. Three more Type 10s returned to base with varying degrees of battle damage. No losses were suffered by the CR.32s, although several pilots from XVI Gruppo returned with bullet holes in their aircraft.

In late September, a series of daily battles began, culminating in fierce combats on 2 and 3 October. Grupo 3-G-3 escorted bombers over the Manzanera front. Polikarpov fighters were encountered, and a probable kill was claimed by Teniente José Larios Fernández from Escuadrilla 6-E-3, who later recalled,

> A large formation of Ratas suddenly appeared above us, flying high in the blue sky as if they had just come out of the sun. Pilots from our escuadrilla above us waved to signal the alarm, after which we all flew directly at the enemy at full throttle in an attempt to prevent them from reaching our bombers. I desperately tried to position my section above the Ratas before attacking them but I did not succeed, as they fell on us

like an avalanche and we had little choice other than to defend ourselves.

Four Ratas in formation dived like lightning straight towards me in a frontal attack. I rapidly raised the nose of my 'Fiat' and pointed it directly at the leading Rata. I had just enough time to fire a couple of bursts before the 'Red' aeroplane dived straight down towards the ground and the others passed by at high speed over our heads, before banking around tightly so as to attack us from the rear.

Things now took a turn for the worse, as they held all the advantages – a superior number of aircraft, height and greater speed with which to manoeuvre. I had no option but to turn as tightly as possible. The enemy seemed to be everywhere, and again I could hear the classic chatter of gunfire behind my shoulders. Instinctively, I threw my aeroplane into a sharp spin towards the River Ebro, knowing this to be my sole chance of survival. It worked, as the Ratas immediately gave up chasing me, probably thinking that I was on my way to the other world. I recovered from the violent dive upon seeing that I wasn't being chased and started to climb once again with my engine flat out, attentively observing the sky in all directions. I was impatient to regain height and rejoin the battle.

On reaching 13,000ft I felt secure once more. I could see that fierce fighting was still going on. A lonely Rata crossed the brilliant sky some 700ft above me. I was in his blind spot, and it flew on without attempting to take any evasive action. Seizing my opportunity, I was able to fire several bursts right into its belly – one of the Rata's most vulnerable spots. The fighter trembled with the impact and appeared to swing for a second, before dropping on a wing, lowering its nose and entering a spin. I followed for a while, stuck to the Rata's tail, still firing. Climbing back up again, I lost sight of the aircraft as if it had been swallowed up by the uneven ground. I never did find out whether the Rata had indeed hit the ground or not. It remained another combat uncertainty. I turned towards our lines low on fuel. On landing, Rossi and I examined the aeroplane and could count a good number of bullet holes in the fuselage – fortunately no vital parts had been hit. The Fiat was strong and could take great punishment. It would soon be parked, fully serviced and prepared to take off again as part of the next flight.[4]

The Nationalist counter-offensive on the Ebro front resumed on 30 October in the north-central sector between Asco and Cherta, with this attack being well supported by air power. All available Spanish, German and Italian aircraft supported the attack flying several missions daily. The Republicans still had about one hundred fighter aircraft but they had hardly any bombers left. The air battle was very much a one-sided affair now with Bf 109s dominating the skies preventing the Fiats from getting at the Nationalist bombers which were 'making the earth tremble with their bomb-loads'.[5] Each time the Ratas attacked they returned fewer in numbers. A number of new Ju 87 dive-bombers increased the potency of the Nationalist bombing offensive. The onslaught was too much for the Republicans who, after taking a staggering number of casualties, ordered a complete withdrawal back across the Ebro. The dominance of Nationalist aircraft was well demonstrated by the very small number of their aircraft lost, despite extensive engagement. Only by desperate repairs carried out at the Barcelona and Reus SAF-9 factory did the Republicans manage to maintain any sort of air component at all. Their plight was compounded at the end of October when all Soviet volunteers were recalled to the Soviet Union. The radio/gunner Zakhar Savel'evich Skutov was the last Soviet airman to die in combat in Spain on 10 October. Afterwards, the Condor Legion Bf 109s operated with impunity and completely dominated the Republican aircraft, whose crews were significantly less effective than the departed Soviets. On 3 November, Nationalist forces captured the town of Pinell, marking the first major breakthrough at the Ebro and soon the battle came to an end during the night of 16 November, when the Republican army completed its withdrawal beyond the northern banks of the Ebro. The Condor Legion band celebrated with a concert to mark the second anniversary of the Legion in Spain. Although the battle of the Ebro was claimed as a great success by Franco's forces, it had taken a terrible toll on their manpower. The Republicans were decidedly losing the war but the cost on both sides meant that the Nationalists were not strong enough, at this stage, to force a conclusion. Barcelona was now the target, but there were still battles to come before the end.

After the battle of the Ebro the Condor Legion was ordered to rest, with only one Staffel remaining operational. At the end of November, Volkmann was replaced by von Richthofen who brought with him a new Chief of Staff, Oberstleutnant Hans Seidemann. Hauptmann Mölders was also posted back to Germany at this time, his place as commander of 3.J/88 being taken by Oberleutnant Hubertus von Bonin. Discipline and morale had obviously been allowed to slip under Volkmann. When von Richthofen visited La Sénia in December as part of an extended inspection tour he noted:

> Things at J/88 are just about tolerable. The Verbandsführer of J/88 are at the present time quartered far away from their people. Too many personnel were to be seen running around without wearing uniforms, playing during celebrations with priests' hats and they have no communal dining facility. It does not please me at all. It will be remedied and J/88 will soon be relocated.[6]

The attack on Catalonia with the objective of taking Barcelona and closing off the French border began on 23 December 1938. A six-pronged attack was launched, with separate columns from the Pyrenees to the Ebro. Spanish Nationalist aircraft supported the Northern Army Corps, the Aviazione Legionaria with virtually all of its CR.32s operated closely with the CTV on the central front of Lerida and the Legion Condor, with its first Bf 109E-1s at La Sénia supported the army corps advance through the southern Ebro area. von Richthofen moved his command post up to Tamarite de Litera. Most of his aircraft operated out of La Sénia.

The bombers had started softening up the Republican defences on the 17th along the lower Ebro valley in a diversionary attack as the bitter winter weather started to close in. When the main attack started it followed the usual format, now much improved, with infantry following up right after the bombing and strafing of enemy lines. Stuka dive-bombers were very much in evidence, striking at the Soviet tanks. The irresistible power of the Nationalist forces drove them forward against dogged defences. When the Republicans tried to bring up reserves from Valencia to Tarragona by sea with air cover, Bf 109s scattered their aircraft and the ships were attacked with a number being sunk by dive-bombers. von Richthofen tried to degrade Republican air power by hitting their airfields, but the weather meant that few could be located by the reconnaissance flights. This was perhaps not the best use of his aircraft because the targets were difficult to locate at the best of times, many being little more than flat areas of land that could only be identified if fuel trucks were visible and aircraft in occupation. To catch the enemy on the ground in surprise raids at Sabadell near Barcelona, von Richthofen circled and attacked from the north to good effect.

The last Republican counter-offensive on the Pozoblanco front, the Valsequillo Offensive, was launched close to the border between Andalusia and Extremadura in a vain attempt to slow down the Nationalist advance in Catalonia, but by the end of January the Nationalists with overwhelming land and aerial forces, had pushed the Republicans back to their previous defensive positions along the Pozoblanco front. By mid-January, the way to Tarragona was open and von Richthofen had moved his command post up to Valls. Desperate air defence was daily beaten further down by the Messerschmitts. By 24 January Nationalist artillery was within range of Barcelona and the outskirts were entered by the 26th but rain and snow closed down all air activity until 3 February.

The Nationalist rapid advance had over-run many Republican airfields which yielded up large numbers of Chatos in various stages of assembly. They were part of a Soviet shipment of 104 sent from Murmansk after a direct appeal to Stalin in early December. Many of those unloaded in French ports, however, were stopped at the border and were never flown. Just why Stalin had agreed to the transfer of these aircraft when the Republicans were obviously in their death-throes is a mystery. It may be simply that he knew the war was lost but was happy to let the Chatos, which were rapidly becoming obsolete in the face of new fighter models, go in return for full payment in Spanish gold. Even those Chatos that did achieve full reconstruction were basically useless since there were practically no Spanish pilots to fly them and their airfields were becoming murderously unsafe with bomb strikes and Bf 109s waiting to hit any aircraft managing to get airborne. In the end, any that were operational at Vilajuiga and could avoid the Messerschmitts were flown across the border to land in Toulouse.

By the 9th, all Condor Legion activity, air and ground, was paused to avoid inadvertently striking too close to the French border. Franco was preparing for a final attack on the Toledo sector and asked von Richthofen to prepare his air force to support it but by 27 March, the Condor Legion was ordered to 'cease operations!' Its last appearance was a mass flight of all its aircraft in close formation over Madrid, Aranjuez and Toledo. The last farewell ceremony was at León on 22 May with the last of the German personnel departing Vigo by ship on the 28th.

The End

At the conclusion of the war, the German Army, Navy and Air Force volunteers of the 'Legion Condor' were returned to Germany, and on 25 May the German troops began to embark on six 'Strength through Joy' ships that had arrived at Vigo, and shortly afterwards 5,136 officers and men sailed for Germany, where they were to be greeted with parades and ceremonies.

They took with them over 711 tonnes (700 tons) of equipment and most of their remaining aircraft. Before leaving Spain, the German and the Italian Legionaries handed over the remainder of their arms and war matériels to the Spanish government. During their time in Spain they claimed to have destroyed 386 enemy aircraft, of which 313 of them were in aerial combat, for the loss of 232 of their own, of that number only seventy-two were destroyed by enemy action. In addition, over 21,337 tonnes (21,000 tons) of bombs had been dropped by Legion aircraft, contributing in no small way to the Nationalists' eventual victory and 226 members of the Legion had lost their lives.

On 14 April 1939, Hitler instituted an award to recognise the bravery of the men, and also to serve as a campaign distinction. Hitler introduced the award by stating, 'To show my appreciation and thanks for the service of German volunteers during the destruction of Bolshevism in the Spanish Freedom Fight, I establish the Spanish Cross in three classes.' The resultant Spanish Cross was awarded under conditions of pomp and ceremony over the next few months.

The Legion Condor landed at Hamburg on 30 May 1939. At the official reception at Hamburg, the 'Honour Standard' was once again unfurled and carried at the head of the disembarking, sun-tanned Legionnaires, where they received an official welcome from Generalfeldmarschall Göring, who announced that Hitler had instituted a new decoration, the Spanish Cross, in three classes of Bronze, Silver, Gold and a special degree Gold with Brilliants. All volunteers from the Civil War were to receive one of the three classes. It was further announced that the Legion Condor was to be officially dissolved within a few days and that in memory of the Legion, the name 'Condor' had been bestowed by Hitler on a Luftwaffe Wing, an anti-aircraft regiment and a signals battalion. A few days after their arrival in Hamburg the troops of the Legion proceeded to Döbertiz, the military centre near Berlin. Here on 4 June Grand Admiral Raeder, the Commander in Chief of the German Navy, visited them. The Grand Admiral distributed decorations to the naval contingent and Göring presented decorations to his Air force members of the Legion.

Chapter 15

Strategy and Tactics

Having found themselves embroiled in a war that started out as no more than a minor act of political support, the Germans did not waste the opportunities that, albeit inadvertently, presented themselves. The war had cost them dearly in men and machines that would have been most useful when the Second World War broke out, but on the plus side, the experiences of war had informed their doctrine and the reality of combat had taught them valuable lessons. Through confusion and turmoil, the Condor Legion had come to understand that the development of a coherent air power doctrine should include the way an air force is organised, who should control it, and how its command should be structured. In Spain, the belligerents were able to address all these larger questions on a daily basis as a matter of practical necessity alongside evaluating the experiences of aircrews in aerial combat. This inevitably involved discussion of the relative merits of tactical and strategic deployment.

In the case of tactical close support, it was never easy to anticipate when and where aircraft would be needed due to changes in tactical situations. Strategic aviation, on the other hand, could be focused not so much on short-term objectives that might change from hour to hour, but on attacking targets that retained their importance over days or weeks. Given the resources and training of his airmen, Kindelán fought a long campaign to keep Spanish aviation under his control as chief of the air force and spent hours explaining to Franco the difference between 'aviacion de cooperacion' (tactical) and aviacion independiente (strategic).

He knew that close support would have to take precedence at least as far as the Spanish contingent was concerned but warned that strategic doctrine should not be ignored.[1] He persisted throughout to argue for unity of command over all air resources and issued a directive in July 1937 laying out the competing and often conflicting air power doctrines. The aviacion de cooperacion was to be commanded by the air chiefs of the four different air regions into which Nationalist territory was divided and these regional commands would receive and coordinate requests for air support from ground forces operating in the region.

Another key area in which the strategic uses of air power developed during the Spanish Civil War was the interdiction of seaborne commerce. This too was a new and undeveloped concept which opened up a number of questions and points of controversy. Among other things, it involved the question of the coordination of air forces with naval forces and related issues of command and control. This was no easy matter since Nationalist naval commanders, like their army counterparts, wanted control over the air component operating in their areas.

The most significant air power technique to be developed during the Spanish civil war was close support of ground operations. This, like strategic bombing, was in evidence right from the start. A document prepared by a Nationalist air officer for the instruction of both air and ground commanders in August 1936, noted that the intervention of aircraft in ground operations had a profound influence, both material and psychological, on ground troops and so it was of paramount importance to reduce enemy air action over ground forces. Ground commanders were warned to be efficient in their use of air support, however, to ensure that air units were not deployed excessively or for prolonged duration. This meant that ground commanders should be made fully aware of the limited capabilities of aircraft so as not to have unreal expectations of what they can do. Safe and practical airstrips should be prepared close behind a ground advance so that aircraft can keep up and be called upon at short notice. Secure communications between air and ground commanders was of the highest importance and if ground forces were to reap the fullest benefits of close air support, they must be ready to advance immediately following the air attacks.

The conventional combat-patrol formation of all air forces was a three-plane flight, flying in a tight 'V' at least, until Mölders arrived. The Germans called this 'V' a Kette. After flying a few sorties, Mölders observed that the average pilot paid more attention to avoiding collisions with his fellow pilots than he did to actual combat. Mölders suggested replacing the Kette with a Rotte, which consisted of only two aircraft, flying about 600ft apart. This distance gave the pilots room to manoeuvre and also enabled them to cover a larger expanse of sky. In each Rotte, the abler and more experienced pilot and marksman was the leader and assumed the primary attack role. His wingman covered his leader's tail and joined in the attack as required. Two Rotten combined to form a Schwarm.

Each aircraft of the Schwarm flew at a different altitude, and when viewed from above each plane flew in the location of the four fingertips of a horizontally extended hand, palm down, with fingers straight and slightly spread. With this loose and flexible formation, large expanses of sky were no longer cut off from view by friendly aircraft as they had been in tightly packed formations. Now that modern fighter planes were equipped with radio, it was no longer necessary to fly close to the leader to observe his hand signals. The Finnish air force may in fact have adopted this system back in 1935, but Mölders was the first to develop and test it in combat. Every air force has since adopted this system. In the Royal Air Force it is known as the 'finger-four formation', while the US Air Force calls it the 'double-attack' or 'buddy-buddy' system.

Converting operational practices from the tight Kette to the open Rotte system often proved difficult, even for many seasoned pilots – especially when all members of the Schwarm made a sharp turn simultaneously. The long distance between the extreme right and extreme left aircraft would force the plane closest to the centre of the arc to reduce speed, while the plane farthest from the centre of the arc had to accelerate. In order to avoid this problem, the wingman, who flew slightly higher than the leader, was to sideslip over the leader to make both members of the Rotte follow the same arc.

An example of the sideslip crossover manoeuvre danger occurred on 4 April 1938, when Nos. 1 and 2 Staffeln were making a reassignment flight from Zaragoza to Huesca. Leutnant Fritz Awe was leading a No. 1 Staffel Schwarm when he ordered a 90-degree left turn. As his wingman, Unteroffizier Adolf Borchers, overlapped Awe's Messerschmitt, Borchers' propeller sliced into Awe's cockpit, breaking the fuselage in half. The tail spun to earth while the cockpit, forward fuselage, engine and wing fluttered down like a falling leaf. When rescuers arrived at Awe's wreckage, they found the dead pilot sitting in the cockpit, decapitated. Borchers' Messerschmitt overturned upon landing, but his injuries were slight.

By 1938 the Nationalists had one fighter group of Heinkel He 51s and one of Fiat CR.32s as well as two squadrons of Savoia 79 bombers, one squadron of Caproni 310 bombers, two squadrons of SM.81 bombers, and a mixed group of He 70s and Ju 52s. These numbers did not include either the Italian contingent or the Condor Legion and give an indication of the overwhelming Nationalist superiority. Although rarely used in the strategic role Nationalist airpower was highly effective. During the Aragon and Catalonia offensives from March 1938 to February 1939 they were used extensively in ground support and interdiction. The Germans of the Condor Legion evolved their dive-bombing techniques, blooding the Junkers Ju 87 for the first time. The basic tactical technique of the Aragon and Catalonia campaigns was intensive artillery and air bombardment of a small area prior to its occupation by a relatively small attacking force. Against the demoralised Republicans this worked well. When the Republic finally collapsed in March 1939, it could attribute its defeat largely to the effects of airpower.

Strategic bombing of military targets was trialled with mixed results. In January 1938, a joint German-Italian bomber force had attacked the power station near Tremp in Catalonia. In March of the same year using He 111s and Do 17s the Condor Legion struck at the Puebla de Hijar rail yards and destroyed a nearby munitions factory. Rail depots and ports such as Cartagena were raided constantly, but it was the Italians with their superior numbers of aircraft who were more likely to carry them out. The Germans simply had too few aircraft for the many roles they were asked to play.

The effect of the Spanish Civil War on air doctrine was profound. Largely as a result of the Spanish experience the proponents of strategic bombing in both Germany and Russia had the ground cut from under them. From experience with the Heinkel He 111 and the Dornier Do 17 in Spain, the Luftwaffe concluded that unescorted daylight bombardment could be a practical proposition. The advocates of dive bombing in the Luftwaffe found a powerful argument in the spectacular work done by the few Junkers Ju 87s sent to Spain in late 1938. The Bf 109 was still an imperfect machine but showed great promise. The Soviet tactical airmen, in turn, had their faith reinforced in ground support air doctrine. No Russian heavy bombers were used in Spain, and the medium SB 2s, although effective against ground targets, were vulnerable to fighter interception. The Chato had proved to be a truly effective fighter-bomber, but was well beyond its usefulness as a modern warplane by the end. Although still able to cope with the Bf 109B over Spain, the Rata had reached the end of its development potential; it would, however, continue to play an important part in Soviet military aviation in the Far East. The Spanish Civil War had educated the participating countries in the use of tactical air power but observers outside the conflict retained an almost nostalgic affinity to strategic doctrine.

A sub-committee of the British Joint Intelligence Committee had been set up in May 1937 to study the Spanish Civil War. It reported that there had been many difficulties with collecting intelligence in Spain but said that the major use of air power had been against troops and that columns of mechanised transport were particularly vulnerable to air attack. Another feature was the strong anti-aircraft detachment for the protection of the airfields of the Condor Legion. More comprehensive papers on the Spanish Civil War were not available until June 1939, by which time the chiefs of staff were too busy with the European situation to study them.

Chapter 16

The Spanish Civil War in the Context of Total War

'Air Power more than any other arm in the twentieth century epitomised total war.'[1]

The argument that the Spanish Civil War was a rehearsal for the Second World War is based on the idea that it was used by three great powers, Germany, Italy and the Soviet Union, primarily as a testing ground for their new generation of weapons and tactics, but close examination shows that each had their own particular reason for their initial engagement, all of which were for political expediency and ideological imperatives rather than military experimentation. The civil war did, however, set the stage upon which the Second World War was played out by its diplomatic repercussions and military alliances forged at the time. It also brought into focus and exposed to scrutiny the concept of total war which, although it had been practised to a greater or lesser extent since the advent of warfare itself, had seen its first ideological exposition in the writings of Guilio Douhet.

There are two aspects of total war. The first is encapsulated in the idea of whole nations being viewed as culpable for prosecution of the war and therefore subject to collective responsibility and the second is the concept of mechanised or scientific warfare unleashed, without restraint, in the application of massive force of unprecedented ferocity causing mass destruction and devastation. The prime agent of total war and the supreme embodiment of technological revolution was the bombing aircraft, which came to symbolise industrial warfare in the modern era and under whose shadow whole governments quaked. The bombing of urban centres inevitably meant killing civilians but wars, by their nature, had always put military expediency over morality. The difference in the twentieth century was that the killing of civilians was not seen simply as collateral damage but increasingly as a strategic initiative designed to influence the progress of the war.

By looking at the Spanish Civil War in the context of total war it is possible to illuminate aspects of both the war and the concept. The expression 'total war' is not well defined but one interpretation implies that war without limits is one where a whole nation is conscripted in one way or another to take an active part in the conflict whether by becoming a combatant or by contributing to an economy that is totally committed to supporting the war. This process was described by the German General Ludendorf as transforming 'the whole society into a permanently mobilised military corps'.[2] Combined with ever growing sophistication of weapons, the means of complete annihilation of an enemy civilisation becomes within reach. This militarisation of the whole state argued for complicity of the whole population which, in a democracy at least, potentially has the power to call on its government to cease hostilities and therefore must accept not only the responsibility for the war, but also be prepared to suffer the consequences of prosecuting it.

The Spanish Civil War, of course, was not expansionist; there was no external enemy. It was not fought to gain territory but for the conquest of hearts and minds. Although both sides had foreign combatants in their ranks, the opposing forces were of the same nation, making the ferocity of both military and community violence, which left few quarters untouched, somehow more barbaric. Citizens were just as likely to be murdered by a raging mob in the street as they were to be despatched by a bomb from the sky or a bullet from a marauding Messerschmitt. Both sides were prepared to give up as much of the nation's wealth as they controlled to prosecute the war; the Republicans the country's gold reserves, the Nationalists the country's natural resources. The blurred distinction between citizen and soldier; the arrogance to waste the nation's wealth to win a political argument and the willingness to fight to the bitter end were all characteristics of what might be called total war.

The intensity of violence such as that perpetrated by both Republican military and civilians against the clergy and citizens perceived to have right-wing sympathies is associated with 'military backwardness' characterised by 'indiscipline and inchoate organisation'.[3] This is a common feature of civil war as was evident in both the Russian and American civil wars where societies were economically undeveloped and harboured deep-rooted grievances and prejudices which had defied compromise for many years. In the case of Spain, this indigenous social 'backwardness' was in counterpoint to the 'modernity' of the military component exhibited, especially by agencies of the foreign powers involved. Looking at total war from the aspect of mobilisation it is clear that in Spain, the civilian contingent of 'new style warriors' was as important as the military.[4] Few remained aloof from the conflict which engulfed virtually the whole community. The primary aim of the leadership of each side soon evolved into a desire for the systematic destruction of the other through dictatorial control, central planning, control of food production and distribution and the systematic conscription of civilian labour into war industries although evidence shows that these aspirations were never fully realised.

The civil war on the ground had, in many ways, evolved little from the practices of the First World War which had been characterised by trench warfare, massive artillery barrages and slow, methodical troop movements. There were extensive instances of civilian populations outside the immediate front-line war zones committing acts of war against each other and suffering terribly at the hands of soldiers of the other side when advances enveloped their towns and villages and these were the manifestations of 'historical' total war. The war in the air, however, while also exhibiting many of the characteristics of First World War encounters, not only in the aerial battles but also in the limited examples of strategic bombing, saw a dramatically expanded dimension of unwitting civilian participation: that of suffering under aerial bombardment. Of course, the bombing of cities had been a factor of war ever since the Zeppelin raids, but before 1936 the civilian population had never been identified as the 'centre of gravity', the terrorising of which was a prime strategic objective as a means of realising a military objective and not merely an appendage or extension of the war.

The Soviet Union, given the relative geographical remoteness of its 'centres of gravity' and preoccupation with internal and border disputes had only limited interest in strategic bombing and had no appropriate doctrine to bring to its air war in Spain.[5] When it was clear that both Germany and the Soviet Union lost confidence in the strategic bombing concept as a result of their experiences in the Spanish Civil War it was very much because of their inability to offer sufficient protection for the bombers rather than because of the failure to progress their war aims through its application.

It was the application of Douhetist doctrine, above all else, that allows the Spanish Civil War to be seen as a 'laboratory' in which 'experimental warfare' was conducted. It is commonly held that the reaction of civilian populations under aerial bombardment in Spanish cities such as Madrid and Barcelona repudiated the Douhetist theory that civilian morale would collapse, leading to pressure on the military leaders to capitulate. Stories of the wounded defiantly giving the clenched fist salute as they were being carried to hospital have been taken as evidence that the effect of the bombing was the opposite of that expected. The real story, of course, is more complicated. It is probably fair to say that, as in so many cases, advocates of a particular viewpoint bring to the argument only such evidence as supports their case. It is true that far from causing the collapse of society, air attack actually forged bonds of defiance between many disparate strata and groups. Rather than surrender or turn against their leaders, the populations demanded revenge in kind and were swift to deal out summary 'justice' to enemy airmen who fell into their hands.[6] It is no less true to say that the bombing of civilians also caused terror and a sense of hopelessness. If there is any general conclusion to be drawn it is that civilians under bombardment at first respond with fear, fleeing the area in panic, but then survivors – because they are survivors – come to terms with the threat, learn to mitigate the risk by means of shelter then celebrate their survival through defiance and revenge.

The terror-bombing of Madrid in late 1936 was against a city that was totally unprepared and which might, for that reason, be seen as the most instructive in terms of how a populace reacts. With little precedent to inform them it came as no surprise to find that civic authorities appeared quite incapable of intelligent, responsible action. At the start of the war there were no air-raid shelters in any Spanish city and posters put up by local authorities advising people that 'the effects of aerial bombardment are far more feared than real' were no help. The absurdity of this official response was best illustrated by the announcement that 'ten thousand bombs have to fall on an area of one square kilometre to have any serious effect.'[7] The only recourse was retirement to cellars or the city's underground stations. Cities, including Bilbao and Barcelona, to some extent were forewarned when their turn came to face the bombs, but still the authorities resorted to desperate measures to forestall panic. A newspaper in Valencia was later to write about 'the sport of watching [the bombers with] immense curiosity'.[8] The reality of the bombing of Madrid on 16 November 1936 was documented by a survivor, Louis Delaprée, on the 25th of that month.

> The darkness shrouding Madrid is so thick that you could cut it with a knife. We cannot see the sky, but from the sky they can see us. Humming, rumbling, pounding…. The rebel planes appear in an awesome crescendo. Pro-government fighter planes cannot pursue them in this darkness. Defenceless, we hear above our heads the deep musical vibration that is the herald of Death. Blasts, cushioned and then ear-splitting…
>
> Window-panes rattling almost inaudibly…. Windows thrown open by an invisible force…. And all the sounds that will soon become familiar to us. The trampling of people as they escape, the sirens of ambulances transporting the wounded, the sobbing of women beside you as they bury their heads in their scarves, the to-and-fro of men who click their heels to convince themselves that they are not afraid…. And above all – above all else – the sound of your own heart pounding ever faster…. The first bombs destroy the Provincial Hospital and the Hospital of San Carlos.
>
> The elderly who can still fend for themselves rush out of the dormitories and jostle down the stairs, huddle in the depth of the cellars, fiercely dispute the 'best places' with all their diminished strength. The disabled, the sick, slide to the floor and hide under their beds. Next morning, five or six of them have gone mad and have to be dragged away from their flimsy shelters. Bombs rain down continuously on the whole area between the Cortes, Atocha Station and León Street.
>
> In San Agustín Street, a missile has sliced a house open from top to bottom, like a plough cutting through earth. As it burns, the flames spread to the house opposite. Was it aimed at the Palace Hotel, where thousands lie wounded? I don't know. But four hits encircle it. The blast from the explosions shatters windows a centimetre thick. As at the San Carlos Hospital, men throw themselves out of their beds and try to escape, bandages come undone, wounds reopen…

An incendiary bomb falls on the roof of the French Embassy in Villalar Street. The fire is put out in time, but the surrounding buildings burn like torches. At five in the morning, the street is still in flames. A terrible confusion reigns in the night, as it is lit up by deadly flares. We stumble against the stretchers, knock into the wounded who watch as their blood flows on the asphalt by the light of the flames.

The whole city is full of similar scenes, of comparable pictures that seem to have been conjured up on the whim of a macabre genius, a necrophilous god. I have painted this scene in some detail because it was the first that showed me the reality of this butchery, and not the abstract and victim-free bombing from which I fled, like everybody else in the tortured city.

The next day was worse. As it turned out, that night had been no more than a dress rehearsal. The flight squadrons came at five o'clock in the morning. (Madrid was still treating its wounded and collecting the corpses.) They returned at eight, at nine, and then at half past three. It was a job well done, a thorough and meticulous bombing of all the central districts. The San Miguel market, the Red Cross Hospital and Marqués de Urquijo Avenue have been devoured. The bombs explode everywhere: in Martín de los Heros, San Marcos, Monteleón.... By lunchtime, just over three hundred dead were already on the slate.

The rebels strengthen the aerial bombardment – no doubt considered insufficient – by launching artillery fire. Six 75mm shells hit the Telephone Exchange, which rises fifteen stories above Madrid, yet miraculously none explode. Nor does a 155mm shell that slides into the small switchboard exchange. The building shakes under the pressure. But no one moves: the girls, their earphones on, go on marking the connections, the journalists try to get through to London or Paris.

Unfortunately, we cannot say that the explosives in the rest of the city are so accommodating. They explode, thunder, shatter, slaughter. Ambulances endlessly scour the streets in all directions, renewing their cargo of wounds and suffering once they have unloaded the previous haul at a hospital. But night falls. And then the butchery begins, the horror of the Apocalypse: the assassins wheel endlessly around the sky, releasing explosives, incendiary bombs and shrapnel.

A bomb falls into the subway entrance in the Puerta del Sol, near Alcalá, tearing up the road and sinking a crater fifteen metres deep. In San Jerónimo, a chasm opens up across the full width of the street. From twenty different places, the fire starts to consume the city. I am near the Carmen Market with two colleagues when the bombardment begins. Three bombs, two of them incendiary shells, fall close by. Crouching in a doorway, we see how the little market stalls catch fire, lighting up the frantic flight of men, women and children.

During a brief lull, we dash to the Telephone Exchange. From this extraordinary vantage point, the sight is one of unthinkable horror. A circle of flames converges on Gran Vía with majestic slowness. We observe how rooftops catch fire, and houses burn downwards before crashing heavily amidst a splendor of sparks and flames. Some burnt-out buildings remain upright, like tall sinister figures, licked by reflections from the fire that continues its work further away.

The firefighters stop hosing these thousands of homes. In any case, the enemy planes make their task impossible. When they see them aiming the extinguishers, they fly very low, just above the fire, dropping a couple of explosive bombs to teach a lesson to these firefighters who are only trying to fulfil their duty.

A dozen of these valiant men were killed in this way, as they tried to put out the fire at the Savoy hotel, and fell from the top of their ladders into the flames. Nothing can be done about it. We can only wait until the rain of killer meteorites has ended, wait until there have been enough dead and wounded to slake the thirst of General Franco's gods.

300,000 people walk the streets, looking for refuge. Mothers retrace their steps to an area in flames, looking for a child who – although they do not know it yet – is nothing but a small heap of ashes. Children, crazed by fear, call for mothers who have been turned into ashes beneath the rubble. A whole people seeks refuge against the wrath from the sky and finds none. From that night on, it turns in circles, incapable of escaping from the horror, accompanied by its mattresses, clocks, resigned donkeys, and the maddened, terrified, clinging children.

Madrid burns for fifteen hours, and then the fire tires. There is a lull for a day. But the following night, the 19th, at 2.30 in the morning, the killing is renewed. The fire starts again, we are back in hell. There are no military objectives in the area where the bombardments were at their most intense. Nobody has seen the famous pamphlets which rebel planes apparently launched to warn the population that they should seek refuge in the Salamanca district.[9]

Louis Delaprée, 'Bombs over Madrid'
(translated by Martin Minchom)

Secondary evidence supports the hypothesis that political alignments were crucial to selecting those areas of cities selected for bombing. For example, in Madrid on explicit orders from Franco, no bombs struck the right-wing neighbourhood of Salamanca. This pattern appears also to have been seen in the bombing of Barcelona. When the Republicans also bombed localities within the territory of Catalonia, this happened almost exclusively in places located on the war frontline such as Gandesa, Horta de Sant Joan, Móra d'Ebre, Valls, Serós and Sort, or in places affected by battles at the end of the military struggle.

Nationalist bombings in Catalonia were against Barcelona and Tarragona and other predominantly urban locations on the coastline, locations close to the French border, or locations near the Ebro frontline where battalions of soldiers or spare troops were positioned during the Battle of the Ebro. Support for the Left in the 1936 elections also had a significant positive effect on the likelihood of a locality suffering from a lethal bombardment.

Bombing civilians could have been an instrument for Francoist military authorities to punish localities where the anarchists and other militiamen had dealt severely with the rightists, namely a form of collective retaliation. These cases of retaliation very often involved the execution of prisoners. This is what happened, for example, on the ship *Aragon*, where prisoners were being held by the Republican army. As a result of a bombardment of the Nationalist air force over Mahón, all the prisoners in the ship, even the doctors, were executed in reprisal.[10]

At first bombing was carried out by single aircraft but very soon air commanders began experimenting with raids of up to squadron strength. The increased intensity of the bombardment led not so much to fear and panic in the population under attack as a sense of helplessness leading to fury and a desire for retribution. Bombings often led to the murder of people who had previously been imprisoned for political opposition at Jaén, Málaga, San Sebastián, Barcelona, Huesca, Valladolid, Granada and La Línea. By 1938 there was no longer any pretence that the bombings of civilian districts were anything other than terror raids. The diplomat Eberhard von Stöhrer who had stayed in Madrid at the start of the war but who became the German ambassador to Franco, wrote in 1938 of the bombing of Barcelona that 'There is no indication that the targets were military.'[11] John Langdon-Davies, who witnessed the Barcelona bombings also wrote, 'the aim was not casualties but the creation of panic … I was unable to find anyone who did not frankly admit that he was reduced to a state of impotent terror by the end of the period.' The Republican commander Andrés García Lacalle said, 'the terrified people fled in mass from the city'. After two weeks of intense bombing, Franco's troops entered Barcelona against little resistance.

The Republicans, although using terror bombing on a smaller scale, through their Minister of Defence said: '[we must] use the same methods as our adversaries … terror against terror. We have waited in vain for the enemy to desist from the predatory conduct it inaugurated in Madrid … I have ordered our aircraft to answer the bombing of Barcelona, Tarragona, Reus, Valencia … by bombing Salamanca, Seville and Valladoid.' It is true to say, however, that Republican bombing of Córdoba, for instance, was on a much smaller scale and caused many fewer casualties when compared to the 113 Italian and 60 German attacks on Barcelona alone.

There was a crucial difference in approach between Spaniards and their allies over the bombing of towns, cities and civilian populations. The Italians operating out of the Balearic Islands, and even Italy itself had greater opportunity to participate when the battlefront moved to Aragon and Catalonia. The Aviazione Legionaria bombed Lleida on 2 November 1937, Barbastro on 4 November and other towns such as Bujaraloz, Caspe and Alcañiz before the end of the year.

Almost all the larger cities along the Catalan and Valencian coast such as Tarragona and Reus, Gavá, Badalona and Mataró were bombed regularly during these months by both German and Italian aircraft operating out of Logroño. However, it was in the bombing of Barcelona that the campaign reached a crescendo. The Italian air commander, General Valle, wrote that the aerial terror campaign was designed both to demonstrate clearly that Italian planes could carry a tonne of bombs for over 1,000 kilometres and to 'give the Reds in Barcelona a New Year's welcome that will cause them to meditate on the Teruel defeat'.[12] In complete radio silence the SM.79s approached and each dropped their 850 kilograms of bombs from 3,000 metres. General Valle thanked il Duce for the 'high honour' of having been chosen for this mission.

This terror campaign on Barcelona reached its greatest intensity with the attacks of 30 January and especially 16–18 March. Italian planes bombed the port and city centre for up to eight days in January, destroying aerial defence shelters such as the Església de Sant Felip Neri. During the civil war the convent was used as a home for evacuated children. On 30 January 1938 a bomb exploded directly in front of the church killing thirty of the children who were sheltering inside. Shortly afterwards, while people were trying to rescue survivors, a second bomb exploded in the square bringing the death toll to forty-two. Ciano confessed in his diaries that the report which described the 30 January bombing raid was the most horrifying one that he had ever read, despite the fact that the attack had been conducted by only nine SM.79 planes and had lasted only one and a half minutes: 'pulverised buildings, interrupted traffic, panic that turned into madness.... A good lesson for the future ... the only means of salvation against aerial attacks is to abandon the cities.'

On 16 March, Mussolini directly ordered his air force to 'initiate from this evening [a] violent action on Barcelona [in the form of] rhythmic hammering', with thirteen flights organised in such a way that the city centre would experience the bombs and sirens from beginning to end.[13] It is clear from this that the Aviazione Legionaria exercised considerable independence of action almost as a separate force.

The Aviazione Legionaria chain of command was channelled directly on the government in Rome. The bombings of Barcelona, Alcañiz, Granollers, Alicante, and later Sitges or Torrevieja were indiscriminate attacks on military and civilian targets; their random nature was intended to terrorise non-combatants and decrease resistance. The prime motivations seems to have been to prepare the ground for subsequent land occupations by Italian forces. It cannot be a coincidence that the Aviazione Legionaria bombing focused on the places around Maestrazgo where the Frecce Nere, Spanish troops under Italian command, were in action. The occupation of Tortosa on 19 April, which divided Republican territory, was facilitated by an intense bombardment that broke bridges and the defensive lines of the Republican Army. The intensive use of the aerial weapon in the Douhetist fashion was directly connected to the Italian fascist idea of war which was directed from Rome and paid little heed to the requirements of Franco's war except where the two happened to overlap.

Chapter 17

Lessons Learned and Lessons Ignored

'The Luftwaffe experience in the Spanish Civil War had an enormous impact on Luftwaffe doctrine, tactics and technology.'[1]

During the Spanish Civil War, the Luftwaffe had been given the opportunity to experience every type of air campaign from strategic bombing to anti-naval campaigns. It had operated over static battle fronts and in support of rapidly advancing ground forces and shown, at every turn, how important aviation was becoming in modern warfare.

Throughout the war it had been a major preoccupation of Condor Legion commanders to maintain discipline. Excessive consumption of cheap and freely available alcohol, something that the personnel may not have been exposed to in Germany given the less liberal attitude to drinking, was held to be responsible for the high number of traffic accidents which accounted for more than half of the 167 fatalities in during the war. For the pilots it was a release from the stresses of combat and the traumas of seeing comrades killed. There were long periods between major operations such as at Brunete or on the Ebro when air operations were little more than routine reconnaissance and this may have led to bouts of boredom.

To help retain focus and also to inform military analysts in Berlin, pilots would be required to write up detailed reports after every sortie and were encouraged to discuss experiences as a means of optimising future operations. Aerial engagements were normally between large formations in which individual action was set against a generally chaotic background. Aircraft speeds were increasing all the time and tactics were evolving in the light of experience. After the first period of Nationalist dominance in the skies, the appearance of Soviet fighters had caused an abrupt rebalancing of air power. Professional pilots on both sides maintained a certain parity of effectiveness for a short time until the Chatos and Ratas with elite Soviet pilots proved their worth and tipped the scales in their favour. This came as a shock to the Germans who had grown used to fighting Spanish Republican pilots in obsolete machines. For fighter pilots it became a matter of surviving an engagement rather than counting their victories, and for bomber crews the sight of their own fighters in close support became of crucial importance. What Harro Harder called the 'sheer madness' of sending He 51s up against the Polikarpovs illustrated the 'stupidity of the orders'.[2] A war-weariness had starting to take hold of the Legion ever since the first combat death when the Ju 52 of Leutnant Oskar Kolbitz was shot down over Getafe on 4 November 1936. The first two fighter casualties, Leutnant Oskar Henrici and Oberleutnant Kraft Eberhard were killed on 13 November and five more bombers were shot down on 8 December, four over Arenas de San Pedro and one over Alcalá de Henares.

The Soviet fighters that had so altered the aerial balance of power caused a major re-evaluation of Condor Legion air tactics in the spring of 1937. The first Bf 109s arrived in March and, although hardly ready for combat, were a great morale booster. The new He 111s were not far behind, but like the 109s were still in the development stages. Gradually the Nationalist air forces, the Germans with their new models and the Italians with their Fiats, regained dominance of the air and began to turn the war inexorably in Franco's favour. This was especially the case since the Soviets had handed over many of their aircraft to be flown by Spanish crews who were much less experienced and not competent enough to fly the high-performance aircraft. German pilots now went into battle 'trusting in the superiority' of their aircraft allowing them to 'think more of the prospect of victory than of death'.[3] Their Spanish foes described them as 'machines of murder'. For the German pilots, as no doubt for many of the other nationalities, the reality of combat with its spectre of death unnerved some, especially when called upon to strafe the ground. Lothar Keller remembered initially feeling uneasy at the 'sight of figures collapsing' under his guns, but by the attack on Lérida he was 'caught up in a kind of fever' as he strafed again and again 'men who were running about like crazy', and concentrated on firing 'as accurately as possible'.[4]

For the bomber pilots, death was delivered at arm's length as they perfected their new tactics of 'chain formation' ground attack with aircraft sweeping at closely timed intervals to maintain a murderous barrage on ground forces. As far as the bombing of towns and villages, Egbert von Frankenberg accepted that the bombs would strike 'defenceless civilian populations', but the crews were simply 'doing their duty' not caring over much about 'what the bombs and bullets wreaked in detail', and returning with a brisk 'order executed, mission accomplished'.[5] The fighter pilot Harro Harder, however, recalls his shock at seeing the results of the Guernica bombing and called it 'an outrageous, swinish act'.

Despite misgivings over some acts, the rationale for fighting 'against the global enemy' of communism was never questioned although international criticism of, especially Nationalist, tactics could not fail to affect them. The vast economic disparities in Spanish society which clearly marginalised huge swathes of the population for the benefit of a wealthy minority must also have been clear as something that could not lie easily on their conscience given that they were fighting for the latter to help them retain their stranglehold on the peasant classes. One high-ranking German officer was impressed with the enthusiasm the Reds employed in their battle against 'the Church, the ownership of large states ... which for centuries have oppressed and tormented the people in a terrible way'.[6] As Franco's forces made inroads into Republican territory, the Germans were made very aware of the hostility felt towards them by the occupied communities and saw at first hand the brutal murders of local dignitaries and socialists committed in the name of their cause. Some pilots began to think that they might be fighting on the wrong side after all, or at least should not be taking part in the war, but did not extend that unease to opposition to their government's policy. Officers like Harder, who was not shy of voicing his disgust at the use of terror was at no time given to questioning his allegiance to National Socialism.

A study of the Condor Legion conducted by German General Karl Drum concluded that daylight bombing missions required formation flying and fighter escorts. Against strong fighter defence, daylight operations were too costly, leading to an emphasis on night missions. The bomber group of the Condor Legion was thus the first to develop and demonstrate the principle and the practicality of the concentrated employment of bomber aircraft during the night. An article on bombardment in the Italian aviation journal *Rivista Aeronautica* emphasised the importance of speed, formation flying, and defensive armaments, and the need for fighter protection.[7]

A Soviet article stressed the critical relationship between pursuit aviation and the bomber. The Soviet writer concluded that the modern pursuit craft must be considered a most formidable weapon, both as a means of anti-aircraft defence and for control of the air. Regardless of efforts made to increase the speed of the bomber, it could never match the speed and performance of the pursuit plane, and the firepower of the pursuit plane would always be greater than that of the bomber. This meant that the advantages in aerial combat would be on the side of the pursuit craft.

The US attaché for air reached similar conclusions. The Spanish war gave an interesting reply to the question of whether more importance should be given to bombardment. Spanish aviators and military chiefs were unanimous in stating that pursuit must come first. The entire army benefited from the superiority of a pursuit air force. The widely held peacetime theory of the invulnerability of the modern bomber had been disproved in Spain, the attaché said. The lesson taught in Spain was that to operate in daylight, bombers must have fighter protection.

All through the war, German personnel had been encouraged to write up all their experiences and send reports back to Berlin. Sperrle was assiduous in complying with this request and all of these reports were instrumental in defining Luftwaffe doctrine as it entered the Second World War. Unfortunately, given that there was no precedent in the modern Luftwaffe of combat-based doctrine upon which to build, the conclusions drawn were sometimes unhelpful based, as they were, on the particular circumstances of the civil war and the experiences of what were, at that time, the cream of the front-line personnel. Not sufficient notice was taken of the fact that many of the conclusions arrived at would not necessarily be applicable to a much wider, more complex conflict with a huge range of experience and capabilities within its ranks. Other conclusions which informed future doctrine were gathered by high-ranking officers from Berlin who made fleeting visits to Spain and felt competent to draw far-reaching conclusions from their brief interaction with the war.

When confronted with impending disaster in 1937 as the Soviet aircraft and tanks took a heavy toll of the Nationalist forces the Germans felt they had little choice but to shore up the Condor Legion with new aircraft upon which the paint had barely had time to dry. It is doubtful if they had intended to sacrifice so much at the outset. It is also reasonable to suppose that raw materials from the Spanish mines would still have found its way into the German military economy without the deployment of the Condor Legion. Germany had, in fact, retained diplomatic relations with the Republican government right up to the end of 1936 as an insurance. That Soviet power had forced the Germans into risking their precious Bf 109s does not support the view that either country had chosen to use Spain as a testing ground for their new breed of weapons. Rather they had used the experience forced upon them by circumstances to make an evaluation of their own and their enemy's capabilities.

The final report on the Condor Legion was written on 20 May 1939 and drew a number of conclusions. The effectiveness of the bomber was confirmed but the designs used in Spain showed the need for improved defensive armament and more fighter protection. The Bf 109 proved to be a significant success but the later versions with the Oerlikon 20mm canon were vastly more effective than the earlier types fitted with machine guns. The concept of Blitzkrieg was eagerly promoted by von Richthofen but there were very few occasions when it was possible to put it into practice, either because of the difficult terrain or the slow, methodical way that Spanish ground forces followed up the aerial bombardments. The bombing of industrial targets was thought to be sufficiently encouraging to warrant more emphasis, but it was clear that the poor accuracy of bombing meant that only sizeable targets could be hit. Success with the bombing of bridges at strategic points was particularly elusive even by low-flying aircraft.

Among the notable benefits to flow from Spain that realised by Werner Mölders with his innovative 'Rotte' and 'Schwarm' tactical formations stands out as the one that was to have the biggest influence on aviation both in Germany and elsewhere. The tactical employment of ground-support aviation was very much appreciated by infantry commanders for its psychological benefits as much as anything else and was, for that reason, called for in preference to strategic bombing whose effects were not apparent to front-line fighters. It was, however, a precarious enterprise with aircraft drawing ground-fire unless the tactic was applied in the manner of a 'chain' attack which suppressed anti-aircraft fire most effectively. Ground support had long been an essential part of Luftwaffe doctrine and pilots in training schools had been drilled in its application, but the Spanish war gave them a crucial opportunity to apply it under combat conditions. Luftwaffe Chief of Staff Hans Jeschonnek was convinced that close air support was 'the most difficult mission [requiring] the closest liaison between [air] commanders and supported army units'.[8]

Precision bombing of front-line targets proved to have disappointing results at first but that was because the Hs123 aircraft that was used carried such a puny bomb-load that even when it struck home the effects were not worth the risk. Only when the Ju 87 came through at Teruel did dive-bombing offer the potential for bringing a seismic shift in ground-support aviation. This was quickly appreciated by von Richthofen, who had originally opposed any investment in dive-bombers when they were first suggested in Berlin. The downside of this was that a number of new aircraft, such as the Ju 88, that were in the early prototype phase underwent substantial modifications to incorporate a dive-bombing capability into the design so that their development was delayed to the detriment of the Luftwaffe campaign in 1940.

When the He 111 was deployed in Spain it was so fast compared to the Republican fighters that it was often able to operate without fighter protection and it was, at one point, believed that bombers in mass formation might be fast enough and sufficiently well-armed to hold their own against fighter interdiction. This theory was not borne out by experience but the Luftwaffe analysts, including von Richthofen, retained faith in the strategic bombing concept which had really not been given much scope for application in Spain. The Spanish Civil War would have been an ideal laboratory to experiment with bomber-fighter coordination techniques but that opportunity was never taken. The fighter pilots who served in Spain, however, gained invaluable combat experience and many of them, such as Herbert Ihlefeld and Walter Oesau, went on to become combat leaders and prolific 'expertes' (Luftwaffe Aces) in the Second World War:

In 1936, the first aircraft in Spain had to navigate using old road maps until they learned to recognise landmarks, which in fact were few and far between given the monotony of much of the Spanish terrain. Hauptmann Handrick's experience was typical in the early part of the war:

> The maps which were available to us volunteers in Spain at that time were rather poor. The scale was as a rule, 1:1,500,000, and on top of that, the maps were highly unreliable. It was therefore no wonder that on my first flights I never found my way![9]

Photographic reconnaissance was the tool applied to correct this shortcoming and it became axiomatic for the Luftwaffe that future battle zones were to be extensively photographed for the purposes of modern map-making. When the potency of Soviet fighter aircraft condemned German bombers to night-flying, it spurred the Condor Legion to develop techniques of navigation and night-landings that would prove invaluable in the future. By the start of the Second World War the Luftwaffe was the only air force in Europe that was even moderately competent at night flying and bad weather navigation.[10]

Strategic terror-bombing, although carried out predominantly by the Italian Aviazione Legionaria, was studied closely by the Germans who concluded that a large-scale civil defence organisation would blunt the edge of attacks on civilians and act as a major contribution to the maintenance of the morale of a city under attack.

Appendix

Deliveries of Aircraft to Spain from the Soviet Union[1]

	Arrival date	Vessel	Tupolev SB	I-15 Chato	I-16 Rata	Polikarpov R5	Polikarpov RZ
15	October 1936	*Stari Bolshevik*	10				
19	October	*KIM*	10				
21	October	*Volgoles*	10				
28	October	*Lepin (from Sevastopol)*		25			
1	November	*Andreev*		15			
3	November	*Kursk*			15		
4	November	*Blagoev*			16		
19	November	*Aldecoa*				31	
30	December	*Darro*		10			
16	January 1937	*Sac-2*		20			
16	January	*Mar Blanco*		30			
14	February	*Aldecoa*					31
1	May	*Cabo Santo Tomé*					
7	May	*Cabo Palos*			31		
21	May	*Sac-2*					31
21	May	*Antonio de Satrústegui*				17	
31	May	*Artea Mendi*	10	23			
21	June	*Aldecoa*	21				

	Arrival date	Vessel	Tupolev SB	I-15 Chato	I-16 Rata	Polikarpov R5	Polikarpov RZ
30	June	*Cabo Santo Tomé*		8	14		
10	August	*Cabo San Agustín*			62		
2	April 1938	*Bougaroni*			31		
6	April	*Winnipeg*	16				
17	April	*Bonifacio*	10				
27	June	*Ain el Turk*			25		
24	July	*Winnipeg*			32		
11	August	*Bougaroni*			33		
	TOTAL		87	131	276	31	93

Soviet Aircraft Losses

	Total
Aerial combat	266
Destroyed on airfields	44
Anti-aircraft fire	42
Accidents	201
Landings in enemy territory	14
Total Aircraft Losses	567

Soviet pilots killed in Spain

	1936	1937	1938	Total
SB	9	6	4	19
I-15	3	3		6
I-16	6	19	20	45
Others	2	5		7
Total	20	33	24	77

Notes

Chapter 1: Background to War

1. Drum, Karl *The German Air Force in the Spanish Civil War,* (USAF Historical Research Studies No.150, 1957) 5
2. Larrazabal, Jesus Salas, *Air War over Spain* (Ian Allan, 1974) 40

Chapter 2: International Reaction

1. Alpert, Michael, *Franco and the Condor Legion* (Bloomsbury Academic, 2019) 7
2. Kowalsky, Daniel, *Operation X: Soviet Russia and the Spanish Civil War*, (Hispanic Studies and Researches on Spain, Portugal and Latin America, Volume 91, 2014) 1
3. Leitz, Christian, *Germany's Intervention in the Spanish Civil War and the Foundation of Hisma–Rowak* (Oxford University Press, 1996)
4. Proctor, Raymond L. *Hitler's Luftwaffe in the Spanish Civil War* (Greenwood Press, 1983) 17
5. ibid 19
6. Stone, Glyn, *Italo-German collaboration and the Spanish Civil War, 1936-1939,* (Cambridge Scholars Publications, 2009) 4
7. Proctor 13
8. Leitz
9. Proctor 21
10. Alpert 34
11. Gustavsson Håkan, *Air War in the Spanish Civil War*
12. Rankin, Nicholas, *Telegram from Guernica* (Faber & Faber, 2003) 113
13. Gustavsson

14. Howson, Gerald, *Arms for Spain; The Untold Story of the Spanish Civil War* (John Murray, 1998) 19
15. Stone 21
16. ibid 23
17. Howson 21
18. ibid 57
19. McCannon, John, *Soviet Intervention in the Spanish Civil War* (Russian History, Summer 1995 Vol. 22, No. 2, pp. 154-180) 158
20. Howson 126
21. Watt, D.C., *Soviet Military Aid to the Spanish Republic in the Civil War 1936-1938* (The Slavonic and East European Review, June, 1960, Vol. 38, No. 91, pp. 536-541) 538
22. Moradiellos, Enrique. 'British Political Strategy in the Face of the Military Rising of 1936 in Spain.' (*Contemporary European History*, vol. 1, no. 2, 1992, pp. 123–137) 127
23. ibid 130
24. Stone 4

Chapter 3: First Moves

1. Larrazabal 56
2. Gustavsson
3. ibid
4. Proctor 23
5. Hooton E. R., *Phoenix Triumphant; The Rise and Rise of the Luftwaffe* (Brockhampton Press, 1994) 123
6. Gustavsson
7. Leitz, Christian, *Germany's Intervention in the Spanish Civil War and the Foundation of Hisma–Rowak* (Oxford University Press, 1996)
8. Beevor, Antony, *The Spanish Civil War* (Cassel, 1982) 148
9. Alpert 56
10. Proctor 253
11. Richardson, R. Dan, *The Development of Airpower Concepts and Air Combat Techniques in the Spanish Civil War* (Air Power History, Spring 1993, Vol. 40, No. 1 pp. 13-21) 15
12. Goss, Hilton P., *Civilian Morale under Aerial Bombardment* (Air University Press, 1948) 149

13. ibid 151
14. Mitchell, Peter Chalmers, *My House in Malaga*, (The Clapton Press, 2019)
15. Goss 152
16. Steer G. L., *The Tree of Gernica,* (Faber and faber 2012) 25
17. Gustavsson
18. Rankin, Nicholas, *Telegram from Guernica* (Faber & Faber, 2003) 117
19. Preston, Paul, *The Spanish Holocaust; Inquisition and Extermination in Twentieth-Century Spain* (Harper Collins, 2013) 287
20. Goss 159
21. Westwell, Ian, *Condor Legion; The Wehrmacht's Training Ground* (Ian Allan, 2004) 18
22. Goss 158
23. ibid 160
24. Howson 36
25. ibid 60
26. ibid 66
27. Warner, Geoffrey, *France and Non-Intervention in Spain, July-August 1936* (International Affairs (Royal Institute of International Affairs 1944-) , April 1962, Vol. 38, No. 2, pp. 203-220) 211
28. Howson 76
29. ibid 91
30. Harvey 94
31. ibid 97
32. ibid 99
33. Leitz
34. Hubbard, John R., *How Franco Financed His War* (The Journal of Modern History, Dec., 1953, Vol. 25, No. 4 pp. 390- 406) 393

Chapter 4: The Condor Legion

1. Proctor 36
2. ibid 43
3. Goss 160
4. Steer 77
5. Corum 186

6. Stone 6
7. Howson 279
8. Gustavsson
9. Howson 116
10. Larrazabal 95
11. Howson 117
12. Gustavsson
13. Richardson
14. Gustavsson
15. ibid
16. Del Vayo, J. A., *Freedom's Battle*, (1940, p 35)
17. Goss 165
18. Proctor 55
19. ibid 57
20. Schüler-Springorum, Stefanie, *War as adventure. The Experience of the Condor Legion in Spain* (Campus Verlag, 2008) 212

Chapter 5: Franco's First Attack against Madrid

1. Richardson
2. Proctor 64
3. Hallion 97
4. Kowalsky 6
5. Gustavsson
6. ibid
7. ibid
8. ibid
9. Preston 343
10. Corum 187
11. Goss 166
12. ibid 167
13. ibid
14. ibid 168
15. ibid 170
16. Hooton 126

Chapter 6: Foreign Aid Increases

1. Gustavsson
2. ibid
3. Schüler-Springorum 213
4. ibid 217
5. ibid 218
6. Proctor 75
7. ibid 79
8. Stone 7
9. Richardson
10. Proctor 85
11. Hallion 110
12. Richardson 20
13. ibid 15
14. Kowalsky 2
15. ibid 12
16. Hooton 128
17. Kowalsky 35
18. Howson 216
19. ibid 151
20. Kowalsky 45
21. Howson 167
22. ibid 183

Chapter 7: The Battle of El Jamara

1. Proctor 85
2. Rankin 136-138
3. Goss 172
4. Steer 186-187
5. Goss 172
6. Koestler, Arthur, *Dialogue with Death* (1946), p 13
7. Gustavsson
8. Proctor 91
9. ibid 108

10. Coverdale 55
11. Proctor 113
12. Coverdale 69
13. Hallion 101
14. Stone 8
15. Howson 212

Chapter 8: Franco's Drive into Vizcaya

1. Rankin 131
2. ibid 156
3. Proctor 119
4. Corum 216
5. ibid 193
6. Proctor 122
7. Beevor 239
8. Gustavsson
9. Steer 161-162
10. ibid 223
11. Hooton 130
12. Preston 434
13. Rankin 157
14. Preston 434
15. Rankin 169
16. ibid 170
17. Beevor 244
18. Corum 199
19. Rankin 173
20. Patterson 44
21. Corum 199
22. Alpert 126
23. Patterson 47
24. Preston 435
25. Gustavsson
26. Richardson 18
27. Howson 231

28. ibid 232
29. Goss 205
30. Proctor 135
31. ibid 136
32. ibid 143
33. Richardson 18

Chapter 9: The Battle of Brunete

1. Alpert 148
2. Proctor 150
3. ibid 153
4. Gustavsson
5. ibid
6. ibid
7. ibid
8. ibid
9. Graham 24
10. Gustavsson
11. ibid
12. Kowalsky 5

Chapter 10: Santander Falls

1. Hubbard 86
2. ibid 88
3. Gustavsson
4. ibid
5. ibid
6. Proctor 163

Chapter 11: Condor Legion at the Crossroads

1. Schüler-Springorum 221
2. ibid 216

3. Gustavsson
4. Proctor 171
5. ibid 172
6. Alpert 153
7. Guilmartin 84

Chapter 12: The Battle of Teruel

1. Gustavsson
2. ibid
3. ibid
4. Bonilla Carno 360
5. ibid 369
6. ibid 359
7. Gustavsson
8. Proctor 182
9. Stone 9
10. Kowalsky 120

Chapter 13: Franco's Drive into Aragon

1. Proctor 187
2. Corum 205
3. Proctor 194
4. Preston 457
5. Rodrigo
6. Beevor 332
7. Lloyd 85
8. Beevor 332
9. Richardson 19
10. Gustavsson
11. Proctor 207
12. Gustavsson
13. Richardson 19

Chapter 14: The Ebro Offensive

1. Proctor 217
2. Corum 206
3. Gustavsson
4. ibid
5. Proctor 234
6. Gustavsson

Chapter 15: Strategy and Tactics

1. Richardson 20

Chapter 16: The Spanish Civil War in the Context of Total war

1. Buckley 21
2. Ranzato 236
3. Chickering 32
4. ibid
5. Buckley 8
6. ibid 15
7. Ranzato 238
8. ibid 239
9. Delaprée, Louis, '*Bombs over Madrid*' (translated by Martin Minchom), (albavolunteer.org , 23 Nov. 2010)
10. Balcells Laia, *Death is in the Air: Bombings in Catalonia, 1936-1939* (2011)
11. Ranzato 240
12. Rodrigo
13. ibid

Chapter 17: Lessons Learned and Lessons Ignored

1. Corum 219
2. Schüler-Springorum 226
3. ibid 227
4. ibid 228
5. ibid 229
6. ibid 231
7. Richardson 17
8. Corum 223
9. Gustavsson
10. Corum 223

Appendix

1. Howson 279-301

Sources

Alpert Michael, *Franco and the Condor Legion* (Bloomsbury Academic, 2019)

Alvarez del Vayo Julio, *Freedom's Battle, translated from the Spanish by Eileen E. Brooke* (A.A. Knopff, 1940)

Askew William C., *Italian Intervention in Spain: The Agreement of March 31, 1934 with the Spanish Monarchist Parties*, (The Journal of Modern History, vol. 24, no. 2, 1952, pp. 181–183)

Balcells Laia, *Rivalry and Revenge: Violence against Civilians in Conventional Civil Wars* (International Studies Quarterly, vol. 54, no. 2, 2010, pp. 291–313)

Balcells Laia, *Death is in the Air: Bombings in Catalonia, 1936-1939* (2011)

Baughen Greg, *The Rise and fall of the French Air Force* (Fonthill, 2019)

Baumeister Martin, *Spain's Multiple Wars; Mobilization, Violence and Experiences of War 1936-1939* (Campus Verlag, 2008)

Beevor Antony, *The Spanish Civil War* (Cassel, 1982)

Bonila Diego Navarro and **Cano** Guillermo Vicente, *Photographic Air Reconnaissance during the Spanish Civil War, 1936–1939: Doctrine and Operations* (War in History , July 2013, Vol. 20, No. 3, pp. 345-380)

Chickering Roger, *The Spanish Civil War in the Age of Total War* (Campus Verlag, 2008)

Cortada Janes W., *Ships, Diplomacy and the Spanish Civil War* (Il Politico, December 1972, Vol. 37, No. 4, pp. 673-689)

Corum James S., *The Luftwaffe; Creating the Operational Air War 1918-1940* (University Press of Kansas, 1997)

Coverdale John S., *The Battle of Guadalajara* (Journal of Contemporary History, Jan 1974, Vol. 9, No. 1 pp. 53-75)

Del Vayo J. A., *Freedom's Battle*, (1940)

Goss Hilton P., *Civilian Morale under Aerial Bombardment* (Air University Press, 1948)

Guilmartin John F. Jnr., *Aspects of Air Power in the Spanish Civil War* (*The Air Power Historian* Vol. 9, No. 2, pp. 83-86)

Gustavsson Håkan, *Air War in the Spanish Civil War (http://surfcity.kund. dalnet.se/scw.htm)*

Hallion Richard P., *Strike from the Sky; A History of Battlefield Air Attack 1911–1945* (Airlife, 1989)

Harvey Charles E., *Politics and Pyrites during the Spanish Civil War* (The Economic History Review, Feb. 1978, New Series, Vol. 31, No. 1, pp. 89-104)

Higham Robin, *Air Power; A Concise History* (The Military Book Society, 1972)

Higham Robin & **Kipp** Jacob W., *Soviet Aviation and Air Power* (Westview Press, 1977)

Hippler Thomas, *Governing from the Skies* (Verso, 2017)

Hooton E.R., *Phoenix Triumphant; The Rise and Rise of the Luftwaffe* (Brockhampton Press, 1994)

Howson Gerald, *Arms for Spain; The Untold Story of the Spanish Civil War* (John Murray, 1998)

Hubbard John R., *How Franco Financed His War* (The Journal of Modern History, Dec., 1953, Vol. 25, No. 4 pp. 390- 406)

Kilmarx Robert A.A., *History of Soviet Air Power* (Faber & Faber, 1962)

Koestler, Arthur, *Dialogue with Death* (Pan Macmillan, 1987)

Kowalsky Daniel, *Operation X: Soviet Russia and the Spanish Civil War*, (Hispanic Studies and Researches on Spain, Portugal and Latin America, Volume 91, 2014)

Larrazabal Jesus Salas, *Air War over Spain* (Ian Allan, 1974)

Leitz Christian, *Germany's Intervention in the Spanish Civil War and the Foundation of Hisma–Rowak* (Oxford University Press, 1996)

Lloyd Nick, *Forgotten Places; Barcelona and the Spanish Civil War* (2015)

McCannon John, *Soviet Intervention in the Spanish Civil War* (Russian History, Summer 1995 Vol. 22, No. 2, pp. 154-180)

Mitchell Peter Chalmers, *My House in Malaga* (The Clapton Press, 2019)

Muñoz Juan José De Arriba, *The adaptability of the German Condor Legion in the Spanish Civil War, 1936-39* (Global Strategy Report, 2020)

Murray Williamson, *War in the Air 1914–1945* (Collins, 1999)

Musciano Walter A., *Spanish Civil War: German Condor Legion's Tactical Air Power* (Aviation History, September 2994)

Plummer Joni J., *France and Portugal in the Spanish Civil War* (Indiana University, 1988)

Preston, Paul, *The Spanish Holocaust; Inquisition and Extermination in Twentieth-Century Spain* (Harper Collins, 2013)

Proctor Raymond L., *Hitler's Luftwaffe in the Spanish Civil War* (Greenwood Press, 1983)

Rankin Nicholas, *Telegram from Guernica* (Faber & Faber, 2003)

Ranzato Gabriele, *The Spanish Civil War in the Context of Total War* (Campus Verlag, 2008)

Richardson R. Dan, *The Development of Airpower Concepts and Air Combat Techniques in the Spanish Civil War* (Air Power History, Spring 1993, Vol. 40, No. 1 pp. 13-21)

Rodrigo Javier, *A fascist warfare? Italian fascism and war experience in the Spanish Civil War (1936–39)* (War in History, Sept. 12 2017)

Schüler-Springorum Stefanie, *War as adventure. The Experience of the Condor Legion in Spain* (Campus Verlag, 2008)

Steer G.L., *The Tree of Gernica* (Faber and Faber 2012)

Stone Glyn, *Italo-German collaboration and the Spanish Civil War, 1936-1939* (Cambridge Scholars Publications, 2009)

Warner Geoffrey, *France and Non-Intervention in Spain, July-August 1936* (International Affairs (Royal Institute of International Affairs 1944–), April 1962, Vol. 38, No. 2, pp. 203-220)

Watt D.C., *Soviet Military Aid to the Spanish Republic in the Civil War 1936–1938* (The Slavonic and East European Review, June, 1960, Vol. 38, No. 91, pp. 536-541)

Westwell Ian, *Condor Legion; The Wermacht's Training Ground* (Ian Allan, 2004)

Index

Agafonov, Pavel, 42
Aguirre, José Antonio, 40
Alar del Rey, 112, 117
Alcala de Henares, 62, 83, 86, 106, 174, 180
Alcázar de Toledo, 20
Alfambra, 131, 133
Almendralejo, 23
Almirante Cervera, SS, 89
American Traveller, SS, 77
Amiot 143, 13
Amorebieta, 98
Aniene, SS, 22, 88, 125
Antonov-Ovseyenko, 54
Arado 65, 9
Arado 68, 9
Araujo, 11
Arganda del Rey, 85
Arrondo, Fidel Dávila, 102
Asturias, 5–6, 90, 117–18, 120
Aviación de El Tercio, 11
Aviazione Legionaria, 11, 39, 69, 96, 103, 117, 125, 140, 154, 156, 159, 176–8, 185
Ávila, 1, 56, 59, 83, 106

Babb, Charles Harding, 77
Badajoz, 5, 20, 23, 101, 146
Baldwin, Stanley, 17

Banque Commerciale de l'Europe du Nord, 74
Barcelona, 1, 5–6, 16, 22, 25, 27, 32, 43, 47, 69, 101, 117, 120, 127, 139–40, 147, 149, 158–60, 171, 175–7
Belchite, 118, 136–8
Berlin, SS, 51
Bernegg, Hubertus Merhart von, 63, 82
Bernhardt, Johannes E.F., 7–9, 34, 44, 116
Berti, Mario, 134
Bf109, 41, 44, 56, 63, 72, 82, 88, 91, 106–107, 110, 112–13, 117, 119–20, 122–6, 128–30, 132, 134, 137–8, 142–51, 154, 158–60, 166, 180, 183
Bilbao, 1, 27, 35, 39, 45, 79–80, 90–8, 102–103, 116, 171
Blagoev, SS, 16, 55, 186
Blomberg, Werner von, 8, 37–8, 65–6, 112, 134
Blum, Léon, 12–13, 17, 29–30, 99
Boddem, Peter, 110
Bolín, Luís, 11, 29
Breguet XIX, 6, 20, 22, 26, 129
Brigadas Internacionales, 46

Brunete, 103, 105–16, 179
Burgos, 1, 35, 40, 91, 106, 115, 122, 150

Cáceres, 5, 38
Calamocha, 128, 132
Campeche, SS, 15, 42
Canarias, SS, 78
Canaris, SS, 16
Cardozo, H.G., 24
Carney, William P., 61
Cartagena, 16, 39, 41–2, 45–6, 48, 61, 74, 99, 139, 141, 146, 166
Ceuta, 24
Christ, Torsten, 130
Churchill, Winston, 17, 30
Ciano, Galeazzo, 12, 30–1, 134, 140, 153, 177
Ciudad de Alicante, 11
Ciudad de Alicante, SS, 11
Ciudad de Cádiz, SS, 74
Ciudad de Ceuta, 11
Ciudad de Ceuta, SS, 11
CMT, Confederaclon Nacional de Trabajadores, 39
CNT-FAI, 40
Condor Legion, 6, 49, 51, 54, 61–2, 67–8, 71–2, 79, 88–97, 101–104, 109, 112, 116–25, 129–33, 136–43, 146–7, 151–4, 158–63, 166–7, 179–85
Cot, Pierre, 12–13, 30, 99
Cowley, Malcolm, 101
Cox, Geoffrey, 60
CTV, Corpo Trupo Volontarie, 36
Cuatro Vientos, 27, 49, 56

Delbos, Yvon, 30
Dewoitine D.372, 13, 22–3, 41, 47–8

Dornier Do17, 83, 102, 109, 137, 166
Dornier-Wals, 2
Douhet, Guilio, vii, 25, 61, 168
Durango, 94–5, 97–8

Eberhardt, Kraft, 26, 180
Ebro, 136–8, 147, 150–61, 175, 179
Ebro, SS, 22
Eden, Anthony, 17
El Burgo de Osma, 124
El Jarara, 85, 87, 89
El Prat de Llobregat, 6, 22
Emilio Morandi, SS, 22
Escalona del Prado, 21, 106
Escuadrilla Rambaud, 21
Estracón, 137

Faupel, Wilhelm von, 65–6, 104, 112
Fernández, José Larios, 156
Fiat A.30 R.A. V12, engine, 21
Fiat CR.32, 11, 21–2, 47, 54–6, 69, 85, 88, 124–5, 148, 151, 154–6, 159
Flight Pablo, 41–2
Fokker F.BIIb, 32
Fokker F-VII, 2
Francia, Ramón Puparelli, 103
Franco Bahamonde, General Francisco, 1–5, 7–9, 11–15, 18–19, 22–9, 33–41, 44–8, 53, 55, 57–61, 65–7, 72, 78–9, 83, 85–95, 97, 99, 101, 103–106, 115–17, 122–7, 130, 133–9, 141–3, 145–9, 152, 155, 158, 160, 163, 174–8
Frank, Hans, 41

Frick, Dr. Wilhelm, 52

Fuerza Aérea de la República Española, Spanish Republican Air Force, 6

Galland, Adolf, 65, 97, 106, 117, 119–22

Gandesa, 150–6,

García-Morato y Castaño, Joaquín, 88

Getafe, 6, 19–21, 27, 48–9, 53, 55–6

Gijón, 89, 117, 119–20

Giral, José, 12, 14

Göring, Hermann, 7–9, 33–5, 41, 44, 50–1, 66, 123, 161

Gourdou-Leseurre GL.32, 89

Graf Spee, SS, 91

Grupo de caza No 11, 6

Grupo de caza No 31, 6

Guadalajara, 73, 85–7, 123, 128, 140

Guadamara, 107

Guernica, 40, 92, 95–8, 101–102, 180

Gusev, Aleksandr, 129

Hamsterley, SS, 91

Handrick, Gotthard, 107, 110, 118–20, 123, 128, 154, 184

Harder, Harro, 64, 82, 98, 110, 123, 126, 132, 152

Hassell, Ulrich von, 12

Hefter, Ekkehardt, 48

Heinkel He 46, 41, 56, 59, 102

Heinkel He 50, 41, 44

Heinkel He 59, 41

Heinkel He 60, 41

Heinkel He 70, Rayo, 42, 83, 106, 129

Heinkel He 111, 83, 91, 96, 106, 109, 118, 125–6, 130, 136–8, 141, 146–8, 151, 166

Heinkel He 46C-1, 41, 56, 59, 102

Heinkel He 5I, 9, 21, 41, 48, 82, 88, 95, 119

Henschel Hs 123, 19, 41–2, 47–8, 50, 54, 56, 59, 63, 71–2, 79, 82–3, 85, 88, 91, 93, 95, 98, 106, 109, 111, 117, 119, 122, 131, 134, 138–9, 147, 165, 180

Henz, Helmut, 145

Herrera, 22, 112, 117

Hess, Rudolf, 7

Hispano-Marroqui de Transportes Sociedad Limitada, HISMA, 9, 34–5, 115–16

Hitler, Adolf, vii, 2, 7–8, 12, 14, 16–18, 33–4, 37, 49–50, 66–7, 76, 104, 116, 124, 134, 139, 144, 147, 155, 161–2

Holle, Alexander, 50, 64, 83

Höness, Guido, 110

Hordena, SS, 89

Hossbach Conference, 134

Houwald, Wolf-Heinrich von, 19, 56

Huesca, 24, 138, 165, 176

I./JG 132 'Richthofen', 9

I./JG 134 'Horst Wessel', 9

Ibai, SS, 78

Ibiza, 26, 39

II./JG 134, 9–10

International Non-Intervention Committee, 98

Irún, 27, 37, 39–40, 79

J/88, 50, 63, 82–3, 91, 93, 96, 106–107, 112, 117, 119–20, 123, 128, 137, 148, 154, 159

Jaime I, SS, 20, 29

Junkers Ju-52, 23, 29, 41, 50, 53, 55, 59–61, 83, 106, 111, 125, 134, 180

Kamerun, SS, 20
Kampfgruppe, K/88, 50, 61, 79, 111, 118, 125, 137, 147, 151–2, 154
Katz, Walter, 112
Keitel, Wilhelm, 67, 134, 139
Kesselring, Albert, 112
Kholzunov, Mayor V., 46
KIM, SS, 42, 74, 186
Kindelán, Alfredo, 21, 24, 30, 40
Kirovabad, 74, 76, 99
Knüppel, Herwig, 19, 26, 47, 63
Kolesnikov, Konstantin, 99
Komsomol, SS, 16, 42
Kopets, Ivan, 42
Krivitsky, Walter Germanovich, 89
Kursk, SS, 55, 74, 186

Labauria, José de, 95
Lehmann, Siegfried, 63, 83
León, 6, 83, 123, 128, 161
Lepin, SS, 42, 45, 186
Lesnikov, Dmitri, 99
Líneas Aéreas Postales Españolas, Spanish National Airlines, 6
Litvinov, Maxim, 31
Lleida, 138, 176
Lockheed Orion, 77
Loire 46, 13

Macgregor, SS, 91
Málaga, 20, 24, 26, 36, 39, 81, 85–6
Maquedas, 47
Mar Cantábrico, SS, 77
Melilla, 21–2, 62
Menant, José Miaja, 109
Menéndez, Leopoldo, 130
Milch, Erhard, 8
Mitchell, Peter Chalmers, 24
Mitrofanov, Petr Aleksandrovich, 56

Mola, Emilio, 2, 4–5, 8, 23, 37, 40, 91–4, 101–103
Monks, Noel, 95–6
MONTANA, 35, 115–16
Montegnacco, Brunetto di, 110
Morato, Joaquín García, 21, 88
Moreau, Rudolf Freiherr von, 29, 96
Mount Monchetegui, 93
Mussolini, Benito, 2–3, 10–11, 16, 33, 38, 41, 67, 87, 116, 133–4, 140, 153, 155, 177

Negrín, Dr. Juan, 74
Nereide, SS, 21
Nesmeyanov, G., 46
Neurath, Konstantin von, 31, 41, 67, 88
Neva, SS, 46, 74
Nieuport Delage NiD 52, 6
NKVD, Soviet Secret Police, 15–16
Non-Intervention Committee, 31, 45–6, 98

Ochandiano, 93–4
Onaindia, Alberto de, 97
Operation Guido, 49
Operation X, 14, 72
Ordás, Félix Gordón, 77
Osorio, SS, 51

Palm, Werner, 63
Pau, 100
Pidonque bridge, 85
Pingel, Rolf, 110
Pitcairn, Douglas, 119, 124
Plocher, Hermann, 50–1, 124, 131, 146, 155

Polikarpov I-15 'Chato', 15, 42, 57, 72, 75, 80, 108, 120, 155, 166, 186
Polikarpov I-16 'Rata', 15, 53, 55, 57, 59, 72, 76, 82, 102–103, 110, 113, 118, 120, 126, 128, 130, 132, 134, 142, 148, 151–6, 158, 166, 180, 186
Polikarpov R5-SSS, 72, 186
Polikarpov RZ, 71, 186
Porto Crispo, 26
Potez 25, 12–13, 89
Potez 54, 12–13, 99
Potez 540, 22, 42
Potez-Bloch CAMS, 13
President Harding, SS, 77
Prestele, Ignaz, 119
Priebe, Eckehart, 128
Puenta de Renteria, 96
Puigcerda, 37
Pumpur, Petr, 42

Queen Elizabeth, HMS, 29
Queipo de Llano, Gonzalo, 2, 4, 40

Rambaud, Luis, 21
Reus, 100, 113, 158, 176–7
Riaño, Ángel, 130
Riaño, Luis, 32, 89
Ribbentrop, Joachim von, 17, 139, 147
Rio Tinto, 34–5
Ro37, 54
Roatta, Mario, 38, 86–7
Rohstoffe-und-Waren-Einkaufsgessellschaft, ROWAK, 34
Roth, Jürgen, 63

San Juan airfield, 22, 73, 101
San Sebastián, 26, 39–40, 79, 94, 176
Sanjurjo, José, 4–5, 8, 137
Santander, 6, 100, 102–103, 117–22
Sarabia, Hernández, 130
Sarkani, SS, 88
Savoia, 6, 11, 24, 29, 54, 101, 165
Schacht, Hjalmar, 33
Scheele, Alexander von, 9, 20, 27, 38
Schmidt, Karl Gustav, 80
Seidemann, Hans, 156, 159
Serov, Anatoly, 106, 111–12
Sexton, Cyril, 111
Shakht, Ernst, 46
Sharov, 56
Sheaf Garth, SS, 91
Skutov, Zakhar Savel'evich, 158
Smirnov, Boris, 118
Smushkevitch, Yakov [General Douglas], 105
Sociedad Financiera Industrial Ltda, SOFINDUS, 35
Societé Française des Transports Aériens, 89
Sonderstab W, 8, 41, 151
Soria, 24
Sperrle, Hugo [General Sander], 35, 50–1, 59, 62, 64–6, 68, 79, 87–8, 91–5, 101–104, 106, 112, 117, 122, 182
Stalin, Josef, 15–16, 74, 76, 100, 160
Stanbrook, SS, 91
Steer, George, 27, 80, 94–6, 155
Stern, Manfred, 113
Stesso, SS, 91
Stöhrer, Dr Baron Eberhard von, 104, 176

T-26, tank, 15, 49, 53–4, 59, 79, 85
Tablada, 5, 22, 46, 53, 63–4
Tercio Extranjero, Spanish Foreign
  Legion, 11, 69
Teruel, 68, 127–36, 177, 184
Tetuán, 1, 4, 7, 9, 16, 20, 24, 29
Tharsis, 34
Thomas, Norman, 101
Timiryazov, SS, 16
Tinkler, Frank, 110
Toledo, 15, 26, 40, 49, 53–4,
  160, 161
Trautloft, Hannes, 10, 19, 26, 72
Trijueque, 86
Trueta, 140
Tupolev SB Katiuska, 15, 42–4, 46,
  49, 53–4, 56–8, 71–2, 75, 98–9,
  113, 131, 134, 186

Untenehmen Feuerzauber,
  Operation Magic Fire, 8, 37, 49
Usaramo, SS, 9, 19, 37

Valencia, 1, 5, 16, 25, 27, 47, 69,
  78, 90, 96, 100–101, 120, 127,
  132, 146–7, 149, 151, 153, 159,
  171, 176
Vansittart, Robert, 17
Versuchskommando, 45
Vickers Vildebeests, 6

Vigo, 22, 123, 161
Viiu, SS, 89
Vigón, Juan Suero diaz, 92
Vitoria, 48, 79, 83, 91, 96, 106
Vizcargui, 98
VJ/88, Versuchsjagdstaffel –
  Experimental Fighter Squadron,
  63, 93
Volgoles, SS, 74
Volgoleson, SS, 42
Volkmann, Hellmuth [General
  Veith], 112, 123–4, 126–7, 131–3,
  136–8, 147, 150–1, 153, 156, 159
Voroshilov, Kliment, 15
Vultee V1-A, 77

Waalhaven, SS, 77
Warlimont, Walter (Guido), 37–42,
  44–5, 48–50, 65–6
Wigbert, SS, 20, 44
Wilberg, Helmuth, 8, 50–1, 82
Winterübung Rügen, 50
Wolf, Daniel, 77

Yagüe, Juan, 23, 32, 58–9, 90, 133,
  138, 150–1
Yakushin, Mikhail, 106, 108, 111

Zaragoza, 24–5, 47, 100, 125–6,
  128, 138, 165